LUCY DANIELS

with a woman's voice

a writer's struggle for emotional freedom

Also by Lucy Daniels:

Caleb, My Son

High On A Hill

LUCY DANIELS

with a woman's voice

a writer's struggle for emotional freedom

Madison
B O O K S

published by Madison Books

Cover drawing "La Peine" by Louise Bourgeois,
courtesy of Cheim & Read, New York. Photo: Eeva-Inkeri.

Published by Madison Books
4720 Boston Way
Laham, Maryland 20706

Designed and produced by Ruder·Finn Design

ISBN: 1-56833-250-5

Printed and bound in Iceland.

contents

acknowledgments

I want to acknowledge with warmest gratitude those who, in different ways and at different points in my journey, were able to understand or at least assist me in my struggle. These include Leanna Ingram, Dr. Wilmer Betts, Dr. Harley Shands, Dr. John Howie, fellow staff members at *The Raleigh Times*, classmates and professors in the clinical psychology training program at the University of North Carolina at Chapel Hill, and my children.

In addition, as the struggle gave way to writing again, I have been fortunate to have the editorial and moral support of Sally Arteseros, Virginia Holman, and Holly Peppe.

Telling my true story brings in many people associated with me at different periods. The identities of some of them, such as people with whom I was hospitalized and patients in my practice, I consider it unethical to reveal. Other identities I've simply thought it wise to conceal. Where patients in my practice are mentioned, I refer to composites of experiences with several people. As a result, numerous names and identities in this book are fictional. My rule has been to eliminate, wherever possible, any pain from exposure. There are, however, people whose names could not be changed: my sisters, cousins, children, and first husband. I hope that this telling of my story will not cause them hardship. Not telling it would have been damaging to me.

To all those whose emotional struggle still keeps them silent.

In my dining room there is a beautiful bowl of purple glass. I bought it in Venice the first time I went there with Rudy, my second husband. Because of how perfectly it symbolizes Italy, that bowl made me love it at first sight. Its thick glass is amethyst in color but frosted on the outside with a thin, splotchy white-gray crusting that makes it look rugged and weathered like a mountain misted with ash. Near the middle of its sloping sides, a crude river of darker purple suggests molten lava or deep cool water varying wildly in breadth. Beckoning one, as it seems, to richness buried or swirling through space, that river refutes fragility.

In sunlight these blended purples evoke a multitude of reflections: of beautiful old Italy with its mists, mountains, and chapel-studded countryside; of how deeply in love I was at the time; and of the man who has since shattered and vanished from my life. I still remember leaving St. Domenico with him early that August morning to catch our flight home from Milan. Looking up at the mountain lit by a single star in the fading night sky, we found its peak already white with the first snow. I felt terribly sad that dawn because our trip was nearly finished and I feared the relationship might be, too. Recently I've been sadder still.

But beyond that memory, this bowl embodies feelings I was once denied but have come to recognize as the very essence of my being: conflict, choice, and struggling between the two; the strain to discern clarity from confusion and to bear the inextricableness of beauty and brutality, strength and delicacy, sweetness and sadness.

Today when I focus on these feelings, in my habit of striving for self-understanding, I never know what will happen. Sometimes there is nostalgia for the sweetness of feeling loved best of all by Father.

Or Rudy. Sometimes there's aching sadness from knowing the impossibility of such wishes. Surprising images and, occasionally, brainstorms, can come to mind, whereas once I didn't dare to be so open. Because then I was afraid to see — the truth, perhaps, or some forgotten pain. But growing older has weathered me in a way that's no longer burdened by apprehension. It allows me to look and look and to occasionally have the delicious experience of seeing for the first time something remarkable that's always been there. I do this with everything now—dreams, music, patients, works of art, and friends, as well as myself. I call this being alive.

He who knows not, and knows not that he
knows not, he is a fool. Shun him.

He who knows not, and knows that he
knows not, he is a child. Teach him.

He who knows, and knows not that
he knows, he is asleep. Wake him.

He who knows, and knows that he
knows, he is a wise man. Follow him.

– Arabic Apothegm

chapter one

THEN AND NOW

My earliest memory is of snow. Bibba, my nine-year-old half sister, pointed at the white feathers from the window, claiming them as one more piece of her own hocus-pocus. She opened the front door so I could reach out and catch the cold tingling flakes in my hand. Twenty months old, I was truly mystified, swirled up in that sea of white myself and wondering if this — like our new house — was yet another permanent alteration of the world in which I existed. I felt delighted and uneasy all at once, because Bibba had a way of exulting over things that turned out to be forbidden by the adults.

That was the day in December 1935, when Mommy brought Adelaide, my new baby sister, home from the hospital. In celebration, our black nurse, Bea, had dressed me in the lavender gingham dress that was Mommy's favorite. I liked that dress too. It was familiar, and I liked looking ways that made Mommy happy. That morning splotches of wet from the snow made some of the gingham checks darker than others.

Another strong recollection from that morning is of the empty, helpless feeling of having lost my voice. Like the snow, it was a change that had taken place overnight. My voice had been there at supper, asking Bea for cookies; it was gone when I woke that morning and tried to say the name of the as-yet-unseen baby. And this loss was particularly disturbing because my voice and my growing capacity to shape it into words was a relatively new and treasured possession.

Bibba's explanation for the problem was as puzzling as her

announcement of snow. She said I had a frog in my throat that was making me hoarse. I will never forget climbing up on the sink in the front hall lavatory to peer into the mirror in search of that frog. I stretched my mouth wide to look into the black cavern of my throat, and the fact that I couldn't see the frog was little help. Bibba could do all kinds of magic, and "invisible" was something she accomplished routinely. I don't recall how that ever got settled. Maybe my voice just came back. Maybe Mommy and the baby arrived and distracted me. But what I most remember from that day is the snow they would be arriving in, the snow that was swallowing the world I knew.

Memories of Adelaide herself begin with her walking. Halfway through her first year I had my second eye surgery, which could have been traumatic enough to erase anything. But probably Adelaide was even more devastating to my sense of personal importance. As the first baby after me, she required all the time and attention of adults who didn't have enough for either of us. Pain about her that I do remember from later makes me suspect that at first ignoring her felt essential for survival.

But I have one early recollection of myself in her presence before my bed was moved to what had been Mommy's sewing room. Lost and searching were the feelings. In the pitch-dark nursery where Adelaide had the crib and I slept in a sideless bed, I struggled with all my strength to jiggle and pull out the huge bottom drawer of the bureau so I could climb in and have a crib too. And those needing feelings are still stronger in another recollection from a little later, one of those middle-of-the-night times when we both were taken to the toilet. Father carried Adelaide and I stumbled behind, holding my arms up and begging Mommy to carry me. "No," Father scolded. "You are big enough to walk," in that deep echoing voice so worshipped in our household. His warm and wonderful face scowled. Glancing up at Adelaide whose chubby little arm securely circled his neck, I hated her and wished she would die, but also knew how wicked I was to wish that. Then, straining to not cry lest I be scolded for that, too, I longed for magic like Bibba's to make me a lovable child who wasn't greedy.

Hurts like that intensified my sense of being lost. And lostness — that sick feeling of blurred worthlessness that, by then, I already knew too well — was both unacceptable and uncalled for in a family and house as perfect as ours.

Nor were those despairing tears ever completely staunched. The only changes would, in time, be in their intensity and, eventually, in my ability to see my misery, as now, from the outside. Lostness has been the river of my life, slamming me now desperately, now determinedly, in time hopefully, in pursuit of myself. And, yes, also, in pursuit of my voice.

But consciousness of this feeling of lostness was never constant. That's what caused me shame and sometimes a blown-away sensation. I had been born cross-eyed. And Mommy, who took this personally, did everything she could to correct it. However, there was a period — before the War and first grade — when on the rare occasions that I left our yard, unfamiliar children would whisper, "What's wrong with your eyes?!" Then the horror in their voices would engulf me with the realization that something was terribly, terribly wrong with me.

Later, but still before starting school, there was another very different but equally disturbing eye experience. Raleigh, North Carolina, was our home then, too, and small enough for strangers to know each other. One day Bea took Adelaide and me on a walk all the way to Pine State Creamery at the corner of Tucker Street and Glenwood Avenue. That was farther than we'd ever walked before; Bea spurred us on with the promise of ice-cream cones. And inside that cool, sweet-smelling shop the lady said, "Oh, my! You have the Daniels eyes! . . . Who's your father, Frank or Jonathan?" Perhaps you'd call that feeling "found!" or something in between "found out" and "discovered." Only because she was referring to Adelaide as well as me did I know she wasn't just talking about my messed-up eyes.

I didn't understand how anyone could recognize us so many blocks from home, let alone what it was about our eyes. Her recognition seemed to contain a mixture of bad and good, a mixture I grew used to later when people talked about our family's outspoken newspaper, *The News and Observer*. In any given situation people might praise and condemn it at once. Many friends and foes called it The Nuisance and Disturber, and Grandfather and Father both declared, "It's the people who hate us that buy the most newspapers."

If you were to look for me in Raleigh today, it would be both difficult and easy. Although I live only a few miles from the house we grew up in and from where Pine State Creamery grew huge at its old corner only to close down and be replaced by swinging night clubs, most of "old" Raleigh doesn't know me or, at best, wonders what caused me to disappear thirty-five years ago after the publication of my second novel. Since that time my identity has been complicated by two husbands and four children, and I made the news most significantly only when I sold my minority share of our family-owned newspaper, *The News and Observer*, in 1990. Furthermore, I've been educated and changed careers. Nowadays I spend most of my time in a consulting room, where, as a psychologist, I help children and adults pursue emotional freedom. I used to do this as Dr. Lucy Inman, still using the name of my children's father. After becoming a millionaire in 1990, following two years of negotiations with my family for a fair price for my newspaper shares, I used the proceeds from my stock to establish the Lucy Daniels Center for Early Childhood and the Lucy Daniels Foundation, which is dedicated to helping other creative individuals gain freedom from unconscious conflicts. And with this name in the phone book and on the outside of our building, people began to ask, "What is your name? Lucy Inman or Lucy Daniels?" So, finally, to end months of confusion, I took back the name from my childhood which is also my writing name.

chapter two

MOMMY'S HOUSE

Our house at 1540 Caswell Street had the appearance of a citadel. It combined the qualities of church and prison, with exotic grandeur veiling alienation. Its massive red brick and ivy-draped Charlestonian presence dispelled any doubts about the richness inside, even as its high wall, closed gates, and double black-green garage doors made it clear that admission was by invitation only. But for us growing up there, it was simply called "your Mother's house" and praised as "beautiful" by everyone who visited.

I also knew—from listening to our cook, Eunice, tell Bea in the kitchen—that it had been a misfit from the start, back when even Bibba was too young to know. Unlike any other house in Raleigh, this one had quickly set people talking—from the digging of its red clay foundation, through the completion of its towering brick exterior, and especially with the erection of the awesome wall which ultimately enclosed its grounds. "They all knew it was fo' Miss Lucy," Eunice said while I lingered in the doorway to the back stairs. ("Miss Lucy" was my mother.) "She was determin' to have a fine house, like ev'ythin' else, to prove she's not only different, but bettah than otha folks in Raleigh. 'Specially, y' know, bettah than Mistah Jonathan's first wife."

But that was only part of the truth. Like other stories in our family, it did not give Father his share of responsibility. That house, like their marriage, had come into being to contain the fears and conceal the inadequacies of them both. Mommy probably saw the house as a chance to prove her own worth by embellishing her prominent and affluent husband. But for Father, Mommy and her house were meant both to erase past failure and to provide impregnable protection against future losses. The problem was that this protection also made their marriage an exquisite prison—in which Mommy, straining to be invulnerable and need-free, appeared cold and unlovable; while Father's sense of deprivation made him angrily exciting and lustful. Only much later did it occur to me that they were probably both depressed. My image of them is mythic: Mommy, as Sisyphus, eternally pushing the stone of her needlessness up the hill; and Father, as Tantalus, locked into hunger due to unconsciously condemning the very aspects of himself that he touted. Each was oblivious to the pain of the other.

And each of us daughters strained to fix this. A woman as pretty as Mommy should have been lovable and happy; a man as powerful as Father should have been generous; and married people are supposed to love each other. Rigidly — unconsciously driven, I'd say now — I was an angel, Adelaide a mess-maker, and Bibba a prankster whose catastrophes kept Mommy and Father at odds. Later Mary Cleves, the last born, also tried to fix things by remaining the baby. But none of this worked. While our efforts to pacify or drown out their pain and seductive neediness distorted us, nothing else changed. Ignored pain was the norm, ensconced in lust and propriety.

Nor was my parents' the first generation of sufferers. For their forebears, death had been a much more common part of life than it is now. The grandparents, who told me stories about when they were little, each told of one parent who had died in their childhood. My mother's mother told me sadly of her own mother—the first Lucy—who'd died of tuberculosis when Granny was only sixteen. She also told me story after story about her beloved first-born son, William, who had died at age eight of mastoiditis.

Other deaths were not discussed, however; and these, I now know, cause the most pain. I never knew my mother's father; he died of a heart attack one month before my birth. Nevertheless, he owned my mother until her death at seventy-four. Granddaddy (as I was taught to call him) had grown up in Charleston, S.C., which my mother always considered a center of gentility second only to Paris. There the perfection her father exacted was practiced with the same daily elegance she would have liked to hold sway in our house. Besides having such an exemplary heritage, he had been educated in Germany and ended up in New York City as a brilliant chemist who invented Wesson Oil. I never heard my Granny, who'd grown up in Montgomery, refer to him as anything but Dr. Cathcart.

My mother told me all her life what a wonderful and astute man Granddaddy had been, and how proud he would have been of me. But at Mommy's funeral, her first cousin told us that this same man had been a cruel perfectionist who allowed his only daughter no frivolities. Required by him to major in chemistry (which she hated), she flunked out after her first semester in college and never went back. Only in recent years have I become able to see what a tormented and terrified woman my mother was. In Raleigh she flaunted both her Charleston and Montgomery blue-bloodedness and her New York sophistication and upbringing to force others to recognize her worth.

My father, instead, had a locally respected heritage. His father, Josephus Daniels, had grown up poor, the second of three sons raised in Wilson, N.C., by their postmistress mother who'd been widowed during the Civil War. Her husband, a carpenter and conscientious objector, had been killed while repairing a Union ship. My father's mother, Adelaide Worth Bagley, was the granddaughter of Jonathan Worth, North Carolina's Civil War governor. By the time I was born, her husband, Josephus Daniels, was known worldwide as Woodrow Wilson's Secretary of the Navy who had taken wine rations away from sailors, and as Ambassador to Mexico under Franklin Roosevelt. He was also the plain-spoken, fighting-for-the-common-man editor of the Raleigh *News and Observer*. I suspect, but do not know, that his lack of a father and his dedication to his ideals, which included the Methodist Church and Prohibition, made him a somewhat distant and awesome father and husband. I also suspect this contributed to my grandmother's being excessively close and domineering with her four sons.

As a grand lady who had entertained elegantly in both Washington, D.C. and Mexico City, Adelaide Worth Bagley Daniels was used to being able to control her surroundings and quality of life. Among other things, she wanted all her sons to live close by. My father and two of his brothers, Frank and Joe, built their houses on the adjoining land she gave them. My mother always hated this arrangement and built the high brick wall around our lot to live with it. No matter how respected the Danielses were in Raleigh, Mommy considered them "nouveau riche" and "common" to live in this manner. My father's brother Worth was the only son who did not work at the newspaper. He became a respected physician in Washington, D.C., and the discoverer of "cat scratch fever."

Today families like this are called "enmeshed," and John Bradshaw talks on television about how children in them suffer. But many people didn't know about that then. The Danielses certainly didn't. "The family" was a sacred unit that included all of us living on those four connecting lots, as well as Worth and his physician wife, Josie, who lived in Washington, D.C. with their sons, Worth and Derick. The Raleigh components were: Nanny and Grandfather, in their grand but somber stone house in the midst of a few acres; their youngest son, Frank, and his wife, Ruth, with their children, Frank and Patsy, on their lot just northeast of Nanny's and Grandfather's; their oldest son, Josephus, with his wife, Evalina, and their adopted son, Edgar, on a lot just north of Frank's; and their next-to-youngest son, Jonathan (my father), with his wife, Lucy, and their daughters, Lucy, Adelaide, and Mary Cleves, as well as Elizabeth ("Bibba"), who was the daughter of Father's first marriage, on a lot just north of Nanny's and Grandfather's.

Such close quarters easily resulted in strong disagreements about the all-important minutiae of our lives. In that fray Mommy and Josephus's wife, Evalina, frequently raised objectionably shrill and opposing voices that brought ridicule or silencing from others, which inevitably also escalated their unreasonableness. Frank's wife, Ruth, in contrast, said little, but over the years she grew fatter and fatter. To a little girl who achingly longed to be worth something, it almost made sense that only male voices were respected—made sense but felt demoralizing.

Furthermore, poorly disguised, unclaimed, often vicious anger bounced about among us all the time, as "the family" strained to show its "respectable" face to the community. In my generation, the third one, the damage from this is mainly evident in mixtures of sadism and masochism pieced together with sufficient blandness to prevent explosions. In other words, we have problems that modern psychology would expect to develop in people pent up and kept destructively dependent. Some of us have worked as adults to change this, but such change is difficult and only possible on an individual basis.

Bibba protested the house's confinement long before anyone else dared to admit it. "Your mother has such a lovely house," the ladies would coo when they came to call. "Don't track mud in you' Mama's house," Bea said on rainy days. "Yeah, this is her house," Bibba would lash back either way. "Everything in it is hers. Except me!" Then she'd take the chewing gum out of her mouth and stick it on the dining room's gold leaf mirror. And Bea would yell, "Stop aggravatin' me, you li'l vixen! You want to fight wid her, you do it! But don't drag us in fo' not cleaning up after you!" As a small child I never understood those interchanges as involving anything but Bibba's anger at Bea and Mommy. I never grasped Bibba's reference to the fact that she was not Mommy's daughter.

Bibba seemed free to go anywhere she chose—as long as she asked permission, came back in time for meals, and wasn't being punished. Whereas I was expected to play in the yard alone most of the day, while Adelaide stayed inside with Bea. The only exception to this was when we went for a walk. On those afternoons, Bea would wear a freshly starched uniform and expected me to comb my hair and put on a clean pinafore while she dressed Adelaide. Then off we'd go, down Caswell to Harvey with Adelaide in the stroller, me straggling behind, and Bea's maid friend, Callie, and the children she nursed, joining us at the corner. Sometimes we went to the railroad yard, sometimes to the haunted house, sometimes just around one block and then another. But we were always back for baths by five o'clock.

The sharp contrast between life inside the house and outside always puzzled me. Caswell Street's tarred surface was potholed and dusty. Father liked it that way because it kept down the traffic; Mommy considered this superior to the busier streets the other Daniels houses faced. Only a few scrawny pin oaks shaded its sidewalks. The other houses on the street, though comfortably middle-class, looked flat-footed and unremarkable next to ours, embellished as it was with ornate ironwork balconies and railings and antique carriage lanterns. Seen from the sidewalk across the street, our house's many polished window panes had the appearance of startled eyes whose green shutter lashes were blinking with dismay at its mundane neighbors. There was so little traffic on Caswell Street that other children frequently played there, making noises that I sometimes heard from inside the wall: "Red Rover! Red Rover!"; "May I take a giant step?. . ." I never played with those children, though. And I believed they wouldn't like anyone who lived in Mommy's house.

On the way home from our walks, however, the contrast affected me differently. I could see our house long before we got there, red brick walls and slate roof rising above the trees and the other houses. And from that perspective, it always seemed comforting, a haven where Mommy's order was so pervasive that it vaccinated us against diseases like diphtheria and smallpox and subjugated the very seasons of the year. I think I knew then, and even in a way accepted, that there was also a formidable price for this order. The very forces in Mommy that imposed such unfailing structure made her unable to hold or comfort a baby. She was allergic to a vast array of foods and fabrics, and unable to tolerate or enjoy many things, including picnics, friends, and sadness.

From the street, our house looked beautiful, rich, and enticing, with ivy traipsing over its brick, and lush green glimpsable through the garden gates. But those heavy gates and the closed garage doors were forbidding as well. Furthermore, in keeping with the Charleston civility my mother loved, the side — not the front — of the house faced the street. And the brick wall, high enough to conceal the downstairs windows, totally excluded outsiders while seeming to hug and protect the house.

The two gates on either side of the garage doors contributed to this disdainful demeanor. Facing the house, the gate on the right opened into the little "back" courtyard, with its garbage cans, clothesline, and mint bed. That was the way black people, children, deliverymen, and workmen entered. There was very little grass and no trees; you could sometimes smell the garbage. The other gate led into what we called the "front yard," which surrounded the house except at the southwest corner. Inside that gate, following the brick walk bordered by periwinkle, the impression was one of sacred serenity. This area was rich with expansive green lawn and stately sheltering crepe myrtle, sycamore, and oak trees.

On the "back" side of the house (but still in the "front yard"), away from the walk and the front door, were three other contributors to the grandeur that alienated Raleigh: a border of formal flower beds; a wide expanse of rectangular brick terrace, formalized by French doors opening out onto it at either end, and ascetically uncomfortable in its unprotected exposure to rain, insects, and baking sun; and, above this, a charming wrought-iron balcony suitable for Shakespeare's Juliet, but otherwise cramped and utterly impractical. In time the espaliered pear tree was added to this list. Mommy tacked it to the wall separating the front yard from the back soon after Adelaide started walking.

The front door at the end of the walk also looked rich but formidable—dark green double doors punctuated by polished brass knocker and door knobs. For those who entered, the contrast with the world outside the wall was even sharper. High-ceilinged rooms and halls, elaborate wallpaper, oriental rugs, gold-leaf mirrors. The mingled scents of camphor, floor wax, and sherry made the house seem remarkable in its exoticness. There were larger, richer houses in Raleigh, but none with such apparent devotion to being extraordinary. Circular staircase, astutely flawless hardwood floors, elaborate moldings, and wall sconces. People who had been inside talked with awe about these and other details. So did others who had not. Grandfather was quoted as saying he thought it was wonderful that his son Jonathan had married a woman who could help him learn to enjoy such finery, but that he himself was too accustomed to being ordinary to fully appreciate it.

Eunice described being "full o' buttahflies" when she first came to see Mommy about a cooking job. "She tol' me to come to the back through that l'il dusty yard with the clothesline. I did. An' I won't surprised fo' her to be pretty with her black hair piled up or about that queen ice way of hers. But I was spooked by the pitifulness under it, that nobody hain't mentioned. She nevah did show me the house that day. Jus' aftah we talk heah at the table, she ask me fo' 'reference' and say I'll heah in a few days." In the end both Eunice and her middle daughter, Bea, had been hired at $15.00 a week instead of Raleigh's usual $13.00, because "Miss Lucy was expectin' quality service."

The most glorious time in Mommy's house was winter with its smells of wet wool and wood fires. Those scents have ever since evoked memories of the huge glistening tree at Christmas and jingling ancient sleigh bells tied to the front door with red ribbon. But fall was the time when order was most obvious. Then the wooden floors were waxed in preparation for oriental rugs to be brought back from storage. Door knobs were shined, too; and the secure smells of brass and floor polish permeated every room. Then, especially, Bea would remind us not to track in mud.

With floors, brass, and windows shining, Mommy's house glistened with hospitality that I realized only much later was as intimidating as it was inviting. Yet, long before I had the words to say it, my thoughts strained to decipher and obey the subtleties of that contrast. And inside the house, these two came together in a simple directive: substantial perfection that was off limits. Like it or not, the priorities were clear and dependable—the house and its furnishings first, the food served there second, the people last. Adelaide disregarded these, leaving messes in her wake, screaming when she was supposed to be silent, refusing food. Bibba ridiculed and defied them. But for me these priorities were venerable facts of life, like such others as being run over by cars or drowned by water if you weren't careful; facts that, if heeded, could also be counted on to make one feel a little more in control.

Some of Mommy's most inviolable canons had to do with which people were allowed in which rooms when. The living room was closed off most of the time, and only used on Christmas and Thanksgiving or when Mommy had a dinner party. With the exception of Christmas Eve, children had to be dressed up to enter it. But even on Christmas Eve I dreaded the living room because most entries there involved having to kiss the ladies.

Though Mommy and Father went everywhere, most of the house— aside from the kitchen, children's bedrooms, and back stairs—was off limits to children and servants. The main difference between these classifications was that, when doors were closed or locked, servants were expected to knock, whereas children were not even allowed to do that.

Mommy and Father spent their days in the library with typewriters clicking and the door bolted. (While Father wrote, Mommy copied his manuscripts.) The servants rarely knocked there, and children were most strictly forbidden to. Bibba liked that because it made it easier for her to do what she wanted behind Mommy's back. Adelaide didn't care; if she got loose, she'd run and kick that door or lie down and scream through the crack. Then they'd get mad at Bea or me while only laughing at her, and joking "That's Adelaide for you!" I was expected to be "reliable Lucy," however. The one time I did knock, Father yelled, "You thoughtless brat!" while Mommy alternated between, "Now, Jonathan—" and "Lucy, you're big enough to know better." After that I mainly stayed away from the front hall, or if I did sneak there to eavesdrop, I was careful not to make a sound or touch the knob.

During the day we had to use the back stairs so as to not disturb Father. But we were allowed in the library during drinks and required in the dining room at suppertime. The logic of these rules was never explained, but it seemed pretty clearly to be a way of putting up with children who were difficult to have around. There was very little sense, aside from our not being allowed coffee and Coca-Cola and being nursed when sick, of children requiring particular caretaking. Rather, the predominant focus was on protecting house and parents from our intrusions and destructiveness.

One of the strangest things, I only realized much later while raising my own children, was how, in contrast to the library, our parents' bedroom door was never closed. Nor was there any protection for us there against the assault of their naked bodies. In the mornings when Adelaide and I traipsed in and out to get our shoes tied or hair unsnarled, they walked about naked, referring to their room as a "goldfish bowl," but seemingly oblivious to a child's need for them to be clothed.

As a little girl I saw nothing wrong with that, of course; only something wrong with me for being squeamish, the same as when Father pulled out his penis and peed without closing the bathroom door.

The best defense was to not look, but even though my bad eye could automatically slip to the side, my good one usually caught a glimpse. And it was in those stunned moments that my first theories of sexuality took shape. Disgust was the feeling, I think, and horror. The sight of Father's ugly penis in its nest of scrotum and pubic hair made everything in me go away. "Let me be wrong," the somber whisper inside me pleaded. Whether seeing it there or listening to him urinate with the lavatory door wide open despite Mommy's scolding, I would go lightheaded with unconsciously imposed distance, and wonder how she could love anyone with that awful floppy snake attached to him. Sometimes that snake was still inside my head at breakfast.

But in a way, Mommy was worse. I could shun Father and cross my heart and hope to die as extra insurance. But I knew that her grotesque flopping breasts and crinkly, crawling hair were doomed to overtake me. "Yeah, you'll be a lady, too," Bibba declared. And when I asked Bea if I would be like Mommy when I grew up, she said, "Prob'ly. Prob'ly be the spittin' image." Disgust and horror!

One of the most difficult things for me in early childhood was controlling my tongue so that it didn't say the wrong thing in the wrong place. Being both very verbal and a curious listener, it was easy for me to hear something startling, to which would quickly be added, "Don't tell _____." The two most frequently repeated phrases that I could understand made silence seem essential for survival. "Don't tell you' Mama," Eunice and Bea cautioned regularly. "Now remember," Mommy extorted, with a dimple tic going in her cheek, "The servants are not to hear this." Bibba made it equally urgent that I not tell Mommy what she told me. So, from an early age I strained to not repeat the things I heard; but despite this, my occasional failure would set people yelling at each other perilously. Yet, staying silent felt almost as bad because the people I most admired and wanted to be like were Father and Bibba, who seemed to speak freely.

Thus, conversations and efforts to understand the differences among their participants continually preoccupied me. At times, this attention even seemed to be needed for safety or to protect those I loved. Oddly, too, there were some similarities between the library and the kitchen. Eunice and Bea's way of telling stories and laughing was a little like Father's. The main differences were that Mommy sat in stern judgment in the library and Father talked louder and less physically than the black people did. In both places, though, much of what was said sounded like a foreign language to me with phrases that were incomprehensible or vaguely disconcerting. Typical of the kitchen were words like "hex," "vixen," "weasel," "two-timing," "ha'nts." The black voices saying them were slurred and strident. While in the library I heard Mommy call me her "eyeballs" or her "heartstrings" and talk about Ruth (Frank's wife) being "in a swivet," or this woman she'd met being a "grass widow." And Father used terms like: "wet blanket," "by the balls," "fuck," "crap," "speakeasy," "holy roller," "slewfoot." Mommy's voice was cool and persuasive when she was pleased or tearful and terrifying when she was mad and screaming at Bibba for being an "inconsiderate hood-lum." Father's voice was deep and rich, hinting at forbidden mysteries even more exciting than his words. The words came faster and louder when he was mad.

Listening in either room often made me feel uneasy and shamefully stupid, yet I was barred from voicing either of these states. Most of what was said in both places was adult conversation, but Father, more than Bea or Eunice, would sometimes speak directly to one of us children. Whenever that happened, it was exciting for the person singled out. Father's interest was never half-hearted; his energy and clever voice could make you the center of the universe in an instant. And to a little girl who was one of four in a family that typically ignored or banished children, such personal recognition was intensely and positively charged. By the time I was three, however, being noticed or even appreciated by Father also set me quivering with anxiety. I didn't understand or perhaps even think about why. He was powerful and important, as well as our family's one source of genuine warmth. I both longed for his affection and felt a shame-ful sissy for fearing it.

Father had a way of saying things that was pleasing and confus-ingly painful at once. To me as a preschooler, for instance, he sometimes said, "Lucy, you are a sexless highbrow. All brains and no feelings." "Sex" and "highbrow" were both words I didn't understand, but Bibba had told me about "brains" and we were always being admonished to not "hurt so-and-so's feelings." I also heard him tell Adelaide that she was "all feelings" and knew that that was what made her a better person. My worry about the difference between being "all feelings and no brains" and "all brains and no feelings" made me feel ashamed of my strengths, as evidence of coldness, just as, I believe now, it made Adelaide feel bad about her feelings and ashamed that her brains were "deficient." I doubt Father knew the destructiveness of his words.

One of my worst speaking quandaries had to do with Adelaide when I was about three and a half. She'd had her tonsils out a few days earlier. Mommy was having one of her elegant dinner parties during which Adelaide and I were supposed to stay upstairs and leave Eunice and Bea free to serve. Those parties were wondrously rich spectaculars that took days to prepare for because they required all the silver to be polished and all the crystal to be glistening clean. Even from upstairs the parties were mesmerizing experiences due to the mixture of clinking glasses, rumbling male voices, laughter, and female shrillness.

At that point Adelaide and I couldn't really play together; at two she talked minimally and became oppositional quickly. However, I went into her room (which was then called the "nursery" and where we had to play on rainy days) and found her in the closet.

"Adelaide, what're you doing?" I asked.

No answer.

"Adelaide . . ."

Her wispy blond-haired head was averted, but when I stepped closer, I saw blood pouring out of her mouth! Gripped by terror, my first thought was to run tell Mommy. But remembering the dinner party and the prohibitions against going downstairs made for a terrifying struggle between letting Adelaide die or having Mommy scream at me for messing up her party. Fear of Adelaide's dying won out, however. It sent me running downstairs as quietly as possible and into the glittering candlelit dining room full of laughing, talking grown-ups in party clothes.

I whispered in Mommy's ear and she left the table to take care of Adelaide. To my great relief, she didn't get mad after all.

chapter three

GOOD VS. EVIL

Adelaide was always being nursed or worried over. Even when well, she continually got into trouble so that she had to be watched, taking all of Bea's time and, on Bea's afternoon off, most of Mommy's. The rest of the week, except when she was bossing Bea and Eunice, Mommy stayed in the library with Father who got mad if he had to write by himself. Bibba was always gone — either to school or to all the other places she went with her friends. So I stayed in the yard alone each morning until lunch and naptime and most afternoons until baths.

On the hottest afternoons I made myself a bed under the crepe myrtle tree. Lying there I could look up and see patches of blue sky through the tangled pink-flower branches — blue sky which made me wonder and try to understand but always end up bewildered instead. Despite envying the children I heard playing together at a distance, I knew, with shame, that I'd never dare join them. Conceptualizing my unacceptableness was, in fact, one of my earliest attempts at problem-solving. It took the form of a straightforward list with causes and effects mixed: a person would only be locked up or out if hateful. Beloved Adelaide and Father weren't locked out. My weird blue eyes, which, even after operations, black eye patches, and looking at pictures in Mommy's slide box, still strayed in different directions, were a major mark of wrongness. But being "good" for Mommy and being like her in staying clean and in having her name seemed the worst defect of all. Evidence of this was the excruciating humiliation I felt whenever Mommy praised me.

"Come in, sweetheart," she would say when she wanted to show me off to a visitor. I always hung back shyly, in a way that I only realized decades later probably aggravated her. "Come on, darling. Speak to Mrs. Jones."

It was all I could do then to pull my eyes up from the floor, let alone get my voice out.

"Lucy is such a wonderful child," she'd continue to the visitor. "See how clean she is? She can stay in the yard all afternoon and still be as clean as when she first went out. I wish she'd talk to you. She's extremely bright and . . . Lucy, please talk to Mrs. Jones."

But, by then, I couldn't even glance up. My skin would have braced itself against the shrillness of her words as though they were acid or ice water capable of dissolving me on contact. I knew that Mrs. Jones, or whoever, must despise anybody so bragged about, and there seemed no way to save myself. In fact, this felt even worse when the people Mommy extolled me to were family. My sisters knew what I was like, and they knew Mommy only praised me that way, while she tended to complain about Bibba, and later Adelaide, just as vociferously. From very early on, I feared this would make Bibba not like me. Adelaide never did anyway. A complicating factor was that each of us labored, without knowing it, to make what Mommy said true so as to feel less violated by her words. And for me, Mommy's praise, in addition to its excessiveness, seemed to clutch me to her with a potency that somehow forged me into her image as it drove others away. Eventually this belief that my most heinous wickedness had to do with resembling Mommy grew to a horrible conviction that froze me in manner and word.

This sense of badness became even more malignant as my various attempts to compensate for it failed. One of my earliest efforts was to remodel myself after some loved person. Bibba, for instance, who seemed generous and warmhearted, was allowed to run free, and stayed in conflict with Mommy. And Adelaide's perpetual naughtiness seemed to make her all the more valuable. However, my attempts at deliberately misbehaving only brought scoldings: "Stop being ugly"; "Start behaving like the big girl you are." Even when I eked out the rare courage to contradict Mommy, my words tended to be misheard as sweet or instructive so that somehow our alliance was even more sickeningly affirmed.

Consequently, I resigned myself to being a hateful person who had to look good. And though this closed the door on ever being lovable, it also made it clear who I was and how I had to conceal it from others. In the yard I experimented with ways to manage this: only sucking my thumb there and in bed with the covers over my head; learning to take off my underpants and wee-wee behind the fir tree rather than getting yelled at by Father for asking to go inside. One day when the pants got so hopelessly tangled that I feared being caught without them, I speculated about whether his belt against a bare bottom could cause lovableness. I also pondered "inside" and "outside" a lot — the other children laughing and calling to each other in the street, how squirrels could scamper up and over the wall, but rabbits apparently couldn't. Confined and timid both came to seem shameful evidence of worthlessness.

One afternoon, I discovered some ants moving in a thin trickle from a patch of yellow dust across a short stretch of earth to the wall and up two bricks to where faulty mortaring had left a tiny hole straight through to the other side. Amazed, I knelt down beside the wall to see where they were going and was incredulous to discover an imperfection in Mommy's wall that allowed this interchange with the outside. And though I could see only a speck of the yard across the street, peering through that crack always made me feel secretly and wonderfully powerful.

Another type of inside-outside capability that fascinated me was that of caterpillars turning into butterflies. I did not buy Bibba's magical tale which had to do with caterpillars making and sleeping inside cocoons all winter to come out as butterflies in the spring. But doubting this metamorphosis, I nevertheless remained on the lookout for it, sometimes keeping caterpillars in a mayonnaise jar for that purpose. My own theory eliminated the cocoon and saw caterpillars as butterflies in disguise or as captors holding the beautiful filmy flutterers hostage inside their ugly worm-like bodies.

My eyes worried Mommy constantly and were the one wrong

thing about me that I couldn't hide. Besides taking me for ophthal-mologist exams every few months, she determinedly put me through the daily regimen of eye exercises he prescribed. There was a certain life-and-death exigency about all this that I know now was fueled by her own guilt and need to feel in control. As a most diligent participant, I "understood" that Mommy's urgency and anger (which interfered with her being happy and lovable) was due to this perversity in me that I hadn't learned to master. Thus, each evening when she had me look at pictures in the hand-held stereoscope, I labored to do what would be "right." My efforts were rarely sufficient, however, because I had no way of knowing whether my eyes were focusing together or not.

"Stop it!" she'd snap at me with no warning as we worked over that slide box. "Stop it! And look at me straight!"

I could see that her dimple was ticking angrily. And though I didn't know how to "look straight," I did soon learn that when Mommy asked if I saw one thing or two, the right answer was "one" regardless.

"Now, Lucy, look into the box and tell me what you see. . ."

"A house."

"Just one?"

"Yes m'am, one."

Saying that always made peace. On the outside, that is. Mommy's dimple would stop jutting in and out and before long she would look composed and satisfied. By the time all the slides were run through, she'd be telling me how good I was and how hard I was trying. If I said "one" for a slide that had two different pictures, that error was tiny in comparison, simply something she'd ask me to look at again. But inside I felt guilty and fake, an early experience of something I came to feel constantly later on — that I was a very bad person and much worse than Mommy knew.

In spite of those exercises and learning to give that calming answer, it was a long time before I understood about my eyes. Aside from Mommy's exasperated sighs and labor to correct them, their defects seemed to be unmentionable at home. But one afternoon, during our walk, Bea and her maid friend Callie talked more openly about this than anyone I'd overheard before. The children Callie nursed were with us — a baby and a boy Adelaide's age who didn't talk. I was walking ahead that day, listening.

"What's wrong with her eyes?" Callie asked.

"They been messed up . . . ever since they brung her from the hospital. Used to be they was both twisted 'round, cockeyed looking, like in a crazy person. Poor Miss Lucy; they say she like to died, her wantin' nothin' that hain't perfect."

"Is her head all right?"

"Oh, yeah. She's as smart as anybody. Dress herself while I'm tendin' the baby. You min' how she is when you see her — always clean, always still, like a li'l grown person. An' her eyes is a heap better. They taken her to this doctor in New York. He operated twic't, last time since the baby."

Callie leaned forward to gape at my face. "That what you call cock-eyed?" she said more softly to Bea.

"Cross-eye," Bea corrected.

"They still don't look right."

"Yeah, but they better. . . An' Miss Lucy, she still work on it with this movie box she make her look in. Works an' works like. . . well, you know how Miss Lucy is. . . an' poor li'l thing, she don't da'st say, 'no.' Don't anybody say 'no' to Miss Lucy. But I don't believe all the movie boxes in the world is gonna fix that eye now. I think Miss Lucy jes' do it to keep from givin' up hope."

I remember myself going hollow as they talked and my pinafore ballooning out like a tent. That hollowed-out feeling was a form of lost-ness that has remained at hand ever since, swallowing me up in any situation where, even if I don't consciously recognize it, there is some-thing I can't bear.

In that particular instance it wasn't just Bea's saying that my eyes would never be right that swallowed me up. It was hearing about those operations, which brought to mind the terrifying bleeding and, thus, the "two" operations of Adelaide's tonsillectomy. And the horrible realization that all "that" had been done to me without my having any recollection of it. The most concrete memory I could relate to Bea's story was having to wear the black patch over my good eye for months after the second surgery.

From today's perspective, however, I do wonder if some of the blown-away sensation of that afternoon wasn't also due to memories of the surgery experience that my unconscious believed I couldn't bear. As an adult I've learned more about those surgeries — from Mommy and clinical reading — than I ever could have remembered. At that time, in order to prevent crying, parents were not allowed to stay with their child in the hospital. A mother simply deposited her child before the surgery and went back the next day to pick her up. A child regained consciousness after the surgery with eyes bandaged and both hands in sacks tied to her side!

In those early days my automatic reaction to feeling lost or afraid or ashamed or hurt was desperate wishing to become as brave as Bibba. Bibba did say "no" to Mommy and sometimes acted "no." I'd hear Bibba yell "martyr" and see Mommy bristle in silence in response. I'd also seen Bibba make faces and shriek, "Snob! Social-climbing priss! Too good for everybody!" and watched Mommy's pretty manicured hand slap her across the mouth. Fear always paralyzed me when Mommy lunged at Bibba and shook her so hard that her head knocked the wall. Fear not only of Mommy's destroying Bibba, but of me intervening. Two equally awful possibilities loomed — Mommy could turn her rage on me or fall down and die, mortally wounded by my disapproval. Once terror did pull a cry of "Stop! Stop!" right out of my mouth, but usually Mommy and Bibba just came to a screaming stalemate themselves, leaving me feeling weak and bad for not getting them to love each other.

Nevertheless, my wish to be lovable stayed strong. So much so, that getting this and other good feelings dishonestly — as in lying about what I saw in the slide box or sucking my thumb in secret — became an ever-present motive. One good feeling that I came on first quite by accident also had to do with seeing. After the second surgery I never could understand having to wear that black patch over my good eye. But despite the resulting shameful sense of clumsy weakness, I did wear it, even in the yard. Until one day, while wee-weeing behind the fir tree, I pulled it off and was literally thrilled at all I could see. Blades of grass, grains of sand, details of my doll's face. Such seeing felt wonderfully exciting and powerful. After that I sometimes hid behind that tree to sneak off the patch and look at things even when I didn't need to pee.

Enterprise and intelligence were characteristics Mommy valued. So were self-sufficiency, originality, and beauty. She took particular pride in using her power to shape such qualities into showpieces of excellence. My best chance to observe this was with the espaliered pear tree. Mommy herself planted it against the segment of wall that separated the large yard in which I was kept from the small dusty kitchen courtyard with its clothesline and garbage cans. I watched some of her tacking of splayed branches into the brick, but wandered away whenever the ticking of her dimple and the air sucking between her teeth intensified.

And from then on that little tree was an object of fascination for me. Something akin to real-life magic — that an ordinary sapling could be made to take on and keep such an unnatural but beautiful form. Mommy clearly took great pride in it, and most of the time after the planting beamed at it instead of sucking her teeth. Since pears were one fruit I liked, it pleased me to think we could grow our own. But therein lay another surprise. The purpose of this trained tree was not to bear fruit but to look beautiful.

There was a hammock for a while when I was three, the only reason I can recall for other children ever coming to our yard. That hammock was green with sufficient width to completely wrap yourself up when being pushed high. It was tied to the trunks of two pecan trees, which Bibba had told me had to be boy and girl in order for the trees to bear nuts. When I was alone in the yard, the hammock just hung there, limp and useless. But when Bibba and her big friends came to use it they'd give me turns, too. Those trees looked very tall to me and were lush with their leaves clumped together like bushes. And the big kids played a game of reaching out to bring leaves back as they took turns pushing each other as high as they could go. The winner was the person who brought back the most "money." It was scary, but also thrilling. And when I finally worked up the nerve to reach out and grab some leaves, too, I felt as exhilarated as if they really were $1,000 bills!

But that pleasure was short-lived. One morning when Bibba came to the yard alone, I wanted her to stay and play. To humor me while still remaining free to leave, she bargained to push me high in the hammock if I'd swing there and not come after her. I agreed. But once up there, I changed my mind and fell and broke my collarbone. Mommy blamed Bibba and a few days later had one of the pecan trees cut down. She said it was diseased, but Bibba and I both knew better. My guilt over this was multifaceted and enduring. Because of Mommy's way of using any excuse to do what she wanted, I believed this accident was also the cause of Bibba's eventually being sent away to boarding school and never again being a regular member of our family.

Besides stealing good feelings wherever I could, I carefully hid from Mommy the more serious ways I did so. Because these had to do with loving Bea and Bibba, when I knew there was an unvoiced rule that I was to love no one but Mommy. Also, Bea and Bibba both did things that Mommy would have called "leading Lucy on." For instance, sometimes Bibba visited the yard to tell stories or complain about Mommy. During the school year when she was supposed to be doing homework, she'd smuggle me into the house to hide under dirty clothes in her closet while she read Oz books aloud instead. And sometimes Bea would take us to the railroad yard where her laborer brother would give us candy. Or to the Pine State Creamery for ice cream that was also against the rules. Then she'd admonish me (since I was the talker, compared to Adelaide), "Don' tell Miss Lucy."

Besides not wanting Mommy to find out about how I loved them, I also wanted to keep Bea and Bibba caring about me even though Mommy was my controller. Bibba's visits to the yard made me feel temporarily more lovable and wanting to do whatever was needed to keep her liking me. So, besides listening intently to her stories about elves, I strained to see the elves when she pointed at and talked to them. When I later admitted that I couldn't see them, Bibba said I'd be able to if I believed enough. After that I pretended I did.

My only consistent company in the yard was Hansel, a brown dachshund puppy Mommy's brother Dick had brought me when I was three. He grew to be a stolid, patient, quiet companion who was perhaps even masochistic in letting me dress him like a baby. Hansel spent most days curled up in shade in summer or sun in winter, just looking up with dark, containing eyes when I touched or spoke to him. And because of how "unfree" I was to really play in those days, he was mainly just a comforting presence.

Often scared at night, I sometimes gave in to the urge to go to Bea's bed. The servants' room was far away, but Mommy would have punished Bibba for letting me in hers. We were not allowed in anyone else's bed, as was well demonstrated by Mommy and Father's angry shouting the few times Adelaide tried to get in to theirs. So—especially in winter when the dark house was cold—I stealthily picked my way down the hall to the bathroom, then around the corner and along the other long hall to the backstairs. Holding my breath all the while, I listened for snoring from Mommy and Father's open door, snoring that eased fears of Mommy over-hearing the creaking floorboards. Vigilant for the ghosts and boogey men lurking in corners and door jambs, I only relaxed when the sound of Eunice's louder snoring told me I'd arrived safely. That room had its own distinct smell — a mingling of starch, white shoe polish, and hair grease, an aura of primitive sensuality, magically powerful in the unpredictable extremes of black "badness" and docility. Bea slept in the bed on the right; the lump her body made was smaller than the huge snoring one in Eunice's bed. When I huddled at the bedside poking Bea's shoulder and whispering her name, Eunice's snore would falter and Bea's heavy breathing would startle to a stop. "What?" Her pigtailed head jerked up. "Who is it?"

"It's me. Lucy. I want to get in bed with you."

Rolling over, Bea held the covers out for me. "Jus' hesh," she whispered. "Don't let you' ma know. . . Don't make no fuss fo' you' ma to hear." And almost immediately, long before I was fully settled against her big warm body, Bea was snoring again. I'd lie there wide-eyed, breathing her smell, harkening to the night noises and creakings, alert for clues like Mommy's slippers in the hall, dreading what could happen if I heard them, until daylight was at the windows and Bea was nudging me. "Get up, Lucy," she would whisper. "Get on back now 'fore you' ma find out." So I would. And though lying close to Bea remained enticing, the risks involved made for long intervals between those visits.

When I was three and a half, Aunt Evalina and Uncle Joe (Josephus) adopted a child who was older than I was. Many aspects of this were perplexing — why, as Mommy said, they couldn't have a baby of their own; why this child's parents would give him away; how he could bear to kiss Aunt Evalina if she wasn't his real mother. But there was one detail that I understood very well: given the chance to pick their child, Evalina and Joe had chosen a boy. And that, of course, was also what my parents wanted. Our household, which had more children than any of my cousins' families, was the only one without a son.

Thus, being the boy became my next major means of stealing the love I clearly didn't deserve. It worked better and longer than any other stratagem, and, in fact, I realize now, involved many intricacies I was unaware of then. It also had many drawbacks. In the first place, even though Mommy and Father wanted a son, they didn't like real boys. What they wanted was a child who would grow up to be a newspaperman and writer like Father and Grandfather. I didn't think I'd ever actually be able to be a newspaper reporter. But in the short run, what seemed to be prized was a child who liked to be read to. Which I really was. And since Bibba had outgrown being read to and Adelaide wouldn't sit still for it, my chance to be the book-loving heir was uncontested. Out of our differences about this, Father, who didn't seem then to care much what Bibba did, used two more foreign-sounding names for Adelaide and me: "My pagan and my intellectual," he chortled over his Bourbon.

"Intellectual" sounded "acceptable" to me. But in time I knew it also meant sexless, cold, unfeminine, too smart, and unlovable. Just as "pagan" meant that Adelaide was warm, lovable, misbehaving, uncontrollable, and stupid. Still, despite this puzzling "praise-for-something-negative" mix, Father taking time to consider us and assign these labels felt not only valuable in itself, but also irresistible. The fact that our stereotypes resonated with his commendation drove us to be like he said we were regardless of the consequences.

Today I still ask, how much of this is reversible? What are the chances of reclaiming one's life?

chapter four

FAMILY WORTH

From earliest childhood the men I most loved and who were most valued in our family were writers. Father wrote in the library with adamant demands for quiet and privacy. Grandfather wrote at the newspaper with the door wide open to visitors. Both published books that proclaimed their knowledge; both wrote editorials with authoritative phrases that other people loved to read and quote. Speaking out with strong voices that declared the truth as they saw it was as dear to Father and Grandfather as life itself. Even though they sometimes disagreed in doing so and often made the lives of those close to them difficult. Nanny declared that she always had to read the paper before going downtown in order to know who would speak to her and who wouldn't.

Both my ex-husbands are writers as well. Though Tom, my first husband, was a farm boy turned photographer when we married, by the time our second child was born he'd graduated from college Phi Beta Kappa with a degree in English and traded in his camera for a reporter's notebook. Like Grandfather, he wrote stories and editorials that often kept him away from home and family. My second husband, literature professor Rudy, worked on his book about Trollope for months on end in the upstairs library. And he wanted me to write there with him.

It seemed to me in childhood that the most valuable writing came from machines. In the yard on summer afternoons I could hear the clicking of my parents' typewriters through the open library windows. Whenever we went to *The News and Observer* building, there would be several typewriters at once clicking on the second floor, and AP and UP tickertape machines printing out stories that seemed typed by ghosts. The building was on Martin Street then, across from the Palace Theater. To reach its first floor you climbed a steep flight of granite stairs and then entered a revolving door. The newsroom and editorial offices were up yet another flight. That building's whole inside was dark and dank. The bathrooms were literally tiny, foul-smelling closets whose doors had to be held shut. In winter it was cold, in summer hot and airless. The entire place was dirty and rundown and permeated with the flat, lethargic smell of paste and copypaper. Upstairs, where the reporters worked and the public seldom visited, was infinitely dirtier, with a black dust coating everything. One of the most puzzling contradictions of my early years was how this powerful institution, revered not only by the Daniels family but also by the Democratic Party, the State of North Carolina, and everybody anywhere who believed in freedom of speech and the rights of the oppressed, could be housed in such a dilapidated building.

Years later a new building with air conditioning and elevators was built on McDowell Street to house both *The News and Observer* and *The Raleigh Times*, which *The N&O* bought in the 1950's. Then Herbert O'Keefe (who had worked for both newspapers but had become editor of *The Times*) said that in the new building people had to get out of the elevator and jump up and down before they could feel in the right state of mind to work. Part of me still understands that, as the writing machines require a lot of muscle! For a small child, an equally curious feature was the pneumatic tube that literally sucked out of your hand whatever you held up to it. Occasionally I was allowed to send an editorial up the tube to the composing room. I did this cautiously, on guard against being sucked in myself. But more often Adelaide did it, gleefully, held up by some male reporter so she could reach. I envied her for that, too. Not just for being held by the man, but also for not fearing the tube.

Sometimes we followed the copy to the composing room where we could see the type for it being made. Usually, too, the kind man who operated the Linotype machine would stop to make a bar for each of us containing our name. On rare occasions we were taken downtown near midnight to see the newspaper "put to bed." We all did that together — Mommy and Father, as well as Bibba, at twelve, me, four, and Adelaide, two. This was an excuse to stay up very late, but I secretly found it more terrifying than exciting. As an adult, I've watched much larger presses operate behind glass and found the experience nothing in comparison with the roar of those huge rolling monsters churning out the newspapers of my childhood. The clanging thunder of their unstoppable process felt like a train charging down the track to mow us down. Despite also dreading Father's scolding me for my fear, I typically clung to the too-heavy closed door while Adelaide would be held by a grownup. Afterwards I was always proud I'd been there and glad we didn't have to go again soon.

Fear about things like the presses made me ashamed. Father thought my fear was sissy. And besides longing for his approval, I didn't want to end up tongue-tied or screeching foolishly like the ladies in our family. Father was hardy and fearless like the presses. If he was mad or excited, his deep voice resembled the roar of the press. When he laughed, it was never fake, though often it was in response to jokes I felt too dumb to understand. His blue eyes, his firm mouth, the thoughtfulness I could see on his solid face when he read a book — all seemed to embody the power required to make mighty machines run. And I wanted that power for myself.

I could see that the most powerful thing of all was words, which seemed more accessible than machines. Listening to the Oz books and the stories about Babar and Madelaine and Ferdinand the Bull, I vowed to become a master of words. This power seemed especially exemplified by the Babar books, printed as they were in cursive script, which was less decipherable for me than regular printing. To be able to read Babar to myself — with all its vivid illustrations of things like the elephants' butts painted like faces — felt like the achievement most needed to put me on the course I meant to follow. My wish was to become so capable with words that people would not only listen to me, but have to, the way they did with Father and Grandfather.

Yet another complexity for a little girl who longed for both love and power was the example set by Grandfather. He had grown up poor and never tired of telling the stories from his hard, but apparently happy, fatherless childhood. There was a glistening white V-shaped scar on his forehead left from the kick of a mule when he was three, and on a chain across his vest was a gold watch which he regularly invited tiny children to blow open. But Grandfather neither drove a car nor used a typewriter; he wrote his editorials with a thick black pencil. He made you feel he did everything that mattered to him that way — by hand and with rolled-up shirtsleeves. No matter what Grandfather did anywhere in the world, people always knew that what mattered most to him was *The News and Observer*. We grandchildren knew it, too. When we went into his office on the first floor to the right of the revolving door, he'd often tell us to go ask Miss Mamie (the bookkeeper) to give us a dollar. Despite Miss Mamie's protests, I didn't understand until I was grown that he was trying to keep us from bothering him. When we did visit with him there, he'd cut out chains of newspaper paperdolls while talking to us. Yet, as editor of the paper, after having been Secretary of the Navy and Ambassador to Mexico, Grandfather was the most important man I knew. It was enough to make me wonder if not having to use machines wasn't a sign of even greater power.

I knew about the power of words. I'd seen Mommy's words cut down the tree for the hammock and remove servants who were the bedrock of my life. And I'd heard about other forms of power like the tragedy of King Midas and his wish for the golden touch. So, as much as I yearned to have the power of words myself, I did not want that power to actually turn me into a boy (as I knew Mommy wished it to). Long before I understood about her father ("Granddaddy") having died one month before my birth, she showed me repeatedly how much she wanted me to be like him and like Father — by the way she praised some things I said and by taking my hands in hers while telling me that I had the big, slender, creative hands of my father and Granddaddy. I'll never forget the sensation of delight and horror that filled me at such moments.

I was less ambivalent and more terrified when Bibba did a spell to make me invisible. My inability to see the elves she said were in the yard was, I knew, due to fear I'd turn into one and not be able to turn back. Once I was openly resistant when both Bibba and Mommy wanted me to put on a court jester's costume to play a part in some play at Bibba's school. I finally did it, though, and pictures of me in that costume still bring back the relief I felt at that snapshot. It shows me, myself, in their costume, not me changed into a boy.

Writing was, in my parents' eyes, clearly the way to have power and worth. This was not only the logic of our immediate family, but the value system shared by the people who visited our home, as well as by those with whom Father worked at the paper. So, discovering that the three cousins who lived on our same block did not share this belief was a source of early and dismaying surprise to me. Patsy and Frank and Edgar, all older than I was by one to three years, had an entirely different value system, including such reference points as the Duke-Carolina game, Wrightsville Beach, Lake Junaluska, and prominent or wealthy Raleigh families. They hadn't read the Oz books, nor were they impressed when I told them that the tallest man in the world, Thomas Wolfe, had come to our house. In contrast with their parents, my parents mainly knew writers, Jews (an anomalous category in the Raleigh of my childhood and one I couldn't understand), professors and publishers, usually from New York or other distant places. It was upsetting to me (in the sense of both "overturning" and "emptying") that my cousins' values were so different from mine.

I never knew my cousins well, and I believe I felt some additional inferiority because of this. In those early days when our grandfather was still Ambassador to Mexico, "Nanny and Grandfather" was a phrase they used with a familiarity that I lacked. Also, they and Bibba and our Washington, D.C. cousins, Worth and Derick, had all visited Mexico City, whereas I never did. Worth and Derick, the sons of my physician uncle Worth and his physician wife Josie, were mainly Bibba's peers, Worth being slightly older and Derick slightly younger than she. When they visited in Raleigh, they were tall, handsome "big boys," who triggered crushes in little girls. Even then the differences between them were quite evident. Worth was shy, serious, conscientious, and scholarly; Derick was a charmer, playful, mischievous, and driven to explore.

According to our family's custom, my cousin Worth was called "Little Worth" until his father, "Big Worth," died when his son was in his fifties. Since my father did not have a son, he was never called "Big Jonathan," but my mother was "Big Lucy" and I was "Little Lucy" until her death when I was 44. Similarly, my father's youngest brother was "Big Frank" and his son "Little Frank." In family discussions it is still sometimes necessary to designate whether the person spoken of was "Big" or "Little" in our experience.

Edgar Foster was the adopted only child of Evalina and Joe. Rumor had it that our grandmother would not let them name him Josephus because he was adopted. I wouldn't know how to determine whether that was true. But it did leave their family out of the "big-little" custom. For a child, that also made it hard to see any connection between Joe's name and Grandfather's, which was always "Josephus," "Mr. Daniels," or "Grandfather." I both pitied and empathized with Edgar when we were little because he was adopted and because his mother seemed even more obnoxious in praising him as her possession than my mother was with me.

Little Frank and Patsy were the cousins I knew best, perhaps because they lived right down the hill from us, with just a high hedge and gate between our yards. Or perhaps because our fathers both had responsible positions at the paper, Big Frank as the business manager and Father as assistant editor, until he became editor in 1948 at Grandfather's death. I almost never played with Frank, but Patsy was the only friend I had before school.

Maybe she was my "best" friend, but she, not being confined as I was, had many friends. Her parents also let her run with the boys, so she had little need or interest in playing in my yard. When we did get together, there were big differences. She didn't play with dolls but knew how to ride a flexy (a sled on wheels popular at the time) and, with the boys, had even walked in the storm sewer under Glenwood Avenue. Patsy was redheaded and freckled and couldn't pronounce R's. I was always pleased to wear her hand-me-downs. Whether due to the Depression or family factors, best dresses routinely made their way down the line from oldest girl to youngest girl in the family.

Because of that I could covet Patsy's dress or coat and know that, in time, it would be mine.

If I were to draw a picture of Raleigh according to my conception of it before World War II, when there were maybe 100,000 people in Wake County, our Daniels complex would surely be the center. It was surrounded by residential streets reaching to Glenwood Avenue, Five Points shopping center and Whitaker Mill and Fairview Roads to the northeast. These extended to the limits of Wake Forest Road and the railroad tracks to the east and to Oberlin Road, a respectable black residential area on the west. Towards the south there was "downtown" with its department stores, the State Capitol, Olivia Raney Library, movie theaters, the professional building where all doctors had their offices, and the *News and Observer* building, then on Martin Street. To the immediate southeast, via Peace Street, there was another, less prosperous black section, where Bea and Eunice lived. Their house was on Bloodworth Street, a name I found particularly spooky. But if at the intersection where Glenwood Avenue deadended into Hillsborough Street you turned right (instead of left, which led to the State Capitol and downtown), you would soon pass St. Mary's College on the right and less than two blocks after it a house, number 1306, that we frequently visited on Sunday afternoons. Hillsborough Street continued a good distance on from there — past State College (now N. C. State University), on the left, and eventually past Meredith College, on the right, to the N. C. State Fairgrounds.

That house at 1306 Hillsborough was the home of Bibba's grandmother, "Tancie" (Annie Cane Bridgers) and her daughters, Ann and Emily, Bibba's aunts. I always knew that Bibba was somehow special there, but I never understood that the Bridgers were anything more than friends until I was four or five. Until then I believed Bibba was my full sister with the same mother and father as Adelaide and I had. Visiting the Bridgers was a lot of fun, because they seemed to appreciate children and to always eat things like fried chicken and home-made ice cream that we seldom had at home. Tancie was a widowed Christian Science practitioner who had raised her four children primarily on her own. The youngest of these, I learned much later, had been Father's first wife and Bibba's mother,

Elizabeth Bridgers. The next youngest was the only son, Robert. I never really knew him until I was well into adulthood; then I found him shy and a little strange.

The oldest of the four children was Ann, a playwright who had once been successful on Broadway. Emily, next to oldest, was also a writer, but she had not achieved any recognized success. She stood out for me in two ways — crippled by polio, she labored through life with braces and crutches, and she was more sensitive and kind than most people I knew.

Tancie was large, heavy, and outspoken. She was distinguished by her wonderful chocolate cake and belly-shaking laughter. Father was clearly even more favored in that household than Bibba. For years I thought it was because of how much he loved Tancie's chocolate cake. Mommy never wanted to visit the Bridgers, but always seemed liked by them when she was there. In short, being at Tancie, Emily, and Ann's presented yet another indecipherable puzzle for me as a small child — a pleasant, benign, appreciative setting we weren't supposed to like too much or stay in too long.

In the 1930's our family had only one car, which Father usually used to go to work and back. On the day my mother did grocery shopping, Father got a ride with Frank; sometimes, too, she needed the car for other things. But Bea was often the one who took us to the doctor or dentist for small things like typhoid shots. On these days, we went by bus. Adelaide would sit at the back with her, and I had to sit up front alone — a circumstance that required considerable pondering. Bea couldn't adequately answer my questions about why being black required her to sit in the back. She pointed to the signs that required this, and I recognized the word "colored." But I still didn't understand. And along with my sadness for Bea about that, there was a sense of despair about myself, that being neither colored nor little I had to sit alone.

In the early years of my childhood (1934-1941), our Daniels grandparents spent most of their time at the embassy in Mexico City. Whenever they visited Raleigh, for Christmas or due to a death in the family or for whatever reason, there were festivities and family gatherings in the big dark stone house next door to ours.

The smell of Mexico (a rich blend of exotic wood and textiles) is strong in all my childhood memories of their house which was called "Wakestone." The gifts they brought back were mostly silver for the adults, sequined skirts and beaded blouses for us girls and serapes and sombreros for the boys. I longed to have a serape and did not understand the "unspecialness" that required me to accept a skirt and blouse.

Other people lived in Wakestone when Nanny and Grandfather were away. Edgar and his parents did, as well as Nanny's maiden sisters and brother, Belle and Ethel and Henry. Perhaps this contributed to the house seeming austere, foreign, even a little frightening. And since Patsy, Frank, and Edgar all knew Nanny and Grandfather and the black people who took care of the house for them better than we did, I felt a strong sense of "outsiderness" during the family gatherings. Being named for my mother, who did not get along well with Nanny, didn't help. But what I remember most is that there, above all, my crossed eyes were noticed and remarked on by Frank and Edgar. There, too, I first learned that boys were more highly valued than girls. Whatever importance I had in my parents' house — as nurse of younger sisters or lover of books — went down the drain at Wakestone. Adelaide was the most valuable girl there because she was the littlest and was named for Nanny. This reinforced the troubled question of my short life: could I be worth something without being a boy?

chapter five

FIRST RITES

That fateful afternoon in my fourth summer was so hot and so long that nothing worked. Some afternoons Hansel would let me pass the time by dressing him in doll clothes. Sometimes he even let me wheel him around in the doll carriage. But that day he wouldn't budge from his spot under the fir tree. Curled close to its trunk, he growled softly without opening his eyes whenever I tried to do anything more than pet him. I went to the crack in the wall and squinted through it. But the yard across the street looked tired in the sun, and there were no ants to be seen. Time stood still. For a while I used my doll as a pillow to rest my head on in the cooler place under the crepe myrtle, to keep my blond hair safe from any dirt that would make Mommy mad. I could hear the other children playing. In spite of Mommy's saying they were "running wild," it sounded like fun.

Then the gate slammed and Bibba appeared from nowhere, riding across the lawn single-handed on her bicycle, balancing a Royal Crown Cola. As usual, we were both eager — me to hear Bibba to tell the latest news. Like when she'd sneaked into Grandfather's house to see the corpse of Uncle Henry laid out to be buried, or when Bea's brother had been sent to prison for breaking and entering. Always stories Mommy must never hear. The day before it had been Billy Thompkins killing a copperhead in the storm sewer where Bibba and her friends played.

But this afternoon, giving me a swallow from her cola bottle, she asked a question instead: "Have you noticed how fat Mommy's getting?"

I nodded.

"That's because she's going to have another baby."

I told her I knew; Mommy had already told me.

Then, wiping the wet from the cola bottle across her forehead and back over her hair, pressing its coolness in turn against each of her cheeks, Bibba looked at me hard, the way she always did when she had something shocking to say. "You know, Mommy isn't my real mother; that's why she's always mad at me. My real mother died having a baby. Father put a baby inside her and it grew and made her fat like what's happening to Mommy. She died from it coming out."

I could hardly hear. Bibba was shouting at me through a wall of clouds, from so many miles away that it was hard to listen. I didn't want to believe — that Bibba's mother was dead, that we weren't really sisters, that a woman could die because of a baby inside her, that I could die if a baby got inside me.

Straining to feel grounded by what I knew and could think about, I remembered Mommy sitting on my bed after prayers and saying in her manners voice, "Lucy, when a man and a woman love each other very much, they may have a baby. It grows inside the mother until it's big enough to come out." I didn't like that either, but it was better than Bibba's story. Still, I needed to know how the baby got in, and I asked Bibba.

"The father puts it there, dummy."

"How?"

"With his penis."

Oh, no!! My mind erased the words. "Do you remember your mother?" I asked.

"Of course. . . She was beautiful. She had short curling brown hair and brown eyes. She used to read to me, and she wore silk dresses. One of them was blue with lace."

"What was her name?"

"Babs. . . Well, really Elizabeth, like me. But they called her Babs. When she died, they changed my name to hers. That's why I'm called Elizabeth now when I used to be Adelaide."

"Adelaide?!. . . But that's Adelaide's name!" I squinted in an effort to understand. I also recalled having heard "Babs" spoken by a variety of people without my knowing who that was. I had the feeling then that I got when I was at the end of the line the time Bibba's friends had let me play Crack the Whip: lost because of the sense being knocked out of me; lost even though still holding on.

"Now it's her name. Because she was born after you, and my name was changed before Father married Mommy."

I just couldn't believe it. Still, other things came together. I told Bibba about the silver cup I'd drunk ginger ale from some time before. It had "Adelaide" engraved on it, but the wrong middle name and the wrong year, 1926. I could spell Adelaide's middle name, W-O-R-T-H, and she'd been born later than me, after 1934.

"Yeah. That's my baby cup," Bibba said. "Adelaide uses it. There's another one, too, with 'Elizabeth Ann Bridgers's on it. My mother's name. Father told me it was hers when she was a little girl. It'll be mine when I grow up."

"I haven't seen it."

"It's in the sideboard. They only use it when they need an extra."

Bibba broke a blossom off the gardenia bush and stuck her nose deep into its creamy petals. That always disgusted me. The smell of those flowers and the way they turned brown when touched reminded me of dying. Like the baby cup of a dead lady. Bibba got back on her bicycle and rode off with the empty cola bottle. I squinted at the dusty pear tree.

I was still mulling all this over when Bea called me in for my bath. In the tub when I let myself urinate and watch the yellow fade into the bath water, I thought about Father putting his penis inside Mommy, like inside Bibba's mother. I thought about how gleeful he was when peeing with the lavatory door open and how he sometimes called that "going to see a man about a dog."

By the time I was drying off and could see myself in the bathroom mirror, another horrible thought had come to me: could Father be a murderer who had fun killing women by peeing inside them to make them break open? Then a sick feeling born of the mirror's wet image re-evoked a suspicion I'd had and suppressed a few times before. Could it be that Father didn't really love Mommy? He did need her — to take care of him, to type and run the house. But what if he didn't really love her? And could it have been that way with Babs, too? After drying the mirror, I practiced looking hard into it, eye-to-eye the way Bibba did. "You should be ashamed of yourself!" I declared like Mommy. But that wasn't how I wanted to be. What I wanted to know was "by accident or on purpose?"

Getting dressed, I put the sunsuit Bea had laid out for me back in the drawer and took my dotted-Swiss pinafore out of the closet instead. Buckling my sandals, I thought about needing to talk to Father alone. Babs was somebody Mommy couldn't stand to hear about. She must be even more jealous of her than of Bibba and Bea. If she knew Bibba had told me about her, Bibba would really be a goner. It occurred to me then that I'd never seen a picture of Babs even though there were pictures of other dead people all about — Granddaddy, Jonathan Worth, Mommy's grandmother. I wondered if a certain photograph I'd seen on the wall at the Bridgers's was Babs.

The library echoed with the clinking of ice cubes in their glasses of Bourbon. I pondered its familiar pungency while anxiously waiting through the interminable grownup talk for the chance to say what I had to say. Though afraid, I was also determined. My worry about saying the wrong thing was even worse with Father because of how easy it was to make him mad. I half expected my question to do that. But also with this news about Bibba and me having different mothers and Bibba's mother dying because of a baby, I had to know.

What I felt I had to know on that awesome evening is impossible to separate out now from the questions and conflicts that I, as a psychologist, know children struggle with even in less traumatic situations. Certainly I wanted many more answers than I had the words to ask for or even the emotional capacity to bear. My very life and its cast of loved ones was at stake. Besides the unfathomable life-and-death issues of babies getting in and coming out, besides the slashed sisterhood of Bibba and me, the nature of love itself was on the line. Despite his sporadic cruelty, I loved Father more than anybody except Bibba. Sitting there, I nervously rubbed the bumps on my pinafore while moving from these to wondering again whether being grown up made Bourbon taste different. In those days I often did that — tried to decipher whether grown-ups really enjoyed things that I found repulsive like Bourbon, cigarettes, and making babies. Or just pretended to.

When Father poured himself more Bourbon, I believed he liked it. When Mommy left the room to help Adelaide change her wet pants, I made myself walk over close to his chair. Then, standing straight, straining to look at him eye-to-eye, I said directly with incredible concentration and power I hadn't known I had: "Did you love Babs?"

He seemed startled, confused, as if I'd said something that didn't make sense. But he didn't yell at me. He looked different from any way I'd ever seen him. Quiet and far away, blue eyes clouding over like marbles, he said sadly, "Yes, I loved Babs, very much."

The dining room was full of eyes. They watched everyone, but I was the person most afraid of being seen. My place at the table was the only one on the side nearest the front hall. I sat in one of the velvet-covered antique chairs that Mommy treasured. A "side" chair, Mommy called it, because it didn't have wooden arms like the ones she and Father used at the ends of the table; my mind called it "plain" for the same reason. Adelaide and Bibba faced me from the other side, also in plain chairs. Adelaide's chair, beside Father's, had volumes of *Who's Who* piled up in it covered with oil cloth to help her reach and not make a mess. Bibba, next to Mommy, sometimes rolled her eyes and made secret faces at me. Bibba was twelve and not afraid; her back was to the mirror over the sideboard. Because of the eyes, I usually pretended not to notice her faces.

On that particular July evening the dining room more eerily than ever resembled the Episcopal church where Mommy took me on Sundays. The evening air was heavy, still, ominous. In spite of the daylight outside, the room itself was dim, because the black-green shutters were closed against the heat and only the chandelier over the table was lit; not the wall sconces, as in winter. This dimness and the smells of cut grass and sickening-sweet gardenia drifting in through the screens created a shimmering mist, which, like the candles at church, infused holy power into things that were ordinary by the light of day. Only here, the power was more threatening than holy, because of the struggle between Mommy's propriety and Father's merry licentiousness. Also because of my need to please them both.

I was afraid to break Mommy's rules:

> Sit up straight.
> Do not speak with food in your mouth.
> Use your napkin.
> Do not use your fingers.

Above all, "Eat, without complaint, whatever is set before you." So I always obeyed. Mommy was very pretty that night. It made me think about how grown-ups called her "beautiful." But also about how horrifying she was when she got mad. Early on, her lovely dimple would turn into a pulsating tic. Then, even before she spoke, a killing look would come into her eyes which seemed like powerful X-ray machines capable of seeing all of a child's thoughts and feelings. Those eyes could make me melt and trickle away to nothing.

But because I couldn't control him by looking good, I was still more afraid of Father. He had never seemed sad before that night. His dancing eyes had touched me a few times in a way that tingled and made my heart beat fast. But always just briefly, because his life was full of people. And his words kept me wary — because they could be kind, but also, suddenly angry. Father had held me only a few times (when I broke my collarbone falling from the hammock; when the car got stuck in the snow; once, terrified and against my will, in the high waves at the beach). But memories of those times always crowded terror with wistfulness when I watched him play with Adelaide.

In the dining room Father's excesses showed in many small ways such as when he helped himself to too much sauce or made fun of the flowered dresses and perfume Mrs. Thompkins wore as president of the Women's Club. Mommy often scolded him about those misbehavings. But when he poked fun — at Bibba for eating too much when she was already fat or at me for being fearful and unadventurous — Mommy didn't intervene. And when he reeled off limericks, whose combination of rhyme and outrageous content was mystifying, Mommy smiled approvingly. He usually recited his favorite about a lady and a tiger with a grin or laughing. I always felt dumb then because I couldn't get the joke. Dumb and afraid because the limerick evoked my feelings about Father eating up little girls:

There was a young lady from Niger
Who smiled as she rode on a tiger
They came back from the ride
With the lady inside
And the smile on the face of the tiger.

Father's spirited displays usually built up during supper, to climax afterward in a romp with Adelaide. He would throw her into the air, then catch her. She would giggle and cry. Sometimes he played the game of roasting her, like a "little pig, with an apple in your mouth!" But usually it was the game where he held her tight and pressed his fist against her squirming belly, shouting exuberantly, "Bore a hole in you! I'm going to bore a hole in you!" Adelaide giggled, struggled, screamed like she was having fun and was scared to death all at the same time. I lurked in a corner or close to some big furniture so he wouldn't see me and want me to play too.

This particular supper time, when I looked at Bibba, her eyes looking back were expressionless beneath her disheveled hair. She pulled out a barrette and put it back more securely. She took long noisy swallows of ice water. But she did not smile or make a face. Only the emptiness of her eyes conveyed that afternoon's terrible secret between us.

Seen from across the table, Bibba always looked very different from the Bibba in the yard. In the yard she was bold and in charge, bursting with the latest story she'd come to share with me, her only confidante, bigger than the grown-up world which she surveyed and reduced to a story. Whereas in the dining room, except for making faces or jiggling her knife blade to reflect a seditious light code on the ceiling, Bibba looked lumpish, grim, defeated. This night I detected the barely perceptible drumming of her fingernails on the underside of the table.

Mommy rang the tinkling silver dinner bell and told Bea to bring the meat. Lulled by Bibba's drumming and by the mingled fragrances of camphor from the silver drawers and gardenias in the silver bowl on the sideboard, I studied the room's reflection in that bowl. It bunched us all up and blobbed our bodies into one, like the funhouse mirror Bibba had told me about. We were not only reduced to silver-bowl miniatures, but distorted like Mommy. My silver water tumbler didn't give a reflection because it was cold and beaded with frost. I knew that I could draw an unfrosted picture on it with my finger, a picture that would run into little rivers before it disappeared.

"No meat for me," Adelaide chimed as Bea set the sizzling roast before Father.

I drew a house on my tumbler quickly, before Mommy could see.

"Just a little, dear," Mommy said to Adelaide.

"No," Adelaide scowled, puckered mouth and fat cheeks braced stubbornly over her napkin.

As Father took up the long silver carving knife and the silver-handled sharpening steel, I watched curiously, but with my usual careful distance.

Seeing him with the roast, his words, "I loved her very much," echoed through my thoughts. The bottom had fallen out of me when I first heard them. There at the table they still triggered an aching longing. And I had the feeling of not understanding either them or their sadness. If you love somebody very much, how can you do what makes them die? In speaking of Babs, Father's voice had quavered with love never reflected when he spoke of Mommy. Maybe the difference wasn't so much in Father as between Mommy and Babs. For the first time I had heard love for a woman in his voice. And I had seen it in his eyes. Maybe he just couldn't love Mommy. Like Bibba said, hateful as she was, how could anyone? As Father sharpened the carving knife, I noticed that his eyes were neither sad nor distant. They focused on the knife and the steel, and his big hands firmly gripped the two and confidently brought them together.

"What kind of meat is it?" I asked. An irrelevant question in light of the sacred rule that everything served must be eaten. But I, dutiful even with revolting things like shad roe, liver, and collard greens, liked to be prepared.

"Lamb," Mommy answered.

"None for me," Adelaide chimed again. The knife blade clanged against the steel.

"Don't be silly," Mommy said. "Adelaide, you know you love lamb. . . You love baby lambs."

"No!"

Bibba was sucking ice and scowling. Mommy glared at her, then at Adelaide. Her dimple jutted in and out. Forcing myself to look directly, I scrutinized her body. And it became instantly, horribly clear that despite the unchanged delicacy of her face and arms, her torso was disproportionately bulky. A sick smothering feeling crowded my mouth and nose. I returned urgently to the house on my water tumbler. But it had bled away.

"You have to be adventurous," Father said to Adelaide. "Live life to the hilt!" Handing me a plate with meat on it and waving the steel for emphasis, he again declared, "Live life to the hilt!" He laughed and winked at Mommy, and she smiled back full of adoration and self-sacrifice. The disproportion between her face and her body had become more glaring.

I liked lamb — especially because of mint jelly — but I held my hands tight together in my lap to keep them from touching a fork before Mommy raised hers. When Father sat down from carving, Bea and Eunice passed the vegetables. They came to my place first, their black dresses smelling of starch, their strong brown hands looking capable and kind, as they offered silver dishes of corn and butterbeans. They, too, were markedly different in the dining room, walking examples of what was meant when they said, "Don't tell yo' mama." In the kitchen they laughed loud and full, showing all their teeth, including the gaps and the gold. Their talk was noisy and earthy; they good-naturedly slapped and shoved each other. Whereas here they were silent, their faces as solemn and still as if carved from stone. I'd religiously obeyed their admonitions about not telling Mommy, due to fearing she would fire them. But to me, even there, Bea and Eunice had the look of endurance, like the water-blackened wood supporting the pier at the ocean.

As the food was passed, I stole another look at Mommy. Her dimple had grown still. The misshapen pink print dress she was wearing I could remember seeing her put on once. Its skirt had a hole cut out in the front; it made me think of the wisteria vine that had grown so thick and tough it had broken through the slats in the shutter for the living room window. A shiver ran through me, and I felt sweaty. In contrast to Bibba's, Mommy's skin was smooth and white: no pimples, just a soft glow on her cheeks where she put the rouge. It was easy to see why Father called her "Beautiful." Still, there was a hardness that had to do with the way she kept order. And no telling when the dimple might start firing. Pretty black hair set in beauty parlor finger waves . . . suddenly alive and menacing. A horrible reminder of how she looked undressed. Black, curly, bristling. Grotesque bosoms falling over bulging belly.

By then my silver tumbler was totally defrosted. Adelaide was dropping pieces of meat into her glass of milk. Bea's black dress and brown arms had disappeared into the kitchen. Father was eating heartily, napkin tied under his chin, and I decided he'd forgotten my Babs question. Nodding at Bibba's empty plate, he laughed and said, "Garbagia, I can see you're champing at the bit. You can win as either biggest or fastest eater."

"Eat your supper, Adelaide," Mommy continued. "At least two bites of everything if you want dessert."

Adelaide didn't answer. She stared blankly back at Mommy while stirring the mess of vegetables around her plate.

"Adelaide couldn't win any prize," Father declared. "Unless for slowness."

I was glad my plate was empty. Although obedient to Mommy's rule, because of how I loved him, Father's stinging ridicule was what I dreaded most: "Casper Milquetoast!" was his scornful epithet for me. "Sniveling sissies don't go far, Lucy!" So my plate was clean.

Wiping his face and hands with the napkin pulled from around his neck, Father stood up to carve some more. "Live life to the hilt!" he exulted. "To the hilt, Lucy!" The knife blade clanged as it hit the steel. Light glinted on it — glinted, danced, leaped off to strike again. The whole room shimmered with a golden haze.

Insulated by a trancelike stillness, I watched with surprise as the lamb seemed to rise to its feet, fluffy and white. At first it lingered at the edge of the table, pawing playfully. The steel continued to strike the blade, over and over like a summoning bell. Prancing, the woolly creature began to run in circles, bleating excitedly, dancing in time. It leapt and spun, captivated by the jingling bells which were at first punctuated by, then gradually gave way to the deeper compelling tones of a sheep bell. With that, its last reluctance was lost and, reassured by the tolling reminder of security, the lamb gave itself to wider, more intricate orbits. Those brought it sometimes closer to the sheep bell, sometimes farther away, with increasing fervor. But then, abruptly, the dance ran out of control, the lamb's steps flying so fast they were only a blur. The bell became ominous, its rhythm no longer related to the pace of the lamb's dance. Rather, the two continued simultaneously but separately — close to each other, sometimes briefly coinciding — but unrelated. Until, suddenly, there was a splash of red in the whirling, bleating blur of lamb.

Or was it Adelaide? Shudders of excitement and horror gripped me. Sweat beaded my palms and upper lip while the rest of me went cold. I found myself completely abandoned to this dimly-lit illusion of silver-reflected mayhem. The swords clattered. The lamb's bleat, now a scream, became more desperate as the blur slowed. The red splashed wider, soaking into the nubby wool; however, no longer just blood, but the very entrails of the lamb were jaggedly spewed out by the knives. Motionless silence followed, with the wool barely visible because it was soaked in blood.

Tinkling the dinner bell, Mommy said, "Bea, we're ready for dessert."

Reflections of butchered lamb and bloodied swords gleamed back at me from my water tumbler. They made me think of dead babies and mothers broken open by the babies' struggle to get out. But the others didn't know. Adelaide was still playing with her food. Bibba glowered at her empty plate. Mommy presided, swollen and beaming, in her armchair at the head of the table. And they all gazed admiringly at Father, who still exulted, "Live life to the hilt!"

"Not me," I resolved in silence. "You all can do it. But not me." I felt safe with that vow. But also guilty. I could not forget the sadness in his voice.

In one sense, you could say that I knew even then what a devastating set of occurrences that day had brought down. My body knew it in the dead ache of waiting in my chair for supper to end. That day's revelations had been far more terrifying than my earlier questions about dates on baby cups. Besides the unspeakable horror of babies killing mothers as they tried to get out, I understood clearly and with grim aloneness why Bibba would be sent away. Also, that while Father didn't love Mommy, there had been another woman whom he still loved very much.

Sometimes after that, I had the feeling that Babs was in the yard with me. She floated at about the level of the second-story bedroom windows, in blue silk with white lace. She never spoke. An intense sadness would well up in me at the sight of her, because, as I understood it, she could see all we did and hear all we said to each other, but could not speak and was invisible to everyone but me. She bore a strong resemblance to a stone statue in Nanny's and Grandfather's lower yard — a sad-faced lady in flowing robes. Neither Bea nor Bibba knew the name of the statue, but with her broken-off arms, she reminded me of the hand-sized Venus de Milo Father had in the library. I'd noticed the same sad light in his eyes holding that broken Venus as when I'd spoken to him about Babs.

When I saw Babs in the yard, she seemed to be weeping as she watched the people she loved go on about their lives ignoring her. Sometimes, too, I had a haunting, barely conscious question about her death. Had Bibba told me the truth or had she simply repeated a lie that had been told to her? Had Babs died in childbirth or had Mommy killed her so she could have Father? I pushed these questions out of my thoughts as "crazy." But every so often, even years later, they'd pop up again.

Something else happened in the months that followed those conversations with Father and Bibba: I became afraid to talk on the telephone. Not that I did a lot of telephoning at age four, but speaking to my grandmother in New Jersey and giving the operator Patsy's number, 4715, or Father's at *The News and Observer*, 4411, had been grown-upness I enjoyed. This fear made it necessary for Mommy to speak for me. And the two together—terror of the catastrophic power of my own voice and dependence on Mommy to contain it—would have far-reaching consequences in my life. Positive and negative.

From Father's response to my question, I came to live according to several overwhelming conclusions at once: although Father didn't love Mommy, he had loved another woman and still did even though his love had killed her. That meant that he could love me, too, and that I could hope to be a woman who wasn't like Mommy. Terror associated with such thoughts led to my oath at the supper table to not live life to the hilt. Yet our family's destructive secrecy seemingly spared my younger sisters. Adelaide and Mary Cleves did not learn about the circumstances of Babs's death until I told them as adults, when it was just one more mundane bit of information. Adelaide said then that she'd been nearly grown before she figured out that Mommy wasn't Bibba's mother.

chapter six

LEAVING HOME

Father would have said that he and Mommy were "Bohemian," and this was, I think, the ideal they shared, even though, like most things, it had different meanings for each. For Father, "Bohemian" was being a gypsy, untamed and unconfined by location, affection, duty or convention; for Mommy, it meant artistic and precious. Together, they warmed to the glory of feeling exotic and wondrously gifted, above conventional standards of behavior. They scorned and eschewed any people or conditions they labeled "common." Those included affluent people who flaunted their wealth (by joining the Carolina Country Club for example), women who wore too much make-up or dressed flamboyantly, and children who lacked manners. I believe now that this Bohemian ideal had been spawned in the rigid circumstances that defined both their childhood homes. Each grew up the favorite child of very successful teetotaling fathers, who were worshipped by and absent for their wives. Rebellions against these controlling, righteous, and/or perfectionistic parents were the bedrock of our household. Both my parents drank too much. But Father extolled the virtues of "living dangerously" by smoking, drinking, and never shying away from risks, while Mommy demanded order, cleanliness, and obedience beyond the capacity of most children. My father's father's plain, Methodist, teetotaling, thoughtful, unhostile righteousness as President Wilson's Secretary of the Navy, Roosevelt's Ambassador to Mexico, and editor of *The News and Observer* formed a shadow which Father struggled to escape by being its opposite. His first book and only novel, *Clash of Angels*, was the story of Lucifer, a redheaded rebel in heaven, who made war with his father, Jehovah. In life's practice, Father was driven to drink and smoke heavily, and he took pride in expressing anger cruelly and in not appearing cautious or diligent.

I've never really known how people outside our family responded to my parents' ways. In the extended family on the hill where we all lived, they clearly set us apart, as did Father's editorials that kept people talking. In the immediate family (which it's hard for me not to see now with psychologist eyes), the cast of staying at odds was established long before my and my sisters' births. And living with the millions acquired through selling my newspaper shares decades later has shown me that my dread of "wealthy" has not been that different from my parents' dread of "common."

Though my life has comprised many leavings — some extremely painful, some literally devastating, a few resulting in benefit — one of the most consciously cataclysmic was in January 1942 when the U.S. entry into World War II moved our immediate family to Washington, D.C. This was an abrupt departure from the powerful entity of the Daniels family, a departure so extreme that both the world as I knew it and my self as I knew me were utterly changed. The losses were sweeping. There could be no going back.

With World War II there was no time to prepare. Not just because of the Japanese attack on Pearl Harbor. Rather, because that attack was only the last of several monumental changes that sickeningly made it seem that life as I knew it was slipping away like sand between my fingers.

The first of these changes had been largely positive. Mary Cleves (named for Grandfather's mother) was born in February 1939, one month before my fifth birthday. And Mommy did not die as I'd feared ever since learning about Babs. When they came home from the hospital, a nurse came with them, and both the nurse and the baby stayed in the guest room, bothering Mommy in her bedroom as little as possible. The baby was big with rosy cheeks and a head full of black curls. Adelaide wanted to poke her blue eyes and pinch her if the nurse wasn't looking. But besides feeling relieved that this new baby was a girl and, therefore, no competition for my position as boy substitute, I also discovered a whole new identity as Mary Cleves's good mother. I soon came to treasure her as a living doll who enhanced my value by secretly becoming my own — Father's real live baby that I could feed and hold and be loved by because nobody else wanted to do the work a baby required. And Mommy and Father so appreciated my helping that they openly acted as if Mary Cleves was my baby, making me more important than ever before and a glowing contrast with naughty Adelaide.

The one drawback in this changed status was guilt because I associated it with Bibba's being forced out of the family. This came to a head in March when Mommy and Father talked to her about boarding school. I wasn't there, but a furious Bibba described the scene to me the next afternoon: "'Your mother and I have been thinking about how to best help you prepare for college,'" she mimicked Father. "Your mother and I!" she snarled to me. "Not my mother! Your mother! And your prep school!"

I gaped in horror. Dead mothers swam before me. Bibba would be put on the train and would never come back.

"I didn't say that, though," Bibba went on. "When he said they'd found a school they liked in Charleston, I said 'What do you like about it?' Even though I don't care! What difference does it make? I'll have to go anyway!"

Her words stunned me. I saw open coffins then — Uncle Henry's with his fat red face gone white and saggy, Babs's with the lovely lace at the throat of her blue dress, Bibba's with a yellowing gardenia against her messy hair.

But she raged on confidently. "He even said, 'I know your mother would want this for you.' Damn! Goddamn! You know why I'll go, don't you, Lucy?! I'll go so Mommy can get me out of her hair! But you know what?! I'm glad! And I'll go in style, with no objection! I wouldn't give her the satisfaction of thinking she hurt me. Besides, I probably will be better off. Either Mommy or I is bound to go crazy here. And I'm afraid it might be me if I stay."

Besides Mary Cleves's birth and Bibba's being sent to boarding school, other events that seemed to set the stage for World War II and to end the life of our early childhood included Nanny and Grandfather returning from Mexico to live permanently at Wakestone, and the celebration of their fiftieth wedding anniversary there.

Vague memories of little-girl times in Grandfather's lap made me hopeful of being special to him again, a prospect that seemed enhanced by my status as Mary Cleves's mother. But after the big Golden Wedding party when Adelaide turned out to be his obvious favorite, I asked Mommy, "Grandfather loves Adelaide best, doesn't he?" And she explained matter-of-factly, "I suppose so. She is the knee baby and named for Nanny."

"Yeah," Bibba added when I reported this to her. "Besides Nanny's old and near dying."

"She is?"

"Sure. When we go there for dinner, can't you see how thin her skin looks and how tired she seems? Why do you think she has the elevator and the wheelchair? That's how people get when they're close to dying."

None of that had reduced the smart of seeing Adelaide in Grandfather's arms. But it did keep me silent and guilt-ridden. It also increased my investment in Mary Cleves.

Disconcertingly, these changes made Mommy's house seem less separate from the rest of the world at a time when the world itself had become more threatening. Across the ocean Hitler was killing innocent people and screaming unintelligibly over the radio. His Nazis invaded Poland and Belgium while an Englishman named Churchill tried to scare them back. Our newspaper had more world and national news than ever before. At family gatherings conversations included such new words as "Hitler," "Nazis," "defense," "draft." Even supper at Mommy's table could be interrupted by urgent calls from the newsroom, where no interruptions whatsoever had been allowed previously.

So, for me at age seven, the abrupt decision for our family to move to Washington felt like a repeat of these other changes, especially the devastating loss of Bibba's company after she left for boarding school.

The frenzy of activity following the Japanese attack on Pearl Harbor galvanized previous worries and threats into the formidable reality of "WAR!" The adults, having lived through war before, seemed knowledgeable about the steps leading from "trouble" to "war" to "World War," and I eavesdropped in pursuit of clues. Pearl Harbor had made "the Germans" and Bea's and Eunice's conversations about "some people are gonna have to fight 'em and even get kilt doin' it" seem more immediate. Also, Bibba's absence and Mary Cleves sitting in her place at the table provided evidence that even though Mommy's house itself had power and permanence, the people in it did not. For months Father had been insisting on quiet at drink time so that he could hear the news on the radio. Static-crackled voices from across the ocean related the "fall" of countries or big cities "before Nazi terror." I wasn't clear about the difference between Nazis and Germans, but I decided that Nazi was just another name for Germans which incorporated their cruelty. When Hitler's voice came over the radio, unintelligible in its language but terrifyingly clear in its frenzied tones of maniacal murder, it reminded me sickeningly of Mommy's dimple. By contrast, President Roosevelt's voice sounded good and brave, but a poor match!

Within days of Pearl Harbor, it was decided that we would move to Washington, D.C. so that Father could help the President with Civilian Defense. Mommy went to Washington to find a house to live in "for the duration" (which sounded like "forever"). Incredibly, Mommy's house in Raleigh was dismantled for use by another family! But there was an even worse blow when near the end of packing, Eunice and Bea announced that they would not be going with us. Eunice said she was too old to leave home; Bea had found out about war factory jobs that paid a lot more than Mommy did. Mommy was furious at first, then tearfully desperate, with repeated sighs of, "What have I done to deserve this?!"

It was then, amongst the chaos of partially packed boxes, with Hansel curled uneasily beside one box in the process of being sealed, that I first glimpsed ending rather than just interruption. The loss of Bea would be worse than the loss of Bibba in several ways. Since Bea couldn't read and write, she wouldn't be able to write me letters, and there wasn't the faintest suggestion we'd ever see her again. Which fit with another black hole in my mind: if the "Japs" and "Nazis" won the war, none of us might come back. They might even bomb Mommy's house!

Only years later, long after "the duration" had faded into the past, would I realize what an important example Bea's ability to leave had been for me. Working for Mommy, taking care of Adelaide and Mary Cleves and me, had been just a job to her, a job she could leave for better pay or better conditions. But our actual departure was so grim that I can only recall smatterings of it now. Father took us all to the train station. After we left, he, with Hansel curled up on the backseat, would drive our car on to Washington. The rest of us couldn't ride with them because of too little space and gasoline rationing.

We'd been to the train station many times before. Always, however, to meet somebody or tell them good-bye, or to travel to New York ourselves, knowing that in a few days we'd return. But, that day had the sick, incredible sense of finality. The last thing I remember is looking out at the station from inside the Pullman. Bea and Eunice were standing there in their winter coats waving to us as the train pulled away. I held tight to Mary Cleves.

3404 Garfield Street in Washington was a square, three-story, yellow stucco house with an eighteen-square-foot patch of lawn between it and the sidewalk. It stood in the middle of the south side of the block just west of 34th Street, its color the only feature distinguishing it from its neighbors. Facing those houses on the north side of the street were the tennis courts for St. Albans School for Boys, behind which — way off in the distance — could be seen the skeleton of the National Cathedral in its eternal state of "unfinishedness." Behind these houses was a network of alleys, which, because there was no gasoline for private cars during World War II, became a gathering place for older children. These alleys, though dirty and somewhat grim, also served as shortcuts and were traveled in summer by the Good Humor man in his cart with its bell and supply of popsicles.

Six blocks north and uphill on 34th Street was John Eaton School, the brick elementary school we attended. Several blocks west and also uphill, Garfield Street dead-ended into Wisconsin Avenue, with its heavy traffic and array of shops. South a few blocks from our corner, 34th Street intersected Massachusetts Avenue, the main thoroughfare to downtown.

Clearly our Washington world was larger and, at times, overwhelmingly larger than Raleigh. And despite the hardships of wartime, there were many advantages. Without either an enclosed yard or an operable car, there was the need to walk many places and, thus, the opportunity to develop autonomy never available to me before. Father's work made him both more important and, in the little time he had at home, more available to children. For the first year of our time there he was director of Civilian Defense. Then he became administrative assistant and later press secretary to President Roosevelt.

Mommy's life in Washington was not only more confined, but arduous. She welcomed our distance from Raleigh, but the demands of wartime, with rationing and without servants, exacerbated her tendency to feel mistreated. In her eyes, both the Garfield Street house and all our neighbors were "common."

In contrast with this, I, and I believe, Adelaide and Mary Cleves, felt more at home in that house than we did in Raleigh. It had three low-ceilinged stories and a basement. On the top floor, where Bibba stayed when she was home, there was a bedroom and bath and an extra-small kitchen which didn't really work. The first floor consisted of living room, dining room, enclosed sunporch, and kitchen. The second floor had three bedrooms, a sleeping porch the entire width of the house, and two baths. The basement, which was only partially finished, we equipped with a small ice box, kerosene stove, and black curtains to serve as our shelter in blackouts or air raids. The whole place was a little rundown, as many houses seemed during the war. Our grey Ford remained undriven in its separate garage throughout the war.

I was relieved to have a room of my own, while Adelaide and Mary Cleves shared the sleeping porch. That long porch had two doors which opened directly into the two bedrooms which were mine and Mommy's and Father's, but the door into my room was kept locked. The children's bathroom was off the hall just outside my room; the parents' was between their bedroom and the large front combination bedroom-sitting room, which we only used for company.

For months after we moved I was miserable. Bibba, at boarding school in Charleston, felt even further away. Her absence and the departure of Bea and Eunice had provided my first awareness of exile and choice. Mommy's terrifying rage and hand-wringing despair simultaneously portrayed what I did not want to become and forced me to be the helper who could soothe her. Though I was terribly lonely, even those children I met in second and third grade felt fenced off by my shyness. Furthermore, without Bea, and in our closer quarters, Adelaide was freer to destroy my dolls and books, and Father's labeling my distress about this as "selfish" and "cry-baby" made me feel both robbed of protection and bad for wanting it. Because showing anger was unacceptable, some of my angry feelings took the form of bedtime distress about how I would manage if Mommy and Father died.

A few years ago I found my third grade mid-year report card; in it Mrs. Stutzman said that I was doing well academically but seemed very angry. Mommy simply wrote back, "I've talked to Lucy about her anger, and I'm sure she will take care of it." In that same period, while being a model child and caretaker of younger sisters at home, I would sometimes lure other small children in our neighborhood out of their yards, then hit them with a switch. The day I almost got caught still stands out as a moment of horror in which the hair on my neck stood up and my hands and legs ached from straining not to shake. I forced myself to look straight back at Mommy as she told me about the call from a neighbor, Mrs. Monroe.

"But I told her she was accusing the wrong person," Mommy said, "that you are a responsible, well-behaved child who would never do such a thing."

Listening, my body automatically braced to fend off her chilling words. Within that shell, everything went cool and still while I grew safely small. But Mommy's words wouldn't let the aloneness hold. I soon felt ravaged instead of small, ridiculously stripped naked and helpless. Like all the other times when her praise refused to see me and, holding me hostage, turned Adelaide and Bibba and others against me. Mommy had told Mrs. Monroe what she believed to be the truth. But I feared she'd have said the same thing even if she'd seen me waving the switch. Just like Father burning my bare bottom when I'd done nothing wrong and yelling, "Goddamn snivelling sissy! . . . If you didn't do it, you should've!" Horrified that I hadn't been able to break myself of the this child-switching thrill, I would have felt even more terrified if Mommy had believed Mrs. Monroe. I couldn't have said it then. Now, though, I believe I was terribly afraid that if Mommy ever saw my badness, she'd disintegrate like the Wicked Witch of the West and dissolve the very basis of my existence. Anyway, her comment ended my cruel behavior.

Except for those escapades, though, I was Mommy's helper. In fact, I was a miniature Mommy who could do whatever was needed: set the table, dry the dishes, mix the bead of orange dye into the white oleo margarine to make it look like the now-unavailable butter, make instant coffee for parents before they got up each morning, fix the breakfast cocoa for myself and my sisters by stirring Nestle's Quik into steaming milk, bring notes home from Adelaide's teacher, tie Mary Cleves's shoes. And Mary Cleves really did make me her mother — she let me dry her after baths, brought her leggings and galoshes to me for help in winter, came screaming for "Wucy" when she scraped her knee or mashed a finger. Because of the war and me being the helper, this didn't make Mommy jealous, and it eventually stopped Father from whipping me like he had earlier when I wouldn't take the blame for something the others had done and wouldn't confess about. Mommy called me her "pride and joy." When angry and distraught about having to do all the work with Father staying gone and everybody else messy, Mommy would shriek, "Nobody does anything around here but me! Me and Lucy!" Then Adelaide and Bibba (if she was home) would hate me.

By late third grade, I turned out to be smart and felt at home in school. And although this drew more heat at home, where Adelaide and Bibba would see it as further evidence of my being on Mommy's side, school became the most satisfying part of my life. There I could do things well, receive praise, and also have friends who didn't hold this against me. When Grandfather printed one of my poems on the editorial page of The News and Observer, I decided I really might be able to become a writer after all. Because times were hard for the newspaper due to the war, I even had the sense that my poem had helped out. Grandfather, in his early eighties, was again doing the job of editor that Father had performed while Grandfather was Ambassador to Mexico. And he had to do it with much less staff because so many men had been drafted into the Army. I knew that he was sad as well because Nanny's health was failing.

The war dominated all our minds. Besides air raid drills in the basement shelter at home and in the school corridors where we bent over with our heads between our knees, we washed and flattened tin cans and hauled them and bundled newspapers to school by bicycle or in Cleves's wagon to help with defense efforts. We also bought U.S. defense savings stamps with some of our birthday and Christmas money, laboring toward buying a bond. With meat and sugar rationed, we ate concoctions of eggs and fish which Mommy presented as "delicious." These were no worse than the exotic dishes we'd had to eat in Raleigh and they felt a lot less strange to me because I helped make them. Also, friends gave my parents shoe ration coupons to use for us children.

Hitler's frenzied voice on the radio epitomized the horror of the war. I believed the crackling static he screamed above was the ocean and our only real protection against the Germans. We all — even Mary Cleves — listened spellbound to that indecipherable screeching. And when alone — in bed or walking to school — I was often obsessed by thoughts of his maniacal murderousness and the images of bomb craters and mutilated bodies that they conjured up. Hitler's staccato invectives still brought to mind Mommy's ticking dimple and Bibba's calling her "martyr." And that had particular intensity for me because I knew Adelaide and Bibba were right: I had become badder from helping — a hateful, weak shadow of Mommy's martyrdom dressed up in obedient neatness. And because I pitied Mommy as well — for being mistreated and neglected by Father and my sisters — I was doubly unfree to drop the role of helper. Instead I identified with a man the newscasters talked about, a Norwegian named Quisling. I understood that he was a traitor who had helped Hitler occupy his country. Having stopped luring children from their yards and switching them just made me feel I was hiding my Nazi-ness.

Hansel was my greatest source of comfort in Washington, providing a much needed sense of continuity. Besides feeding and walking him, I liked his company on my bed when reading. Requiring little fuss, he was always just there — either outside tied to the porch rail in good weather, or curled up in the brown chair in the sunroom that had become his by habit. I can't remember now whether I talked to Hansel. If I did, I'd have wanted to hide it from Mommy and Father, who joked openly about Adelaide's imaginary boyfriend, Bill.

Another presence with whom I felt a strong affinity was F.D.R. His voice on the radio, his pictures in the newspaper, all the adult conversations I overheard about him made me glow with a worshipping warmth. His paralysis from polio made him seem even stronger in character than other people. The mementos Father occasionally brought us from "the boss" made my heart quiver and increased my longing to meet him despite knowing, with reverence, that he was too busy with the war. In fact, I think my one reason for believing that we could beat the Nazis and the Japanese was that Franklin Roosevelt was commander-in-chief.

All three of us younger sisters recall that our years in Washington were characterized by a greater sense of warmth and togetherness than we had ever known in Raleigh. Part of that, I believe, was the war itself — people working together and helping each other more, due to our common enemy. Just surviving required tasks that people had to perform together. Grocery stores and pharmacies delivered; doctors came to the house. They had cars and gasoline which other people lacked. If something was needed from a place that didn't deliver, I was allowed to walk the seven blocks up Garfield Street to Wisconsin Avenue to get it. At such times I felt capable as well as free.

Other aspects of these wartime conditions were pleasurable as well. The house next door to ours on the right was used by Brazilians for some kind of office; they were friendly with children and taught us Portuguese phrases. Many Saturday nights we, as a family, played games like "Michigan" and "Bonanza," which involved anteing up chips and winning piles of them by playing lucky cards. On Sundays we all, including Hansel, listened to Jack Benny, Charlie McCarthy, and Fred Allen on the radio.

Sickness was an organizing principle in our lives in those days, often controlling what we did, sometimes increasing our sense of camaraderie and sometimes our distress. With sulfa drugs available, abscessed ears no longer had to be lanced. Mary Cleves, Adelaide, and I all had mumps, chicken pox and measles together. One bit of trauma for me resulted from Father's having a bad back not long before I had the measles. I was home from school that morning, probably recuperating from something, when I heard his excruciating bellow from the bathroom. I didn't know what to do; I didn't want to see. But when it came again, I was afraid not to. Maybe he'd had a heart attack; I knew he was dying. In the bathroom I found him naked in the shower and still crying out. When he asked me to get him a towel, I did. I also wrapped it around him as he instructed. But I did all that with terror and dismay about his nakedness, and an irrational sense of my own badness nagged me later.

Measles, my worst sickness in that house, hit me a week or so later. That episode stands out now as the first time in my life I believed I was dying. For days I burned with fever and was too weak to sit up or walk to the toilet. For a while my throat was so swollen I couldn't swallow, and there was a sense of death on the brink of plucking me out. When able to walk again, I peered into the unlit bathroom mirror to see the red bumps on my face and feared being blinded for doing so. I also wondered about the possible connection of both death and blindness to my having seen Father naked.

Polio was the most dreaded of diseases for all of us. In the spring and summer months, newspapers ran front-page headlines daily chronicling the number of people stricken. And as the numbers rose, increasingly isolating precautions were taken. Swimming pools were closed, meetings and events canceled. There was a constant somber tension that the disease might strike our family. With pictures of people in iron lungs, I wondered how anyone could bear to go on living with just their head sticking out of a machine. That made it easier to obey Mommy's prohibitions against leaving our yard and playing with other children.

Impetigo was a less deadly disease that we had several times. Part of its pain was the humiliation Mommy suffered because she considered it the result of filth. The treatment for impetigo then was to scrub the sores clean with Dial soap and apply some type of ointment three times per day. But Mommy scrubbed those sores so relentlessly that Adelaide and Cleves screamed like they were being tortured. Once the Brazilians even called the police.

Undoubtedly the best aspects of Washington for me were the ways I ended up feeling competent and confident about all kinds of endeavors (including cooking, school work, jump rope, and Russian handball) and the friends I made. Jane Greenwood and Gary Lee Cox were school friends who were as smart as me. But the friend I played with most was Patsy Parker. She lived next door, and my mother didn't like her or her parents. Patsy was almost two years older than I was and much more knowledgeable about the world. But during the polio epidemics when we were both confined, Mommy didn't stop us from playing together. The game was Tarzan and Jane and their repeated close-call adventures in the jungle. Mostly Tarzan (Patsy) was rescuing me (Jane) from near-death situations. I found myself having strong, loving feelings for Patsy, feelings that I thought about in bed at night in and out of my worries about Mommy and Father dying. Only after I was grown and in psychoanalysis did it occur to me that those feelings with Patsy were sexual and, therefore, at least a partial reason for the death worries. Of course, another was my unaccepted anger at Mommy and Father.

Today as a psychologist, helping patients recognize repressed sexuality and the fears that have driven it underground is one of my main tasks. And when I do this — say, in helping a young woman trade in compulsive overeating for friends and an enjoyable hobby, despite her unconscious conviction that her sexual feelings as a three-year-old killed her father — it often recalls my thrill and sadness over Bibba's dating soldiers in the war. Their being so handsome and just a hair away from death made my heart quiver.

I marveled at Bibba. Especially with David, I think his name was. He was stunning! In the framed photograph on Bibba's dresser, and even more so when she sent me to let him in the front door. Tall, slender, strong, blonde, blue-eyed, in his ensign uniform, he was like a god from the movies! I was grateful Bibba let me greet him, and I couldn't understand why she didn't love him. Or why, given that he was about to be shipped overseas at any minute, she wasn't going to marry him. I knew Bibba liked David and that he liked the way she played the ocarina (which we called the "sweet potato") at USO parties. I also knew David was the reason for her using the hair-dissolving formula on her legs.

Mommy thought that in wartime, without razor blades, you ought to let the hair on your legs go. But that made Bibba mad. After hot wax that was too hard and sand paper that made her skin raw without really removing the hair, she brought the chemical formula in secretly so as to not rile Mommy. Only it stunk like rotten eggs exploding. And even though it was summer with all the windows open, that odor was so strong that it set our eyes watering. Mommy raged about Bibba being "inconsiderate," "common," "under-handed," and "determined to make trouble."

In retrospect, I think it was after the depilatory uproar that I gave up on reconciling Bibba and Mommy. There was nothing earth-shaking about it, just a sense of the two of them remaining at odds, while Bibba no longer needed to belong. She had grown shapely and pretty, as well as good at the ocarina. Young men like David liked her. Furthermore, by 1943 or 1944 Bibba was almost never in Washington, spending what little vacation she had from her board-ing school, Ashley Hall, at camp or with the Bridgers. And at Vassar, after Ashley Hall, wartime expedition was in effect with longer semesters so students could finish in three years. Yet even then, Bibba, when she was home, was very helpful to me. In the nights when I couldn't sleep because of worries about Mommy and Father dying, she took time to listen and talk to me. I also suspect that, sad as it was, Bibba's moving out revealed the same hopeful possibility of escape as Bea's choosing to do munitions work.

In terms of remoteness from home — emotional as well as geographic — camp in Maine at the age of nine was the furthest my parents ever sent me. Besides their forcing it on me against my will, I felt a particularly intense sense of injustice because of how much I helped at home.

"We have a surprise," Mommy made the announcement at supper one night in March 1943. "Lucy, you and Adelaide are both going to

Camp Wohelo for the summer."

She'd already told us about it earlier: a camp that she'd gone to — where you slept for two months in a cabin and learned to swim in cold water.

"I don't want to go," I said immediately.

But, as Father quickly put in, there was no choice. We were going to give Mommy a rest and that was that.

Adelaide dealt with the intervening three months by bragging to company. I strained to manage my dread by looking at the distance on the map at school, getting the feel of two months by thinking about the weeks between Bibba's school vacations, and praying for something to upset the plan. At bedtime, Hitler and worries about Mommy and Father dying gave way to dread of my own nonexistence.

At the railroad station, Mary Cleves screamed bloody murder and hung onto my shorts so hard that it took Mommy and Father to pull her off. My stomach quivered with a sick sinking feeling, and her bawling pushed goose pimples up on my arms. At other bad times I'd helped myself feel better by taking care of her. But that morning, if I even took a step closer, Father snapped, "No! You stay away from her!" So I ended up feeling as sick for Mary Cleves as for Adelaide and myself. As soon as we came upon the crowd of other Wohelo girls, Mommy and Father started saying good-bye, each of them holding onto kicking, screaming Mary Cleves so hard that they couldn't hug us. Adelaide began to cry then, too, and a camp lady picked her up. I just stood stiff beside our duffel bags, watching until Mommy, Father, and Mary Cleves disappeared.

On the train our car was full of babbling girls between Adelaide's age and Bibba's, all dressed in camp uniforms of halter shorts and striped jerseys. Countless faces without names. Except for Adelaide's, dancing up and down as she checked out car and bathroom before coming back to me. But she was no help for my continuing fear of our getting lost and only our duffel bags being found with the name tags Mommy had sewn into underpants, shorts, shirts, and pajamas.

After the dismal lunch of orange marmalade and peanut butter sandwiches with tin cups of milk, I finally dared to teeter to the lavatory at the other end of the jolting, cluttered aisle. The metal door was cool to my hand and so heavy that it took all my strength to push it open. Inside I slumped with relief onto the slamming, swaying seat. I'd needed to urinate for hours and out of fear had postponed going until holding it was no longer possible. But then, to my surprise, tears flowed free at the same moment: warm, relieving torrents that blurred my vision. Rebuttoning my shorts, I squeezed my eyes shut and tried to picture Mary Cleves. But the image of her round pleading face only made me cry harder. Until suddenly, opening my eyes, I was relieved to see that every one of the tear-streaked faces looking back from the little room's mirrored walls was my own.

In Maine, measuring and counting were no longer comforting. Woods stretched forever. Clockless time was portioned out by meals, activities, and the main cabin bell. Still, in a determined attempt to keep track of our eight weeks, I made a pencil mark on the envelope of Mommy's first letter before each Saturday night campfire. I also sparingly meted out the toothpaste in my tube and did without my flashlight whenever possible in order to make its batteries last.

Nor was it certain that eight weeks was all we'd have to stay there. The polio epidemic, which was crippling and killing people by the hundreds, might extend it. For some reason that I didn't understand, there was no polio in Maine. If the epidemic didn't ease in Washington by the end of August, we'd stay two or three weeks longer.

What helped most in getting through our regimented days was the frozen dutifulness I had acquired through eating shad roe and collards at Mommy's table. With that same ruse of self-imposed numbness, I endured learning to swim in a jellyfish-infested lake, and prevailed at tennis practice, canoeing, rowing, hiking, and eventually raising the sail on a sailboat.

At naptime Adelaide sometimes broke free of counselors in her cabin on the other side of the camp to come screaming for me about wanting to go home. Then I'd be surprised at her burying her wet face in my sweatshirt and, even more, by my own arms automatically encircling her without any traces of hate.

Yet I myself never spoke of homesickness to anyone, though I cried into the pillow at night when the others were asleep. Worse than the fears of Mommy and Father dying then was a hulking sense of choking that would not let me picture them at all. Sometimes as the weeks flowed into each other and especially after the announcement that some of us would stay at camp two extra weeks due to the polio, there were panicky periods in which I believed they were already dead. Again, I had no image of their faces. Just a dreadful emptiness exacerbated by realizing I couldn't remember where Bibba was spending the summer. Nor were Mommy's periodic typed letters much help; in the night they seemed no more than cold mile-markers on the road to death. And my worries about Mary Cleves were worse still. By the middle of August, with flashlight batteries used up and toothpaste tube flattened, I was convinced that something dire had already happened. If I had to get up in the night to urinate, searching for the toilet in the dark reminded me of sneaking to Bea's room and of how Bea was no longer there. When I guiltily gave up and used a clump of grass instead, thoughts of Mommy and Mary Cleves being killed in the blackout shelter would not cease. The idea of a bomb falling on our house and reducing it and everyone in it to a blackened hole plagued me. If that had happened, my rumination continued, Adelaide and I wouldn't know until nobody met our train.

All I could see from the train window was a sea of khaki soldiers' uniforms stretching forever. No bomb crater. Though perhaps there was still no one to meet us — the most likely sign of that death hole that I'd been so careful not to mention to Adelaide. But then I detected a tiny red thread which unwound its way through the khaki and turned into Mary Cleves! Phew!! She was scanning the train windows for us but couldn't see me wave. By the time we got out, Mommy was there, too. And after hugs all round, the four of us lugged the duffel bags across the station to a taxi. When Adelaide asked about Father, Mommy said he was at work and might not get home until after we were asleep. Riding along, with her in the front seat beside the taxi driver and me between Adelaide and Mary Cleves in the back, I began to feel safely home. But no sooner had I recognized that easiness than my eyes fell on the scarlet and bruised stripes on Mary Cleves's legs sticking out from her green shorts. Thus jarred, I also realized that those stripes were the width of

Father's belt! One of her arms was bruised too. I felt sick, then disbelieving, before a fleeting sense of agitation about what must be done and who must do it. In the end, I said nothing. Nor did anyone else.

The war helped us feel less isolated. But there were also times — as when I discovered the bruises on Mary Cleves's legs — when we felt clearly unacceptable in a way that had never occurred in Raleigh. For instance, it was everyday life for Father, enraged and ripping off his belt, to whip us with our pants down. One year some teacher called to complain about bruises on Adelaide or Cleves. And, just as when their screams during the impetigo scrubbings had alarmed the Brazilians, a policeman came to investigate. But nothing ever happened. It just became a big joke Father told many times while other people laughed — about how loud Mary Cleves and Adelaide could scream, what strong lungs and implacable wills they had.

We thought nothing of spankings and screaming and Bourbon then; we took them for granted. Probably if I hadn't been away at camp, I wouldn't have noticed the bruises on Mary Cleves any more that night than Mommy did. At the time when beatings were inflicted, I'd cringe inside myself, whether the person being whipped was me or someone else. But afterward, it was as though there had been a thunderstorm we'd had no control over and were relieved to have survived. Yet, in another horrible and unnameable way, all this made us sick. Unable to recognize and condemn these brutalities, we kept on experiencing them as ordinary life. Thus, we all had unbearable unconscious guilt and shame to struggle with any way we could. Adelaide's way was to continuously get into trouble; mine was to be a diligent but depressed shadow; Mary Cleves's was to be the "unblameable" baby; Mommy and Father ridiculed the teacher and the policeman.

I don't recall the teachers ever doing any more than complain. Later, after the war ended and we moved back to Raleigh, life was much different: we had a maid, and no teacher in Raleigh would have complained like that about Danielses. Still, things that had happened earlier — like the bruises and the teacher and the policeman — made an irreparable dent in our sense of dignity. Sometimes seemingly insignificant things can disrupt beliefs so that you can't go back to the way life was or even the way you were before. I think that's what happened to us. Or at least to me. I refused to know some things then, tried to hold onto the way life had been by refusing to know. But that refusal was useless; after the war nothing remained the same.

The feelings about these losses are best conveyed by a dream I had years later:

Cleves and me, little girls at the beach. Dazzling sunshine. Hot sand. And as always, I was the big sister looking after my baby. On an errand? Or an adventure. Running up the sand dune, laughing and squealing, with the sand burning our toes. But then Cleves shrieked, "Lucy! Lucy!" And, horror-struck, I immediately understood: I, Lucy. . .Lucy the big sister. . . the responsible one. . .was blowing away! This stuff. . .whatever. . . liquid. . . it didn't look like blood, but was life water. . .was gushing, pouring, draining out of every pore in my body and being whisked away to nothingness.

chapter seven

THE CURSE

Somehow in the last ten years or so I've learned to be curious about the unexpected rather than automatically disappointed or wary. Maybe I got that in analysis with Dr. Howie; maybe my teenaged children set the stage for it by repeatedly putting me through the wringer. But I mostly credit patients — and all the times they've caught me off guard.

Like the time that four-year-old Jane, after a three-week Christmas trip with her angry mother, announced in the playroom, "I want to drink milk from your breasts." Or when belligerent 39-year-old Alice Jones walked into our session with both my novels (when I'd thought my identity as a writer was lost, never to be discovered) and told me she'd spent Sunday afternoon with a friend I'd had in eighth grade and had never seen since. Moments like that make a therapist feel so powerless that there is nothing to be done but wait and let the patient and your own slowly recovering wits show you the way. I give my patients credit here because I would never personally seek out such confrontations. Yet these have repeatedly led me to new discoveries about both the patient and myself.

I've also had time to learn that what matters most is not the surprise or the loss or a brilliant recovery but just the capacity to keep going. But in Washington in 1945 I didn't know that. Losses, and even changes, seemed simultaneously incredible and catastrophic.

The first loss came in February 1945 — a time in Washington when I was particularly happy and successful in John Eaton School's fifth grade. Hansel became paralyzed and had to be put to sleep. I wept for days. So much had I always taken Hansel's somber, patient presence for granted that even today I can feel that ache in my throat from that sudden incredible emptiness.

The death of Franklin Roosevelt less than two months later had similar impact. We heard it first on the radio in the midst of the afternoon soap operas — at least we heard about the cerebral hemorrhage. Later someone called from the White House to say they expected him to die. For nearly two days after that Father was unreachable. And, again, it was as if I myself were lost. I sat alone on the front steps, staring at the street as my silent tears created a rain-streaked glass which separated me, with President Roosevelt as with Hansel, from a world in which they were no longer present.

Roosevelt's funeral procession was even more poignant for me because it was similar to the first inaugural parade I'd attended in January a few months earlier. At the time of his funeral, I had just turned eleven. I stood stone still at the front of the crowds lining Pennsylvania Avenue. Tears streamed down my face, and, for once, there was no reason for shame. Here and there others wept, too. Nobody was talking. I'm sure someone was with me, probably one of Father's secretaries. But no one could have been a companion at that time. F.D.R. was my personal hero. The small souvenirs he'd sent me had places of honor in my bedroom. As the horse-drawn casket passed before me, my whole body vibrated with a physical dirge, waking to a world that had lost its star, its savior, its reason for being. As certainly many were wondering that day whether the war could be won without Roosevelt, I had a sense that life as I'd known it would not continue without the only president I'd ever known.

As it turned out, Roosevelt's death did end our life in Washington. And that decision, too, was made abruptly. One minute we were busily going about our lives — going to school, flattening tin cans, having air raid drills, talking to friends, making supper — and in the next, Washington and all these things in it, were over. When school ended in the middle of June, Adelaide, Mary Cleves, and I were bundled off to Grandfather's house in Raleigh while Mommy and Father concluded their affairs and moved our furniture.

By August, as we were preparing to move back into the Raleigh house, the bombing of Hiroshima cast a pall on the homecoming. It triggered in me a grim sense of the goodness of our country dying with its heroes. Not only were we, in Grandfather's house grown more dank since Nanny's death, trapped by an envelope of death, but that envelope seemed to have expanded into a huge and catastrophic one for which Americans were responsible, Americans and the Democratic president who once had been the rescuers.

That fall, as our life in Raleigh resumed, it proved to be quite different than we could have imagined. In outrage over the renters' mistreatment of her house, Mommy arranged for refurbishing as soon as the materials could be obtained. But nothing could really restore either the house or our lives. In part, this was because being back on Caswell Street made changes more obvious. Bea and Eunice were missed all over again; so were Hansel and Bibba, who, by then, was grown and living in New York. Cleves, in first grade, became Adelaide's pal instead of my child. Adelaide enjoyed more freedom to do mischief that got them both into trouble and kept Mommy distressed. As the oldest daughter at home, I had skipped sixth grade and would have felt pleased with my success in seventh if it hadn't raised fears of getting nearer to the age when Bibba had been sent away.

Perhaps an even greater diminishment was Father's working at the newspaper instead of at the White House. He had wanted this. President Truman had asked him to stay on and he'd chosen not to. But in Raleigh, where he went to work later and was always home for drinks before supper, Father frequently seemed discouraged or angry. After Washington he more frequently lamented, "It's terrible to have to live your life in another man's shadow." We sometimes overheard him complaining to Mommy about problems with Grandfather's editorials or Frank's "stupidity." Mostly when we were with him, he was drinking Bourbon peacefully or raging at or ridiculing someone — either one of us or a guest.

With great effort and insistence, the renovations Mommy was so intent upon eventually got under way. A part of planning for them was making new room assignments — moving Father's writing room upstairs to what had once been the nursery or Adelaide's room;

moving Adelaide way back to the room that had been used by Bea and Eunice and later Bibba; moving me from the sunny bedroom over the kitchen to the large guestroom with its private bath in the northeast front corner of the upstairs; and moving Cleves into my old room. Downstairs the kitchen and breakfast room were to be completely gutted and reconstructed to provide a modern kitchen with an expansive pantry. By December the renovations were underway: replanking and painting Mommy's prized balcony; restructuring the kitchen and pantry; painting the doors and other woodwork throughout; making preparations for new wallpaper.

In the midst of all this, a couple of months before my twelfth birthday, I came home from school one afternoon to discover blood in my underpants. I knew what this meant. Mommy had briefly explained menstruation to me, complete with such details as periods lasting five days each month and being called "the curse" by some people. Bibba had told me what a drag the curse was and how you couldn't go swimming when you had it. But none of this had prepared me for the sense of physical out-of-controlness that accompanied my recognition that this blood was leaking out of my body and could not be explained away. Now I would label the feelings that flooded me despair and guilt. But what I experienced then was a horrifying sinking sensation, like stumbling across a suicide. A loss I could neither ignore nor accept.

Mommy gave me some Kotex pads and a "sanitary belt." Probably she also showed me abstractly how to adjust it. Perhaps the devastation of that afternoon's discovery distracted me from everything else, because all I can recall of it is a grim sense of straining to cope. Since our family had to go out to supper that night because the kitchen was unusable, I went into the upstairs hall bathroom to change Kotex pads. I had the dread then that, totally outside my awareness, great waves of blood could come pouring out of me and expose all the horrible aspects of me to anyone on hand. So I obsessed over that pad while, from outside the bathroom (which had no door like all other rooms in the house at that stage of the renovation), Adelaide motioned and yelled, "Lucy, Father says come on!"

But I couldn't get it right, and the next thing I knew Father was out there yelling, "Lucy, we're all waiting for you! Come on! Hurry up!"

I can't recall if I responded in any way. Mostly I was straining to attach the pad securely to the sanitary belt. But suddenly Father began screaming and beating on the wall with his fists. "Goddamn it! Come on! Your selfishness is disrupting the whole family!" He rushed in from the hall and stood red-faced and snarling in front of me. I was scared numb and still can't remember if my pants were up or down when he got there.

Father never apologized. But neither did he keep reminding me of how I had inconvenienced the family. Later that evening when we were walking to the taxi after supper, he put his arm around me and said, "Lucy, your mother tells me you have become a woman." His voice was very sad as he said it. He hugged me with one arm and kissed my forehead.

Besides its own distressing presence, menstruation announced to me that growing up was going to happen no matter what and that I had best get myself together to at least look the part. My most immediate behavioral response was to give up sucking my thumb, which I still did in secret while reading or going to sleep. Long ashamed of this indulgence, I now mustered the willpower to stop "cold turkey."

Six weeks later I came down with scarlet fever, which became protracted into a two-month absence from school, characterized by my not wanting to eat and withdrawing sadly and wearily into my new and finer bedroom and bath. Not until late April did I return to school and finish the make-up work started at home. But my teacher, Miss Townsend, was warmly appreciative of my success in catching up and talked with me a lot that spring in a way that made me feel that being smart was not unfeminine. I had a crush on her and didn't feel ashamed of her praise. But the problems with eating and a certain sad withdrawal continued. The comfort of my new room and the realization that it might still be used as a guest room added a painful sense of impermanence.

That spring the house renovations were completed and after Mommy hired and fired a succession of flighty black women who were both poor cooks and unable to do other things up to her standards, she found Leanna Ingram. However, in those months Mommy, who had been relatively healthy all the years in Washington, began to suffer from an array of vague physical complaints that hung about her like a veil much of the time. By fall 1946, when I was a twelve-year-old eighth-grader, all of these problems — Adelaide's and Cleves's troublesome freedom, Father's depression, anger, and lengthier drinktime, Mommy's physical complaints, and my decreased appetite and withdrawal — had become unremarkable habits of life. But, fortunately, so was Leanna. She was a tall, large-boned black woman whose very appearance commanded respect; her voice was soft but clear-spoken. She treated Mommy with quiet directness, but did not cower. When Mommy wanted her to do something she regarded impossible or questionable, she would explain the problems she saw, and if ordered to do it anyway, would obey calmly. Leanna prayed before every meal and had to get off by 6:30 on Wednesday evenings for church. She could make the most delicious bread we'd ever tasted. With all this, she emanated a kind of quiet solidity our family had never encountered before.

By winter 1947 my body held me prisoner. I couldn't get out of bed in the morning without first feeling inside my nightgown to check contour and texture. And I was startled every time by the strange soft mounds of flesh on my chest and by the fuzz of pubic hair. Startled and then whipped by anxiety to jump up and examine myself in the mirror.

The reflection usually soothed those concerns about breasts and pubic hair by making what was there look like less than my fingers felt. In the mirror my bony chest appeared full but not knobby, and the pubic hair wasn't visible at all unless I got right up next to the glass. But disgust would well up in me again whenever I did that: I felt dizziness and nausea, as well as a sudden cold tingling at the roots of my hair, on my arms and legs as well as scalp.

My body changing made me feel as though an alien force was taking me over against my will, turning me into a gross and hateful monster. Worse still, that demon was well known to me. For years, Mommy's image had lurked inside me. Then "the curse" had made it undeniable. After that first time, every period came as an attack by the vicious aspects of my mother inside me, bursting forth against my desperate, prayerful efforts to contain them. Some of the pressure for consulting the mirror was to see if I'd begun to look like her.

After studying my reflection, I would get back in bed and lie utterly flat in order to further persuade myself that the physical changes were minor. That position didn't affect the pubic hair, but it did flatten my chest out evenly and cause my hip bones to protrude in a way that seemed comfortingly less fat. Even so, I couldn't dress before again examining myself in the mirror.

My morning body-checking ritual was only one of the more easily recognizable ways that I labored to contain consternation. With Mommy's fine house refurbished, our lives should have felt restored to orderly perfection. But somehow the very luxury of the house emphasized the way other things were out of control. At supper, which had been re-labeled "dinner" and moved from six to seven o'clock, the same rules of decorum were in force. However, Leanna served the food alone and the rest of us were different as well. With Bibba gone forever to New York, Mary Cleves and Adelaide sat across from me, both of them eating a lot, with Cleves fighting the most with Mommy over things like liver and stewed tomatoes. The growing closeness of Cleves and Adelaide shut me out. So did the teachers' evaluations praising "Lucy's industry and imagination in pursuing her writing ambition." Mommy always delighted in those comments, while Father reacted in ways I couldn't understand. Sometimes he chortled, "You really are my boy, Lucy!" But just as often he would ridicule me for being a "greasy grind whose book-ishness will drive the boys away." Sometimes he did both at once.

The "sides" of Mommy and Father became more bitterly at odds as our growing up caused the outside world to intrude on Mommy's order. That had begun in Washington with Bibba staying out too late with soldiers. But the clashes with Adelaide and Mary Cleves in Raleigh were worse and continual. Adelaide seemed to be increasingly ingenious at finding ways for her and Cleves to "mortify" Mommy. And when Mommy and Adelaide went at it, it reminded me of Mommy and Bibba. Only then I never intervened, and Father usually did, taking Adelaide's side by joking that she was his "irredeemable pagan" and berating Mommy as a "straight-laced ninny." Which usually started her dimple ticking and, soon after that, an argument.

Even after all these years, those quarrels ring through my memory like the refrain of a once popular song or Hitler's voice crackling on the radio. And the reverberations of those harsh voices and withering looks were all the more powerful because there was no telling when they'd erupt. It might be Adelaide's friends, Bibba's forgetting to deposit checks, Adelaide's dress and behavior with boys, Cleves hiding her liver and putting it in the garbage, my good grades, the Bridgers, my not eating. Today, still, the words in my memory fit the voices so well there's no need to see the faces:

"Why do you say that to her, when you know she'll do anything to mortify me?!"

"If you weren't so holier than thou, she wouldn't be tempted!"

"Yes she would! Because you just lead her on!"

"You Goddamned pious martyr!"

"I'm exhausted! You leave it all to me!"

"How can I help it? Nobody does anything good enough for you!. . . China doll bitch!"

"When I'm dead and gone, you'll be sorry. . . "

Or:

"Jane Adams and I got the highest grades on the social studies test."

"Does that qualify you to compete for first prize as 'greasy grind'?"

I didn't know what to say.

"Why can't you be friends with somebody less deadly than Jane Adams?"

"I do have other friends."

"But you're hell-bent on growing up to be a boring, sexless greasy grind."

"Jonathan!"

"It's true and you know it! That's where this Goddamned eating business comes in."

"You are not being helpful!"

"You're being a pious bitch!"

"Well, I wouldn't be if I had a little help around here. . . Nobody does anything here but me!"

The end was always the same: Mommy with face swollen and tear-streaked at one end of the table, Father scowling and silent at the other.

One day when I came in from school, the house was still. That meant Cleves and Adelaide were out. In the kitchen Leanna was preparing dinner and laying out the drink tray. Upstairs Mommy was resting. My part in this, I realize now but performed unawares then, was to practice the piano for two hours before I turned to homework. I did know that Mommy loved to hear me practice; it was yet another aspect of my developing into the "gifted artist" she expected me to be. But as much as I was trying to soothe her, I think the ordered routine also served my own need for control.

"Lucy? Is that you?" she called from upstairs. "Lucy, beautiful, come here a minute, please?"

Climbing the spiral staircase, I made my voice cheerful in reply, "Yes m'am. I'll be right there."

She was stretched out on the bed, with the shades drawn. Her pretty face was twisted in pain or anger.

"What's wrong, Mommy?" I asked.

"I have one of those terrible headaches," she sighed.

"Do you want me to do something for you?"

"Just give me a kiss, dear. . . I've taken some aspirin and a pain pill. I just need to rest."

I kissed her forehead obediently. "Do you know why the headaches come?" I asked.

"Oh yes. It's just the change."

"The change?"

"Menopause. Change of life, you know."

I knew to ask no more. "Well, I'll do my homework instead of the piano," I said.

"No, darling. Please play the piano. Nothing is better for my soul than to hear you play."

"It won't hurt your headache?"

"No, indeed. If anything, it will make it better. . . But, before you practice, ask Leanna to show you about burning the sanitary napkins in the basement. That way you'll know how to do it yourself."

Leanna was setting the table. "What you need, honey?" she asked as I lingered about without speaking.

"Mommy said to get you to show me about burning the Kotexes."

"Sure. You go get 'em from you' room while I finish here."

As I tiptoed back up the stairs to get the three-day accumulation of pads, each neatly and obsessively wrapped in toilet paper, I thought about how much easier burning them seemed after asking Leanna. I didn't understand my foreboding about this burning. It would be a relief to be able to get rid of them myself without having to wait while the trash basket filled up. But I'd been afraid to speak to Leanna about them before, while I now felt unburdened from having done so.

The basement was as dark and damp as ever with the small metal-framed windows near the low ceiling creating the sense of being in a submarine. The only light came from single bulbs hanging from the ceiling at wide intervals. All my life I'd worried about snakes and spiders in that basement. I'd seen a few of the latter. The servants' toilet was down there, too, another detail contributing to my sense of pity and guilt about the way black people were treated.

Leanna never seemed ashamed or afraid of anything. Despite carrying the trash basket as she walked beside me through the basement's dark, her presence made me feel calm and unashamed too. Almost matter-of-fact. "You don' need t' do it ever'day," she was saying as we approached the even darker hole in the wall that was the fireplace. "Maybe wait for ten of 'em." She'd brought a box of safety matches from the kitchen. "I keeps these upstairs so's they don' get wet an' no good. In the cabinet with the glasses."

I emptied the basketful of bundles into the little black grate.

"Heah, honey," she said. "You strike the match."

I did and dropped it into the middle of the white pile.

"An' do one moah, so's we won't have to wait."

With the second little flame, the toilet-paper packages took off. Standing there watching the fire consume them, I thought about the care with which I'd wrapped each one and about the need to burn them so that the garbagemen wouldn't see. I wondered whether if they did see them it could be like a dog smelling fear on you and attacking because of it. I almost asked Leanna.

"Don't evah leave till the fiah's died out," she was saying. "Even a l'il spahk can go wild. So, you need to wait heah till they's nothin' but ashes." We did.

Even after I got to the piano, my mind kept going back to that dark damp basement. Until thoughts of Mommy intervened, filling my practicing with images of her listening and sighing, listening and beaming. She would be pleased that I'd burned the sanitary napkins. But as much as I needed to soothe her, giving Mommy pleasure could make me shudder.

I was a dedicated piano student by then, able to play some pieces with skill and verve, but devoting most practice hours (at least twice as many as required) to scales; always with both hands and at ever-increasing speed. My fingers were so proficient they could do it without direction. The effort involved had to do with keeping myself sitting there and trying to control my thoughts. I knew that menopause meant periods stopping, but I wondered what other terrible things went on to keep Mommy in such agony. What came to mind was a woman's insides rotting away, another reason to dread changes in my own body. Scale after scale I played. Concerto after sonata.

"Anybody home?" Father called out as he entered.

I stopped playing and went to give him a kiss. Piano practice was like "greasy-grind" studying in Father's mind. He hated it at drink time.

"Where's your mother?" he asked.

"She has a headache."

"Jonathan, I'll be down in a minute," she called.

"Lucy, my dear," he said to me. "How about getting your old father some glasses and ice?"

"Yes, sir."

In the kitchen Leanna had the tray set up. All I had to do was empty the ice tray into the bucket. But by the time I got back to the library, Mommy was there with Father. "Lucy, have you seen your sisters?" she asked.

"No, ma'm."

Sucking in her breath, she shook her head as if tortured. "I just cannot depend on them," she sighed.

"Forget them," Father advised. "They'll come back when they're hungry."

"And neither bathe nor do homework!" Mommy fumed.

"Well, I don't want them to ruin our drinks," Father snapped. "Lucy, go call your sisters."

I slunk away half-heartedly, knowing they would hide when they heard me call. Still, I did holler a few times to the empty air, "Ma-ry

Cle-ves. . . Ade-laide. . . Ma-ry Cle-ves and Ade-laide, Mom-my wants you!"

When I went back in without them, Mommy said, "They wear me out! . . . Lucy, you sit here and keep your father company while I look."

In those days being alone with Father filled me with apprehension. I adored him and still longed for him to love me. In Washington I'd felt as though he did, especially my writing and my wanting to be the first woman president. But too often since our return to Raleigh and, as far as I could understand, without any warning, I enraged him instead.

That evening, while sipping his Bourbon, he launched into his usual combined crowing and lament for having four daughters. "Just consider," he preached, "what other man has been blessed with so many beautiful slaves? . . . Why even the Shah of Iran with all his concubines does not know what it is to be endowed with such a gifted and varied selection. So you, Lucy, are the writer and intellectual. The boy for whom my heart has cried! But then there's also Adelaide, the pagan and outrageous sinner I'd have been if I could. And Mary Cleves, forever and always the beautiful baby. Also Bibba, we mustn't forget Bibba even if she is in New York. . . though, I'd have to say that in our scheme she's 'nobody.' Sweet, unconventional, but pathetic 'nobody.'"

Listening with the indulging silence that was expected when Father held forth, inside my head I pictured what he described. Me stiff and feelingless, cold-faced and shy. Adelaide guzzling beer and turning into a "hussy" like Mommy warned. Mary Cleves stuffing herself with chocolate cake. When I got to Bibba, I thought of thin air, big sister as invisible as she'd told me the elves were when I was little. When he finished with his "concubines," Father went on to questions about my writing and where I thought of going to college to learn the world's literature.

"I don't know," I answered slowly. "In the eighth grade, college seems a long way off still. Right now I don't like to think about leaving Raleigh."

"Well, to be a writer you'll have to."

I knew better than to argue. But I also didn't know much else to say.

"Haven't you even thought about it?"

"College? Not really, because getting able to write better is what I work at now. Mrs. Banks says she can see my skill growing steadily."

"Mrs. Banks is nothing but a hoity-toity Raleigh busybody!"

"But she said the paper I wrote about tobacco farming was excellent."

"Tobacco farming! My god! If you don't have any more imagination than that, Lucy, you'll have a hard time being a writer." He sipped his drink and looked at me hard over the rims of his glasses. "Like I always tell you, you've got to take risks and see the world and meet interesting people if you want to have something to write about. Tight-titted librarians can't cut it."

I don't think I said anything. I usually didn't when he was talking that way, because the words would leave my head. . . also, because I was afraid of saying the wrong thing. Even so, he was suddenly shouting at me: "Why is it that you have to be so Goddamned selfish? Self-centered, sexless greasy grind who doesn't give a damn for the feelings of other people! And no feelings at all yourself! Cold and greedy! Consumed by your own self-centeredness, how do you expect anyone to like you?!"

I never could believe it when he started yelling like that. I searched desperately for something to say to appease him, but I felt hopelessly stupid and vile from again having done whatever it was that triggered his rage, from not even knowing my selfish badness well enough to contain it. "I'm sorry, Father," I whimpered at last, "But I don't understand — "

Which only set him off again, red-faced and sneering, "All you are is a Casper Milquetoast mask over selfish greediness that sucks life dry! That hateful mind of yours! You always were intellectual, Lucy, but do you have to use it to destroy life?"

"I'm sorry, Father," I wept. "I don't mean to be that way." I knew what he was talking about, even though I lacked the words for it myself — my terrible wickedness that could be concealed many places — but never from him.

"Don't give me that," he bellowed. "Just cut it out and care about somebody else for a change!"

Reduced to tears, I fled upstairs, where, sprawled on my bed, I once again struggled to comprehend how I'd messed up. "Greediness that sucks life dry!" kept running through my mind as

I sifted through the conversation. Being unable to recollect what I'd said made me feel even worse, because I wouldn't be able to keep from saying it again.

After a while Mommy came to beg me to come back. "You mustn't take him so seriously, Lucy," she pleaded. "Your father's just tired. Whatever he said that hurt you, I'm sure he didn't mean it. He loves you very much."

She certainly did want him to love me, and I wanted to believe her. Because I adored Father and felt his intense expressions of feeling to be genuine and honest, to be loved by him would have made me feel good and deserving. But privately I knew that he had to mean the things he said because he had said them many times before. Also, because whenever I returned to the library, as I did that evening, he always acted as though nothing had happened.

After supper that night I went to see Grandfather. He was writing when I arrived, half buried by the mountain of newsprint on which he scribbled with a thick black pencil. Before he looked up I noted how much older he seemed and how sad without Nanny. Her death from heart problems during the war had left a sense of echoing loneliness in the big house. Hearing my step, Grandfather raised his crooked hand in greeting and cried out more cheerfully than any other person I knew, "How wonderful to see you, my dear. . . Come tell me about your day." Then, pushing the papers aside, he returned my hug and settled back to talk.

At first I did relate a few safe details, leaving out anything as real as Father's anger or Mommy's headaches. But soon Grandfather monopolized the conversation — with the familiar stories from his childhood and of his meeting Nanny. Also, the endless accounts of his adventures as politician and newspaper editor. By then I knew all the characters in those tales: "Franklin" was President Roosevelt; "the President" was Woodrow Wilson; "Mr. Bryan" was William Jennings Bryan. And so on, through the entire cast, including certain Mexicans and beloveds from his rural boyhood.

Listening that night, I marveled again at Grandfather's age. Seven of my lives would have fit into his eighty-four years. His wrinkled face was expressive as he talked, showing, I thought, patience and sadness over the many political causes and valued personages slipped into oblivion. When raised, his eyebrows furrowed his forehead in a way that obliterated the V-shaped scar left by the mule's kick eighty years earlier; I suspected that younger and with fewer wrinkles that scar would have glistened white and large enough to detract from his face. I tried to picture other stages between the ages of thirteen and eighty-four, an effort which his confiding, self-engrossed, timeless voice made easier. He didn't sound like an old man, and I got the idea of his loving to talk, making a ribbon of words that tied together all the times of his life. Until when? I thought. At what point does age give way to death?

"What have you been writing lately?" he asked. "Your father says you're a remarkable writer."

"Mostly just school work now."

"Nevertheless, my dear, God has given you a wonderful gift. Intellect is that, you know, and you must find a way to use it that helps the world. . . ." He then went on to talk about writing being an even more valuable gift than most because of its capacity to touch people in many different ways. "Look at all *The News and Observer* does," he chuckled. "Fights my democratic battles, advertises the grocery store bargains and reports the news and society gossip. . . It gives the people of Raleigh much more than I could on my own."

Months earlier I'd felt counterfeit visiting when I knew he preferred Adelaide. But by that particular evening I had my own place with him. It had to do with a kind of common ground that I recognized but never could have put into words then. Now I'd say our separate lonelinesses were the connection. Also, maybe some of the sexual attraction that I learned much later had probably been what set Father off. But my main feeling with Grandfather was one of being good the same way he was good. And that became a source of hope at times.

I remember his again telling me that night about picking cotton: "One of the greatest blessings of my life," he said, "is that I had the opportunity to be poor before I got rich. I learned many things from that — but especially how it is to be poor and how to get beyond it. As a little boy I helped earn money every summer by working in the cotton fields. Until one year I got a job in the drugstore. After that I never picked cotton again!

"Lucy, you and your cousins have not had that good fortune. So, other lessons will be yours to learn. But I hope you'll all remember 'Noblesse Oblige' . . . that from those unto whom much has been given, much shall be expected."

I never answered when he talked that way. Though deeply stirred by this challenge which seemed to me a sister of the Golden Rule from Sunday school, I never could imagine myself meeting its expectations. Part of my silence was a prayer that I would somehow find a way.

When it was time to leave, Grandfather rode downstairs in the elevator with me so that he could stand at the front door with the lights on to watch me run home through the dark. He loved to look up at the stars and tell the stories of the constellations, calling them by their Latin names with delighting familiarity. But especially from that chilly night, I can remember his hand grasping my shoulder as he pointed up at Ursa Major and said, "You know, my dear, the greatest miracle of all is that we're here."

I kissed him good night then and ran off into the darkness while he waited to hear me holler from home.

"Lucy, your mother and I have found a school," Father said, pouring his Bourbon one evening a few weeks later.

"What?" my voice quavered. "What kind of school?"

"A Quaker boarding school. A co-ed Quaker school in Pennsylvania that prides itself on preparing students for the best colleges."

"It's a quite charming place, Lucy," Mommy continued as he savored his drink. "I know you'll love it. And we can all be satisfied that, for once, your mind will be appreciated."

Once again Mommy's words felt like ice water dousing me. "Your mind will be appreciated" ignored most of me, while at the same time calling me special in this way that everyone but she would despise. Stunned, I tried to find some way to stick up for myself without turning them both against me. "What if I don't want to go away?"

"You will," Mommy answered, beaming. "This is your kind of place, Lucy. A school where sensitivity and intelligence are not only appreciated but cultivated and encouraged."

"And not by developing you as a greasy-grind spinster, either," Father put in. "They expect boys and girls to go to dances together."

"But what if I want to stay in Raleigh?"

Mommy's dimple started up. But before she could speak, Father exploded, "Don't be ridiculous! Lucy, you've got to learn to live life to the hilt! If you can't take advantage of an opportunity like George School, all the brains in the world won't save you! You'll end up a boring, sexless librarian!"

"Let's talk about it later," Mommy said. "Lucy, I don't think you can understand without looking at the catalog and thinking over what your father and I know about the Raleigh schools."

They went on drinking their highballs without speaking, and I retreated into dismayed but obedient silence. Then Mary Cleves and Adelaide entered the room fighting over a skirt.

"For God's sake, take that racket out of here!" Father yelled.

"You two wear me out," Mommy pleaded. "I told you to leave that skirt in my room to be let out."

They were still wrestling with it when the doorbell rang, but then began racing each other to answer it.

"Who could that be?" Father said softly to Mommy and me. We all strained to hear the voices in the hall. Mommy's dimple started again. Father sighed and mumbled, "Woe is me! I can't even have a drink in peace!"

"Grandfather's here," Mary Cleves called from the hall.

"Goddamn it!" Father cursed softly. "Give me your glass! Lucy, quickly, help me put these behind the books!"

I hurriedly obeyed, setting both his and Mommy's glasses of Bourbon on the back of the bookshelf and replacing the volumes in front of them. But I felt all mixed up. Who was against who? Whose side was I on? I'd helped hide drinks from Grandfather numerous times before; I knew Mommy and Father couldn't bear to be seen by him with glasses in their hands. But since I'd also been at Grandfather's when he encouraged visitors from out of town to pay a five o'clock visit to my parents or uncles that implied having a drink, this was hard to understand.

"Hello, children," Grandfather greeted us as he shuffled in. "I felt lonely after my supper."

"It's nice to see you, Mr. Daniels," Mommy said. "Please sit down with us."

"How's your writing coming, Father?" Father asked.

"Fine," Grandfather answered, his crooked hand resting on Adelaide's shoulder. "I can only stay with the book so long at a time, though. . . I brought you two editorials." He pulled some folded papers from his coat pocket and laid them on the table.

From across the room I saw Father grimace and shift irritatedly as he said, "Thank you, Father. I'll have to read 'em. . . I hope I can use them."

Grandfather's face remained bland. "Well, you see, I like to help," he said.

I can't remember any more about that visit. My belief is that Grandfather left soon afterward, probably sensing the tension and lack of welcome. But it may just have been that I left, withdrawing into that insulated, thoughtless state I sometimes conjured up when I couldn't bear what was happening. I never did know whether Grandfather realized they were being mean to him; I never dared to talk to him about it. But it was clear to me that evening that he and I were both people Mommy and Father didn't want around.

And what a painful and surprising thought! Writing had always been the connector between Father and Grandfather, writing and *The News and Observer*. It was also the example I was using to make myself valuable. So, for Father to want to be rid of Grandfather felt shattering. Both Father's words and the drinks behind the books made me sick at heart. So I ached to unhear the whole interaction. Not thinking definitely felt the best choice.

At supper, which was delayed to let Mommy and Father finish their drinks once Grandfather had gone, I had an overwhelming sense of transcience. Pushing the food around on my plate to look like I was eating, I gazed at Cleves in Bibba's old place and imagined her looking back at my empty chair or sitting in it to make the table even. Ruminating over Grandfather's writing to fill up his loneliness and over Adelaide's and my train ride to camp, I tried to plead with Father: "Since I make A's already, why do I have to go to boarding school?"

"Because the Raleigh schools are lousy," he answered fiercely and then shouted, "And because for once in your life, Casper Milquetoast, you're going to have to take a risk!"

"Lucy, you'll love it," Mommy put in nervously.

"Is Lucy going to boarding school?" Mary Cleves asked.

"Yes," Father said.

"Probably," Mommy echoed.

"When?" Cleves persisted.

"We haven't decided," Mommy soothed.

Father shot her a silent sneer. Then he tore the napkin from around his neck and, scowling at my plate full of food, yelled, "God forbid that Lucy might have to do something she doesn't like!"

What I most recall about that summer is sadness and dread. I had grown thinner by then and that, as well as the dinner-table uproar about my not eating, resulted in Mommy taking me to Duke Medical Center. After an array of tests — blood, metabolism, urine, glands — as well as answering questions, Mommy and Father told me that the doctors had concluded that Lucy needs to eat more, and boarding school would be better for her than staying home. So, George School became an approaching reality. Mommy and I bought clothes and talked about academic requirements and roommates. Father held forth about the guiding principles of Quakerism and the fact that some of our ancestors had been Quaker abolitionists.

Probably both of those factors appealed to my need to feel important and special. But at a deeper level they seriously threatened my personal security, leaving no doubt about Mommy's and Father's determination. I would be sent away. Like Bibba, Bea and Eunice. This felt like death to me or more accurately, like execution; invisibility at its "realest." Part of me fought desperately to prevent it, while the rest strained to prepare to cope once it came to pass.

Clearly thinness and not eating would not prevent my expulsion from home. Nevertheless, evidence of these provided a form of personal reassurance otherwise unavailable. As the ledges of my hipbones sharpened under the bedcovers and the corrugation of my ribs grew more defined in the mirror, expanding dread led me to check those vital signs more and more frequently. Despite not saving me from boarding school, such proof of bodily containment suggested that some control of myself remained.

Those personal reassurances were the only protection I had against my repeated somber realizations that summer of "I'll never do this again" or "that won't be here next year." Grandfather figured heavily in this growing awareness of life's impermanence. My fear of death had long been quelled by associating it with old age, which only made matters worse in considering him. I well remember looking over at the lamplight flickering on his thoughtful, tired countenance, and my mind quickening with "I need to preserve this moment in my memory" intensity. We never did talk about dying, though. I was too inhibited, and he was too busy telling me political stories and his ideas about boarding school, which especially intrigued him because he'd never been to one. Yet I questioned whether he'd still have been proud if he'd known I menstruated or that Father hated my selfish greediness; also, whether he knew about my greasy-grindness and didn't mention it out of not minding or trying to be kind. Those were intrusive thoughts that I had no wish to keep. Yet when I look back now, I still have them.

"So by tomorrow night you'll be gone," Grandfather said. "Are you excited?"

"More scared," I ventured. " . . . In some ways I still don't want to go."

He had again come down with me on the elevator, and we were talking outside in the September night. His hand rested on my shoulder the way it always did when we looked at the stars. "You might be confusing fear and anticipation," he said. "I remember when the President asked me to be Secretary of the Navy. I said to your Nanny, 'I don't know if I can do it.' I knew nothing about ships then except that my father had been killed repairing one. Then I believed I was afraid, but now I think that was anticipation. . . of what became a wonderfully exciting and fulfilling part of my life and of history."

He hugged me tight then and said, "I'm going to miss you, Lucy."

I have a permanent memory of that: his stiff arms around me and his lips on my forehead as I replied, "I'll miss you, too, Grandfather."

"But don't you ever forget, my dear, that life is a wonderful

journey with ever-changing, strange and exciting possibilities. . .
Good night, Lucy."

"Good-bye, Grandfather." Running through the darkness, cheeks wet with tears, I wondered if anybody else would visit him.

chapter eight

SILVER METEOR

Trains have all but vanished from the American countryside. Every so often we learn from the television about one that's been wrecked or sabotaged. Rarely do we hear of people who travel regularly by railroad, and when we do, we know they're taking their lives in their hands. Even commuters must worry about this since that gunman ran amok on Long Island. With sadness I can envision a time when our nation may be full of people who've never ridden a train.

I've always been terrified by the things that took me away from home. Including trains. These fears have never stopped me, though. Persevering through them has felt essential to be able to bear myself. Only in recent years have I become more adept at distinguishing external danger from my own inner timidity. Even now where the two are mingled, I may still err in the direction of undertaking a project or pursuing a relationship that less frightened or weak-feeling people would walk away from. Yet, I'm not altogether regretful about this because of the opportunities that the need to overcome fear has brought me. Among the agents that have separated me from home are husbands, psychoanalysis, education, and money. But the first such separators were trains.

In my childhood, Pullman cars transported you everywhere, and I associate most leave-takings with them. Because of the infrequency and significance of my train trips, each one seems to be filed inside me still, ready for review like the videos parents make of events in their children's lives. Train feelings are in my body, too: sensations of swooshing, barreling, straining, lurching, squealing, and clanging to a stop. The most accessible train memories are those of my trips to and from boarding school.

I was at George School in Bucks County, Pennsylvania for three years, starting as a ninth grader in the fall of 1947. That resulted in six train trips each school year, for Christmas and Easter vacations, as well as leaving home in fall and returning in summer. The main route was between Raleigh and Philadelphia, with a change there to another for Newtown. The most memorable of these rides for me now is the one back to Pennsylvania after Christmas vacation in January 1950.

Rushing darkness swallowed the train. And I, feeling like I was hurtling through nothing to nowhere, shivered to feel charged remnants of the self I'd used to know fling themselves into that swirling black and leave me just one more lost star dancing into eternity. Clackety-clack . . . clackety-clack, the cars battered the rails. I knew that sound well from the other trips when its regularity had lulled me like rain on a tin roof. The jolting and joggling were familiar, too. But not the hurtling sensation which possessed me that night for the first time.

It followed from Father's advice that I "take this year by the horns," which meant trying to believe I was as capable and successful as other people said. Thinking of myself that way — Dean's list, assembly speaker, writer of stories praised by Mr. Frescoln — filled me with excitement, which felt very much like the train's hurtling. That night I was being rocketed by both of them into my sixth and what I expected to be my most transforming semester yet at George School. Braced by the straining resolutions of what the Quakers called my Inner Light, I had vowed to not only travel alone that January, but to do so without panic. I also hoped to make this a new year in which I did feel worthy of my accomplishments and in which neither my terrible homesickness nor the sense of living inside an isolating bubble would undo me. Those resolutions had come from Father's quoting F.D.R.: "We have nothing to fear but fear itself" and from my own desperate need to be grown up. But, beneath this resolute show, I still felt hollow.

The berths had already been made up when I boarded. The green curtains hung loose over my lower one as I sat there waiting for the conductor to collect tickets. Despite the plan I'd made, I felt shy with both him and the porter I'd tipped a dollar to wake me one hour before Philly.

"Yes, m'am," he'd said with dependable black impassiveness. "I cert'n'y will. Have a good night."

The year before he'd said the same thing. And I'd laid awake all night — worried over his forgetting, convinced that death crouched ready to pounce at every trestle, dreading being sucked up by nowhere the further we got from Raleigh.

But that night in January 1950, impelled by Father's admonishment and my own determination, I raised the shades and turned out both the lights. Then, refusing to worry over the porter, I gave myself, undistracted, to the light-flared darkness. And doing so brought to mind all the other times when I hadn't been able to — that first fall sleeping in the upper berth because the lower one was Mommy's; the year after that, flooded by tears of fear and loneliness. In contrast, the hurtling felt jarring and unsettling, but not unbearable. It thrilled me to think of Father looking proud.

On the first trip to George School, Mommy wore her gray suit and black shoes and her indispensable hat. Her way of looking more dressed up and proper than other people had always been the outward expression of the cosmopolitan sophistication which made her absolutely certain of how things should be done. "The most important detail of any travel is tipping correctly," she'd lectured as we latched the suitcases. "Then you can depend on the porter to get you up in time and on the redcap to pleasantly manage the luggage. The same is true of dressing well. It lets people know you expect good treatment."

Mommy had to be treated well. At the Quaker school as much as on the train or by the Raleigh black people. The problem was that despite demanding respect, she didn't expect to get it and, therefore, had to shame it out of people — Leanna, the porter, the dean of students. That was why Father called her "Mrs. Purple Plume" to her face and told the joke about only two kinds of people coming from South Carolina — "those who've never worn shoes and those who treat you like you've never worn shoes."

In some ways having Mommy on the train that first year had made it easier. In the lower berth she'd talked to the porter and the conductor. Also, she'd known enough to get off at the right place whether the porter remembered or not, even though her regalness helped prevent his forgetting.

But at the school I'd been mortified by her haughtiness and by the scared clinging that came over me. And it was there, in the lobby of the main building, that I'd first noticed the bubble. A transparent, blunting film that sealed me off from everybody else. Looking back at it fifty years later, that bubble seems to have been protection against Mommy — against the ice water of her praise, against the arrogance with which she offended others, against the desperate sense of having to have my own emptiness contained by her. At the time, though, it felt as disabling as clinging to her. Clutching the suitcase as I traipsed down the corridor after Mommy and our girl guide, everything looked and sounded far away.

Weird as that seemed, the numbing insulation between me and the clearly more intelligent and self-sufficient Quaker students also consoled me. When the guide left us in my room at Brown House, the bubble thickened into a fog that I felt as desperate to embrace as to push off. Probably because I needed it to contain me from the feeling of fading away and because Mommy, in departing, would sever my last tie with home. When she did leave, the fog swelled into a choking mist that engulfed me and made the entire expedition — train, taxi, George School — a mirage viewed helplessly through rain-washed windows.

George School turned out to be as wholesome and picturesque as the pictures in its catalog. Old brick buildings laced with ivy; majestic shade trees arching over walks and roads; acres of woods and playing fields. All with a cameo nobility that symbolized Quakerdom for me. The teachers were strict but in a sensible way that I found surprising. The other students were friendly enough and fascinated by my southern accent. Still, I felt intimidated by what I saw as their intellectual and social superiority. I clung to the bubble for consolation.

In time, I did manage to make some friends and, in fact, two very good friends. Eleanor Magid was a Jewish day student. She had dark eyes and curly black hair and an intense seriousness about her angular face. She was an only child and a wonderful artist who'd been encouraged all her life to pursue the drawing and painting that she loved. Brown House was a cottage some distance from the main building; it grouped together seven girls from all four grades for whom there wasn't room in the main building. Being there my first year, I believe, slowed me down in making friends with classmates, but it probably enhanced my friendship with Eleanor, because it made us both outsiders.

The other friend I made, and with whom I was roommates our junior year, was Liz Starr. She was also Jewish — a tall, big-boned, dark-haired, dark-eyed girl from Nashville, Tennessee. She had a brother a year older who also went to George School. I'm sure that Liz's being a fellow southerner was something that drew us together in the largely northern student body. Also, my needing a good and bright friend and her quiet, substantial willingness to share in that. Liz and Eleanor and I were all in the L sequence, accelerated classes focused on languages. We shared both a certain alienation and the intellectual ability and interests that had made me (or perhaps all of us) misfits in other settings.

Our threesome became devoted. Despite seeing each other daily in class, we had long philosophical talks which mostly occurred by chance on our way to gym or during study periods. Since we were all thinkers and had more to say than time allowed, we often exchanged earnest letters written on notebook paper.

A remarkable feature of these friendships was the discovery that with Eleanor and Liz the bubble almost disappeared. Sometimes, too, I suddenly felt admired and important with them. On the one hand that felt good — acceptable and belonging. But on the other it aroused guilt about my greedy selfishness in academically out-performing Bibba and Adelaide and an urgent need to restrain myself lest I lose these friends as well. Those were thoughts I never shared with anyone.

Not even God. In Meeting for Worship, where attendance was required both Wednesday and Sunday mornings, I earnestly pursued my Inner Light. Mr. Huben's religion class lectures about thinkers like Kant, Kierkegaard, Dostoyevsky, and Thoreau, who had focused on man's innerness, gave me hope — that I, too, possessed an inner self. Some students, I knew, were only concerned with behaving well enough in Meeting to keep the teachers on the facing bench off their backs. But that austere silence came to be highly valued by me. I often closed my eyes during it to better discern what Mr. Huben called "the truth within you."

"The Inner Light is God's spirit entering you," he droned. "Sometimes it will move you to speak, to stand and share your enlightenment with others. When that happens, you become an instrument of God."

"But I don't really want to," the voice inside me whispered. "I want to be lovable and good." (Which was not possible in our household where "bad" made Father lovable and "good" made me "greedy.")

"From those unto whom much has been given much shall be expected."

"A scar is a kind of mark, a stigma," my thoughts wandered. In my mind's eye Grandfather's white V reflected the lamplight. He had forgotten that he was an old man. In his mind's eye he and I had been the same age. . . equals, peers, grown-up children, both people from whom much was expected. "A mirror of respect." But respect can be an isolator, too, an insulator, a quarantine, a wall, loneliness. . . to hide the "me" and the "not me" Father condemned as "feelingless intellectual."

I looked for Liz's dark eyes as I rose to speak: "Thanksgiving is the time of year when we express our gratitude for God's bounty. . . ."

Streaking through the blackness that night in January 1950, the light studs became shooting stars that I could no longer "really see" because of how their flitting heightened my own sense of rocketing. And spun thus into a star myself, I clutched the nightgown to my bony body as all the protection remaining against the relief and exhilaration of no longer being as weak and full of dread as in the beginning.

My suitcase contained a *Seventeen* magazine with one of my stories in it. And at the ride's end, Liz and Eleanor would hug me and talk with excited admiration about my story being published. However, that transformation from lost loner to valued friend felt perplexing. Eleanor and Liz and Mr. Frescoln knew me as a thinking person who sometimes rose in meeting to speak her thoughts and wanted to be able to write as effectively as our heroes: Dostoyevsky, Thoreau, Mark Twain. Welcoming me, they would grin and exclaim, "Now you are a writer! Lucy, aren't you proud of yourself?!"

But I felt fat . . . disgusting, soft, weak, bloated, gross, not vigilant enough against the swelling flesh making me like Mommy. Still flying with the lights, I reached inside the nightgown to find protruding hipbones, corrugated ribs, hollowed collarbones to soothe away the fat, filthy, selfish accomplishment, Mommy-in-me coming out. But uneased, I had to slither flatter to the lying-down position. And my fingers feeling for the hair held back in disgust as much as my mind had earlier prayed to hold my body back from the curse. Before the fat fear, I had reassured myself that if the periods didn't come, I wouldn't be like her. But they had. So I was. And the hair was proof.

Mommy and Father had been delighted with the story. Over the ice cubes, they'd smiled at each other and said to me: "Of course. . . I've known you would write ever since you learned to talk."

"It's always been in your blood, bound to come out eventually. Time proves all."

Mommy had read the introduction aloud: "'Good-bye Bobbie,' our short story of the month, is by Lucy Daniels, a fifteen-year-old high school junior at the George School in Bucks County, Pennsylvania. Lucy says that this story was inspired by the marriage of her sister. Lucy's ambition is to be a writer like her father."

I'd listened, standing in the doorway, blushing from their delight. Father took long drafts from his cigarette. Mommy folded the magazine and held it out for him to see my picture. But I knew they hadn't read the story because they didn't mention what it said. I kept wondering if they would read it and, if they did, whether they would understand what I was saying in it.

"Lucy, we are so proud of you," Mommy declared. "Your giftedness will enrich the world."

"My boy!" Father praised, pouring more Bourbon into his glass. "My wonderful boy! I'll probably have to worry about being in your shadow, too."

All I'd felt was numbness and that there had been some mistake.

The things they kept saying didn't sound like me.

The news of Bibba's wedding had come suddenly, after Mommy and Father hung up the telephone one summer evening.

"Bibba's getting married," Father had said.

"When?" I asked.

"It's not quite decided," Mommy answered. "Probably sometime this fall."

"What will we wear?" Mary Cleves asked.

"Never mind that yet," Mommy said.

Only long afterwards had she told us that no children would go; due to the expense of a New York wedding, Bibba had decided to have only Mommy and Father. I had felt sad and deeply hurt, preferring to see it as Mommy's rather than Bibba's doing, so as to not lose the last shreds of my fantasy about our still being close. From that perspective, Bibba's marrying seemed a final loss of the most treasured guide and hero of my childhood. And later, a confusing note from Bibba seemed to make my preference truth after all. It read: "Dear Lucy, I've really been disappointed to learn none of you can come to the wedding. I've wanted very much for you to know Chick. But I guess I'll just have to think of another way to accomplish this." That letter reminded me of having to help hide the drinks behind the books.

Probably I dealt with Bibba's marriage by starting "Good-bye Bobbie," which was about the painful feelings her loss caused me, and by visiting Grandfather. He had been writing as always that summer but was, also, still glad to stop and talk when I visited. After climbing the wide stairs and breathing the rich mingled scents of Mexico, polished mahogany, and oriental rugs, I often entered the library without his hearing me above the electric fan's fluttering of papers. Again in those visits, he talked about his writing and politics and wanted to hear from me about my writing and George School. I compared him in my mind to Eleanor and Liz. But I didn't tell him about the story I was writing. Perhaps, I decided later when it was too late, because of how sad I might have felt doing so. Even without telling him, I thought about how old he looked. The whirring of the fan was always a comfort as I approached and departed, telling me he was still there.

I never told Father about the story either, but I almost did several times. I didn't because somehow that summer Father despised me more than ever and because I'd figured out that for some reason my excitement over something like writing especially led to trouble. Many an afternoon (because I kept wanting him to love me and because Mommy seemed to, too), I'd go to the library to talk with him at drink time, only to be devastated minutes later because something I said or something about me provoked him. I could never recall — I can only guess even now what it was that set him off. But his words pursue me still: "Goddamn, little shit, do you have to be so selfish?! You and your self-righteous greediness!! So hateful and intellectually insensitive, maybe you don't have it in you to consider another person!"

My part was still to plead, "I'm sorry, Father, what did I say? I don't mean to be selfish. . . ." Then to flee to my room in tears, still trying to figure it out.

In my memory the magazine picture looked fat. The cheekbones were not prominent enough. The eye sockets were less hollow than I needed them to be. Besides that, the chin was too firm, the mouth too confident and full of teeth. Turning to the Pullman window's ebony mirror, I hoped to find a less prosperous reflection to correct it. But the image there was little different.

Grandfather would not have noticed the fatness in either. Or understood how despicable such prosperity was. Rather, Grandfather would have considered publishing a short story, an adventure like going to boarding school. But this January also marked the anniversary of his sudden death from pneumonia. And, as with Bibba's wedding, Mommy had decided that my returning home for his funeral so soon after Christmas didn't make sense.

When I looked outside again, the lights had ceased. The dark gray window framed a landscape that was asleep. Or dead. Darker, hunched, muted forms of ghost towns slipped past, lit only by solitary street lights that deepened the impression of barrenness. They reminded me of the shades of the underworld we'd read about in Latin. Persephone. Odysseus. Aeneas. In religion class, Mr. Huben had said that Kierkegaard and Nietzsche found enlightenment in bleakness. But that night's rocking clacking only seemed eternal to me.

At George School, the things that troubled me most were homesickness, guilt for being a greasy grind, and the fat fear. Calorie counting became an obsessive preoccupation equaled only by ruminations over the food I could not eat. My advisor, Mr. Short, called me in about eating several times. But whenever questioned by him or Mrs. Johnson, the nurse at the infirmary, I'd say, "But I do eat. Like everybody else, I eat what I want and don't eat what I don't like. You don't criticize other people for that." That usually silenced Mr. Short, but not Mrs. Johnson. "Other people don't have your weight problem," she'd retort. And in time she got the doctor to write an order requiring me to rest at the infirmary instead of going to gym and to drink eggnog between meals. When Mrs. Johnson finally came upon me pouring an eggnog down the drain, she said solemnly, "Lucy, this is a very serious matter. You are growing up. But even when a person is your age, when they get as thin as you, responsible adults cannot ignore it."

The homesickness was terribly distressing. It was worse than ever before in my life, and none of the things I'd expected to help, did. The fuller my life at George School, the more outstanding my grades, and the more successful I became in extracurricular activities and leadership positions, the more severely both my grief related to Mommy and Father and my desperate yearning to be home besieged me. This felt especially shameful because of its contrast with my responsible, serene, assertive stance as a student leader. I did mention missing home to Liz and Eleanor, but I never told anyone what a desperate weeping wreck I became during those telephone calls home. After each one I hated myself so much that I wanted to die. Yet I could hardly wait to call again. And nothing helped.

Whereas at the start of George School I'd called home every Sunday morning after Meeting, by my junior year, when I should have been more independent, even calling two times a week wasn't enough. Mommy and Father didn't like it either. Sometimes they'd be supportive. But more often as my despair and weeping increased with the mid-week call, Father would become infuriated and ridiculing, and Mommy would confront me belligerently with my good grades and community contributions as proof of my having no reason to miss home.

The problem was that her confrontations had no more impact on me than my own. I remained desperate and ashamed of myself as a failure. And this seemed both markedly worse in my junior year and out of keeping with my friendships and accomplishments.

Mr. Frescoln and his interest in my writing had provided the main distraction from other worries all along. After reading my freshman copybook journal, he'd asked if I had ever considered writing my thoughts and feelings about Bibba in short story form.

"Not exactly. . . But I have thought of doing something about her."

Mr. Frescoln's freckled round face had brightened with a grin. "I definitely think you should." He reminded me of Father. The way his reddish brown hair curled on the top of his high forehead. The laughter crinkling at the corners of his green eyes. His brusque confident manner that, despite being critical, made me feel all the more important for being valued by him. "If you do write it," he'd said at the end of that talk, "I'd like very much to read it, whether you're in my class or not. You clearly have talent. And if you do work at it, Lucy, there's no telling how far it may take you."

I felt aglow after that talk. Back in the dorm, I told Liz about Mr. Frescoln's praise. But I never told her or Eleanor about how I felt talking to him. Nor, as time passed, did I tell either of them about the thrill I felt when he called on me in class. Those feelings — a singing in my blood combined with goose pimples and light-headedness — seemed all the more exhilarating (and less embarrassing) for being private.

Just two months earlier, in November of our junior year, we'd all taken the Pre-Scholastic Aptitude Test. The evening before, Liz and I had talked while she was brushing her thick black hair. I'd been tired and depressed that night and viewed the next day as the beginning of the end of the friendship shared by Liz and Eleanor and me because these college boards would enable us to leave school and disperse. Though I felt we were almost sisters, I'd begun to realize that fall, with increasingly sad helplessness, that friends lacked the natural permanence of family. And that felt particularly tragic due to how our threesome had been much better than sisters — because we could all belong and because the success of one didn't ruin the others. That night I felt stupid despite the A's I continued to earn from studying every spare minute.

Despite being short, Liz's hair was thick as well as black. I envied her because it looked strong and vibrant. Eleanor's hair was curly and dark, too. Mine was brown and thin. "I'm afraid about tomorrow," I said to Liz. "I feel stupid."

"How can you say that?" she asked. "With your A's and your writing?"

"You know it's only because I work so hard," I replied. "You see me. I won't be able to keep good grades in college. Even if I get in."

"Lucy, you wear me out the way you stay so down on yourself!"

The brush driving through Liz's hair reminded me again of the differences in our bodies. Liz's was soft and full and growing taller. She and Fred were going steady. I envied that but would have been too shy to go steady with any boy. I felt especially grateful that she didn't act superior about it. We were to be roommates the next year as well. In the same room. It wouldn't have occurred to either of us to do otherwise. But after that, I mused, watching her, we'll all three be scattered to colleges we don't even know yet. And I'd be separated from them, as I was from Bibba and Mary Cleves and Grandfather.

"You know, Lucy," Liz said, putting down the brush and turning to face me, "I bet you'll be the one of us who scores highest on the college boards. But I don't envy you. Because I do believe that when I go to college with my lower scores I'll feel a lot more happy and confident than you do."

Tears blurred my eyes. They had to do with losing Liz.

Perhaps I dreamed on that train ride. Or perhaps I just dozed and, waking again in the lightening gray, was struck with how much a berth resembles a grave. There seemed only an instant between that eight-year-old lurching lavatory reflection on the ride to camp and my conflict-ridden, developing, starving adolescent body. My story was about Bibba's leaving. But in the honesty of my heart, I knew that it had to do with my losing Bibba, my causing the loss. Like my causing Grandfather's death by not having gone to see him enough when I knew nobody else listened to his stories the way I could.

Mr. Huben had talked to us many times about an underground railroad in Germany during the war. It had enabled some Jews to escape the Nazis by being smuggled through Catholic convents. He'd used that as an example of "backing your convictions with personal responsibility and sacrifice." Still, despite my having known better, politics and God, William Jennings Bryan and "The Other Wise Man," had all died of loneliness. I thought about Grandfather's no longer writing in the study with the fan on, and I remembered that we had never talked about death.

The sky had become paler gray. Dawn veiled farm buildings and landscape with a misty shroud that allowed only occasional slow, dull lights to glimmer. Stretching so my feet pressed against the end of the trembling berth, I recalled Grandfather chuckling as he talked about his childhood longing to journey to the railroad bridge metropolis of "Capa City." (I had only understood after years of hearing this that as a child he had mistaken "capacity" for the name of a town.)

My *Seventeen* story felt like it had come too quickly, leaving me behind — but also, too late, since Grandfather would never read it. Those two coming together in my mind — the story and Grandfather's absence — created a desperate sense of life running away. And by then, in response to that urgency, the medley of my crimes was automatic — a deep well from which my pleas for forgiveness only drew more resounding guilt: Bibba being exiled for badness while I faked goodness; Grandfather drowning in loneliness; Father's rage about my selfishness; the proof of it in Adelaide's bad grades and my magazine story; eggnog down the drain.

In contrast, I knew that morning that back at George School Liz and Eleanor would shout and hug me. Mr. Frescoln would say, "It certainly is gratifying to discover magazines can recognize a well-written story." But I wondered if even they would really read it. Would it matter for itself, published or not? Would they see me in it and not just my Inner Light? I held up my hands to look at their thinness before pressing them against the solid sharpness of my hip bones.

Because the train was late, I spent a long time sitting upright in the remade berth while looking out at tenements and warehouses crowded together in the outskirts of Philly, weathered gray in the bright morning. Studying that contradiction, I measured the circle of my wrist with overlapping thumb and middle finger, then the circle of my upper arm. The smallness of both was reassuring. The train continued rumbling, clackety-clack, clackety-clack, but had become diligent instead of hurtling.

Taking the magazine out of my suitcase, I again appealed to its photograph for signs of purity and immortality. But they were still absent: Too much fat. Too little bone. Too full to fit the mold of their expectations or my intentions. Too hungry. Too greedy. Too weak. This meant that the means to hold life back, to ward off its cruel shortness, would have to come from Inner Light rather than outer appearance. The sunshine was helpful, though. Its sparkle on the window glass revived my hope that time could be frozen by a bracelet of thumb and forefinger.

chapter nine

BLANC MANGE

These nights sleep eludes me. Years ago depression caused that, and lying awake in the dark made life seem grimmer still. But now I use the awake time to figure out what feelings block the sleep, what my unconscious mind fears it will see if I dream. At the moment, I think it's also afraid of what I'm writing.

Last night I finally got up at 3:30 and played solitaire. Since it doesn't require concentration, I can go on thinking about problems or feelings while the game lulls my unconscious into giving up defensiveness. I've realized, too, that solitaire is a kind of transitional phenomenon for me. Since Mommy played it all her life, this game not only symbolizes my aloneness and denial of feelings about aloneness (in its being "only" a game), it may also help me feel connected to her when I'm afraid. Last night playing seemed a clue that a separation is about to occur.

Putting a red queen on a black king, I thought about my words compared with Father's. I've coveted his wonderful way with words all my life and am still locked out of it, perhaps by my unconscious. Not as cruelly now as earlier, though. Psychoanalysis has shifted me from envying his voice to searching for my own. There's also another comparison — of my own experience of being weak while Father called me "greedy, selfish, soul-sucking" — which made me feel like an abusive monster and hopeless cripple at the same time. But the past tense is wrong here. I can still feel like both when I try to write.

In time I did sleep and had this dream:

The willow outside my office window is lovely in its early spring tenderness. But walking toward it alone over lush, sweet grass, I realized that a noose hung from its branches. Soon other people arrived. A crowd assembled. "What is this?" I asked, turning to a group of them. They looked at me strangely and did not answer. Trying not to look embarrassed, I asked again, "Is someone to be hung?" "Yes," they chorused. But when I asked, "Who?" they looked at me strangely. . . severely? . . knowingly? A single voice echoed, "A murderer."

Even upon waking I knew that dream had to do with writing — maybe with publishing that first story at fifteen or with retelling the next part of my life now. I love that willow tree. From my consulting room chair I've watched it go through its seasons again and again. I wonder why the dream dressed it for spring instead of winter?

Leanna's brown face turned toward me solemnly from beside the sink. "I already separated the eggs for you," she said. "So's you can finish quicker beings it's the day for the doctor."

Her words triggered fury that turned my mouth sour. With my body stiffening to prevent a flinging fit, I delayed answering to control my tongue as well. "I don't want eggs today," I finally stated, "I'm making blanc mange."

"I thought you said 'Spanish Cream.'"

"I did, but I can't." I spoke with careful precision in order to hide the weakness and to keep indecision from churning up again. Spanish Cream seemed temptingly richer. And puffed up with air-filled egg whites instead of whipped cream, it wasn't really fattening. But with my daily self-imposed limit of 500 calories, its 75 more were too many.

I could see Leanna's head shaking as she returned to the sink. "You could put them back in the icebox to use tomorrow," she said in response to her own question about what to do with the eggs.

"No," I said. "I won't be using them. From now on, it has to be blanc mange every day." I could see her head shake some more and thought I detected muttering as well, reminding me of Mrs. Johnson at school and of the eggnogs she'd made that were part whole milk, part cream. At home I would only use skim milk. The day Mrs. Johnson had finally confronted me about pouring out the eggnogs, I had almost talked to her. Despite sounding angry, something about her had made me think she wanted to understand. Now, at home, Mary Cleves still tried to touch my hand when she said, "Please eat, Lucy. I'm afraid of what they'll do if you don't." But I'd known Mrs. Johnson couldn't bear me. And I knew that nobody at home could either. Not Leanna or Mary Cleves or even Dr. Greenhill.

As I stirred the skim milk in the top of the double boiler, Leanna kept on: "I think you has to put some sugar in. I think there has to be some to make it smooth together."

"Not today," I declared, keeping my eyes on the milk. "Only sucaryl today."

"Don't you remember from before how you used half and half, sucaryl and sugar?"

"I remember. But now I have to use all sucaryl."

Leanna went on shaking her head as I replaced the sugar bin. I knew she was fuming about me being "spiteful" and not saying it because they'd told her I was sick. Leanna could only think about the taste and the texture. Pounds didn't matter to her, and she didn't even know what calories were. Whereas they kept insisting inside my head — over and over. To get relief, to prevent a mistake: 200 for two cups of scalded skim milk, 105 for three tablespoons of cornstarch at 35 each. One-third cup of sugar is 1/3 of sixteen table-spoons or 5-1/3 tablespoons times 60 equals 320. Too much. It might taste better, but I couldn't stand the worry of not obeying my plan. The frantic, disgustingly lost feeling of too much, too fat, too bad loomed. So did the feared screaming desperation of needing to shake it off me and not being able to.

Cleves wanted to talk to me. I could tell by the way she tried that she wanted me to protect myself from what Mommy and Father might do. Cleves was almost twelve then and far from being my child, as before. But I knew she loved me and with Adelaide away at George School we might have been friends. Talking to her would have been a relief. Only — there was no way I could have gotten her to see the inside part of me that got overrun with guilt when I tried to eat.

After the quarter-cup of cold milk, I stirred in the drops of sweet clear liquid, then the vanilla. 330 divided into four custard cups made 82-1/2 each. Pouring with meticulous evenness, I was relieved that with only 330 in my midnight meal, 170 would be left for the rest of the day.

In the night I wandered and eavesdropped. Like a werewolf. In the day I was confined by the need to avoid eating temptations. Also, by shyness, discomfort with talking, dread of their seeing my emptiness. The main reason for night wanderings was that they allowed me to find out things I never dared to ask. Lurking in the dark hall, my ears reached out to grasp what they were saying to each other in bed with the door open. Their words resounded starkly against the background of the hushed house.

"Died. . . some movie star's daughter."

"How do you know it was the same thing?"

"It said so. Anorexia nervosa, an eating disturbance."

"What did Greenhill say?"

"It's true. Some do die of it."

"Well, what's he going to do then?"

"Keep bringing her . . . to talk to him and so they can advise us. . . He still wants to see you."

"Lucy, these doctors are stupid! Fools! With people like us at their mercy! How is talking to someone like that going to help? You'd think he'd have the education and the brilliance to see clues we can't, to say things that would make her change. But strutting in his white coat, diplomas lining his walls! Just a lot of show while he's still help-less before a sixteen-year-old!"

"But give him credit. This is no ordinary disease. And Lucy is a remarkable girl. Anorexia is an affliction of the brilliant, the rarely gifted."

"And she is certainly smart enough to outwit him. But you. . . and you say it's with his instructions, support her self-centeredness! I tell you, he's torturing us. And implying it's our fault. Taking our money and confusing us to boot!"

"But, Jonathan, he's well respected and all we've got."

"Which of them isn't?! I can't even argue with her any more for fear of being 'controlling rather than caring.' Whatever that means! How do people die of it?"

"I don't know. From being susceptible, I think. He still wants you to come."

"I don't have the time for such games. Such stupidity! Besides, I want at least one of us to not be destroyed by him!"

As usual, the doctor said nothing. Just sat there with his pen and pad and stared at me in silence. The point was to get me to talk. I wasn't sure about what. I'd asked him early on, because even then I'd been trying to be good. But his answer, "whatever comes to mind," only made me more horribly aware of my mind's emptiness. I thought he meant for me to tell him what was wrong, why I had to keep getting thinner. Only, I didn't know. Besides, if I had, how could I have told him, since, after me, he always talked with Mommy? Especially when the only thing I did know was that I hated Mommy in me coming out.

"Why aren't you eating?" he finally asked. That day and every day.

"I do eat." But inside my calorie-filled head the thought reverberated: Father says this is stupid.

"But very, very little . . . some meals nothing. Why?"

I considered not answering. In that ritual I, too, could be silent. But, instead, I said the other, "Because I'm not hungry."

Early on he'd stayed quiet when I said that. And I would get the relieved and winning feeling of having thrown him off. But nowadays he'd changed to asking, "Isn't there more to it than that?"

His tone of voice was tempting. I kept my eyes away from his, but something about his white coat, pipe, and Adam's apple moving up and down made the idea of talking skitter through my thoughts. 330 for tonight left 170 for today. I didn't talk, of course. Father said he was a waste of money. Afterwards he talked to Mommy. Besides, my head was empty of any words to say. Empty of everything except calories and hunger. Probably what he meant by, "Isn't there more to it than that?" was that he'd guessed about the hunger. Probably he knew I lied about it. And, therefore, that I lied about other things.

Maybe he even knew that hunger had become all there was to me. And calories. He did not say it though.

After more silence, he asked his other question, "How are things with your parents?"

"It's not their fault," I said. "I'm just not hungry."

Riding home, Mommy said nothing. Her eyes were fixed straight ahead. Her hands gripped and loosened, gripped and loosened on the steering wheel. Her dimple jutted slowly in and out, in and out. I kept my eyes on the road or my lap. I knew Mommy wasn't talking because Dr. Greenhill had told her not to. I studied the huge wrists of my skinny arms. I rubbed the sharp hipbones under my dress. 330 for blanc mange. 60 for mushrooms. Maybe 100 for two pieces of diet bread or an apple. Last night's conversation picked at me. Should I ask Mommy? Dr. Greenhill had never said, "You can die of this." Neither did they. I said nothing. Like always.

The typed note attached to my June 1950, report card had read:

George School is proud of Lucy's achievements and appreciative of how her investment of self and energy has benefited the student body as well. But at this point it is the faculty's consensus that Lucy's eating problem is so serious that something substantive must be done to correct it before she returns to school.

"Goddamn fools!" Father had raged. "Since when is eating or weight reason to suspend a child from school?"

"I think they're worried," Mommy said.

"Rigid, blind, unimaginative old-maid clerks!" Father continued. "Taking it on themselves to tell parents of four children how to raise them!"

That had been the end of George School and the start of Dr. Greenhill, whom Father always referred to as "that stupid Jew."

In February 1951, the dining room echoed with the faces and voices of the people sent away. With Adelaide at George School, only Mary Cleves and I remained, opposite each other, but never exchanging words, almost never letting our eyes meet. Before Christmas Cleves had come to the closed door of my room every day after school. But when she started begging me to eat and telling me I was wrong not to, I got mad and stopped opening the door.

In the dining room I thought, Mary Cleves only thinks she loves me. If she knew how mean I really am, she'd hate me. The loneliness of that made me ache.

"Pass your plate, Lucy," Father said.

"No thank you. I'm not eating this."

Mommy looked at him killingly. Her dimple was going.

"What are you eating then?" His voice sounded furious.

"Jonathan!" Mommy's voice pleaded, vibrating with controlled anger.

"What are you eating then?" he yelled.

"Mushrooms." 60 calories. Two cups of liquid and pieces.

At last Leanna brought in the soup bowl filled with the two cans I'd opened and heated and saved from her butter. Nobody spoke. I could feel Mary Cleves looking at me, her eyes accusingly piercing in her fear-flattened face.

"Lucy, your Goddamn selfishness is intolerable!" Father shouted at me again before putting some meat in his mouth. "You, the intellectual! The one with intelligence enough to have some sensitivity! And capable enough to have promise! Instead, you piss it all away! You torture us all with your self-centered selfishness and insensitivity!"

"Jonathan!" Mommy pleaded with another killing look. Her own face had become red and tear-streaked.

"Don't try to play martyr with me!" he yelled back at her. "Doctor or no doctor, I will speak in my own house!. . . Mushrooms?!" he jutted his neck forward and bared his teeth to scare me. "MUSH-ROOMS!" Louder and shriller. "Lucy, your greed and selfishness are destroying this family!"

In my bedroom I no longer cried. I was cold and shaking. But otherwise, Father was right: I had no feelings. And tonight even the hunger had vanished. Despite not eating the mushrooms.

"Please come back down, Lucy," Mommy came in and said after a while. "Father is sorry. He loves you very much."

I gazed back at her without tears. From inside the bubble. My fingers stroked the new peach fuzz on my cheeks as I tried to decide whether to answer and what to say if I did. Does she see this peach fuzz? I wondered. Can she tell me what it means? Is it a sign of death? Or of maleness? Does it have to do with the stopped periods?

I knew that also happened in pregnancy. Such thoughts plagued me constantly. I had learned that the absence of periods was called "amenorrhea" and that it was something that went along with anorexia nervosa. But I wasn't at all sure that either of these was correct about me. I knew that I, not some strange disease, was making myself not eat and grow thin. I'd hated the periods I regarded as Mommy coming out in me, but now that they were gone, I worried that I could be turning into her boy against my will. And there was no way the doctors could really know about any of this because I didn't talk to anyone, not even Cleves or Mommy.

The guilt about what I was doing to the family and the fear of death had driven me to decide to eat a few times. But with each try, the other guilt and self-hatred had come back so fiercely that I'd stopped again. And I hadn't told Dr. Greenhill about this because I didn't want him to know (and possibly tell Mommy and Father) how bad I was. But now I wondered if God, or actually my behavior, wasn't punishing me after all by somehow turning me into the boy they wanted.

Mommy was still there. "Please, Lucy," she begged.

Afraid of what I might say to her, I lapsed into thoughts of Eleanor and Liz. Had they known about all this, they'd have been horrified. Probably they wouldn't even recognize me. They'd written letters that I'd never answered, despite wanting to. Even when I'd tried, I'd balled up the paper and thrown it away. How could I write them? What could I say? Because I no longer felt like the friend they'd written to. If I don't answer their letters, I thought then, still not answering Mommy, they'll forget me. I didn't want to be forgotten, but that seemed the only bearable alternative.

"Please come back, Lucy," Mommy pleaded again. Her dimple had stopped. Her diamond pin was neatly in place. She spoke with the proper patient voice she used when we went to the doctor or to church. "Father wants to talk with you. . . . Leanna has saved the mushrooms."

"Maybe in a little while," I finally answered. "But I need to be alone first."

I went back to thinking about Liz as Mommy closed the door behind her: Liz on her bed, brushing her thick black hair that night before we took college boards. How sad I'd been that night, thinking of college scattering Liz and Eleanor and me. Soul sisters gone forever. How thin and weak and unattractive I'd already felt compared to her and Eleanor with their soft, curving bodies and thick hair.

I could remember my eyes being wet when Liz said, "Lucy, you wear me out the way you stay so down on yourself!" But now, in my Raleigh bedroom fifteen months later, I was beyond tears. Peach fuzz covering cold emptiness.

Downstairs Father was drinking Bourbon. Usually when he did that, he was exuberant and loving. But he didn't apologize for yelling at me. I sat in the corner of the sofa that was dark, and as usual he held forth about "Live life to the hilt. . . Drink deep of the wine of life."

I watched him and listened. His face was ruddy in the lamplight. "I can remember myself, drunk as a lord," he continued, "leading the parade of us up a mountain in this horrendous thunderstorm. . . Of course, the rest were drunk and crazy, too. But they mainly followed me, I think, because of the brilliant words that came to me. I really was a clever skunk! But remember, there are less consequences for boys. . . I'll never forget all the girls Wilson Fennel and I used to screw. Competing. Daring each other on. Each determined to out-man the other!"

Mostly he seemed to be saying all that for himself. But Mommy, sitting catty-cornered to him with her own drink, listened benevolently. Then, stopping to take another swallow, he fell silent while gazing into space and wrinkling his forehead. When he resumed, Adelaide was the subject: "That pagan!" he exclaimed. "Wonderful life-loving pagan! Of course George School can't understand her! I just hope we're lucky enough for her to not get herself pregnant. Remember that, Lucy. At this point, I don't see how any of my daughters can forget what I've said about not bringing any babies home."

Mommy's dimple ticked continually. Her lips puckered, and the eyebrows came together over her nose. "The problem," she said, "is that Adelaide is so pig-headed. She could get pregnant out of spite, because she's heard you say that. . . And after all I've done to teach her! Not to mention the rules this year at George School. It's as if she's determined to pay me back by humiliating me! By doing what she knows is common and vulgar. How can she do this to me!? She wouldn't if she weren't mean to the core, determined to degrade herself and us in the process."

"No, my dear," Father chuckled, taking another sip. "I'm afraid it's not that simple."

I scrutinized him as he twisted his glass. For some reason I expected to hear a new secret. Perhaps something about Babs. How she'd died.

"You have to remember she's my child," he resumed. "Satan's life-affirming temptress. Desire driving through her like a demon. Desire drunk for the whole, the all, the ultimate! And death be damned! Scoffed at! Defied!" Tears glistened at the corners of his eyes. His mouth quivered before taking the next sip. And then, while swallowing, his eyes discovered me; picked me out of the sofa's shadow, and set my heart pounding with fear and excitement. "You are the wise one, Lucy," he continued more softly. "The gifted one! And I love you for that. You would never be stupid. . . or so cheap. . . as to bring a baby home. You're too cold and blue-blooded, too much a lady." His eyes went away again then, glassy without moving, wistful over something I couldn't see. Then, "Come, Lucy," he said, raising his glass and peering into my eyes. "Come sit on an old man's lap. Warm an old man's heart."

I forgot his hating screams when he said that. Or rather, I prayed for however I was at that moment to somehow make up for what it was in me that set him off when he hated me. Also, there was a way that Father's loving me made me want to comfort him, kiss his forehead, and let him kiss me so that he would chuckle and the sadness would drop away from his eyes. But by the time I was on his lap with his hand stroking the back of my neck and his lips brushing my forehead and my ear, other feelings — excitement, dizziness, fear, nausea — slammed me back to the numbness that I knew so well. And that lack of feeling crowded me with distrustful questions: How could Father love me there when he'd hated me in the dining room? How could he when I was not a pagan, when I was careful to not let him kiss me on the mouth? Was he saying it because he thought I was dying?

Mommy stood up and left the room. The boniness of my legs hurt against his hard thighs. He caressed the hair about my ears and the bones of my cheeks. His hand took my chin and turned it to face him so that his moistened blue eyes looked deep into me. But due to the kissing fear, I pulled myself back around. I felt lulled and dizzy from the Bourbon on his breath and from the tingle of his fingers touching my ribs and squeezing my thigh.

"You know you're my boy," he said. "The only child I have with the intellectual sensitivity to continue the Daniels legacy."

He kissed my ear, and I felt wet on his cheek. But by then I was numb all over, cold, like he said, "feelingless." Bad. Even in the face of his love.

"Lucy," he crooned on, "You must remember that. This eating business, these stupid doctors. . .you are bigger than both of them. You have the intelligence and the talent to rise above them. And you must! I need you to be my boy. As you are, as you always have been . . .my wonderful, wonderful gifted boy!" He kissed the back of my neck, sending quivers of longing through its deadness.

The "boy" part felt weird. I tried to think of it as just the intellectualness that was one part of me Father could love. He didn't know it had been lost, that all my mind could think about was food and calories. He jiggled his knees. "Yes, you are. . . and will always be. . . my wonderful, libidinal scripting boy."

The numbness erased me then, leaving only the tingling in my legs from loss of circulation.

In the mirror I felt better: thinner, flatter, ungreedy. Unmean. Looking made me think of Jesus. I wasn't that thin, but I was thin enough not to look like Mommy. Maybe not to keep Mommy out of me, but at least not to let her show. The pubic hair still taunted; even without periods, it resembled her. But otherwise, those thoughts told me, Lucy is thin enough to not be hopelessly greedy: the scales said 53. That was one pound more than that morning. But part of it was soda water and the mushrooms I finally had eaten. The sockets of my eyes looked deep. Was that death? Or just unfat? Things did happen outside my control. The downy hair on my cheeks. The hair on my head thinning, falling out. Eyes hollowing. All unintended byproducts of un-fat. Un-woman. Un-Mommy. My own famine. Or maybe death? Was there a place called starvation? 300 calories? Or 47 pounds? Or a precise hollowing of eye sockets? When did famine become starvation? When there were no longer eyes in the sockets? And if so, was that the same as death?

I tiptoed, doing all I could to carry the tray with its four dishes of blanc mange without making noise. No sugar. 330 calories. 60 more for the mushrooms. But as I stepped gingerly through the darkness, straining to keep the dishes from clinking, their bedroom voices stalked me.

"Dr. Greenhill thinks it's destructive for you to lose your temper with her like about the mushrooms. Jonathan, he even called it 'brutal.'"

"A lot he knows! Since he can't do anything with her, I shouldn't yell! And we have to live with the disruption she causes. I don't want to be brutal, but neither do I want to be sucked down this hole of destruction Greenhill goes along with."

"He keeps saying you need to come."

"I won't.... He's the doctor. My time and strength need to be preserved."

In spite of all my efforts to be silent, my bedroom door squeaked as it opened.

"Who's that?" he screamed. I heard his feet hit the floor.

I didn't answer, praying he'd decide he was mistaken.

"Who's that!?" he screamed louder. Then coming, stomping, "WHO'S that?!"

I stood frozen.

Then the overhead light clicked on. Flooding the hall with blinding glare. Exposing me.

"Why didn't you answer me?!" he shrieked, and started toward me, rumpled and hulking in his pajamas. "What are you doing sneaking around in the night?! Like a burglar or a murderer!" His face was red, furious.

I did not answer.

But he stared me down.

"Just getting my blanc mange," I whispered. "Like I always do."

"In the middle of the night?!" he yelled. "Destroying our sleep as well as our meals with your Goddamned self-centered snivelling!!"

He moved toward me abruptly.

I felt cornered and naked. About to be erased.

And again things happened outside my control. The tray suddenly tilted with a snap of my wrist that sent the glass dishes crashing, shattering into splintered shards coated with milky paste. All my 330 calories! Smeared on the polished floor. Perched in the brass chandelier of the foyer below. And my gnawing hunger! Bulging mounds of splintery white blobbed feebly and too late, barricading my cowering carcass against the onslaught of his passion.

Last night after remembering all this, I had another dream:

A serene white landscape. Ice and snow with no people in it. Observing from a distance, I felt peaceful. The hills, trees, spires, peaks, skyscrapers, which were all white, rose around the edge of its frozen lake like giant teeth around a surreal mouth.

chapter ten

SENTENCED

Focusing on the years that followed is like peering into ruins left by a bomb. For a long time I couldn't look. Or rather, like my brain-damaged patient with visual agnosia, I could look and look without recognizing anything. In an uncanny way that made not only those years, but the underpinning of me, feel erased. Not looking and trying to forget seemed best.

But Dr. Howie's way of doing things is the reverse — seeing and remembering. From the first time I stumbled across him, his pressure to recall and consider, consider and recall prodded me to look and feel. From that beginning, the crater's charred fragments took on life that slowly evoked a wincing wonder and gradually drew me into closer scrutiny amid shifting feelings of fear, guilt, relief, shame, anger, and pain.

It was with Dr. Howie that I first understood that seeing is a discrete and individual capacity that cannot be forced. Also, that some things are easier to see than others. I've always recalled that poignant morning of my first snow, but filling in the memories and feelings of this next life period has required years of arduous and sometimes agonizing work. And, even now, it's short on understanding.

A traumatized person's capacity to see the reality of both him/herself and others changes with life circumstances and with the emotional wherewithal to tolerate what's there to be seen. Time, age, and personal effort have repeatedly altered the external circumstances of my life. Dr. Howie has helped me change internal circumstances.

Still, it has taken more than half my life for experience and psyche to make the seeing I can do now bearable.

So much was lost in that psychic bomb crater. Not only my voice, utterly, and my feelings, but the very basis of my self. As the anorexia tightened its grip, what little psychological insight I'd had vanished. The unconscious terror and rage and the conscious guilt, all of which I strained to contain by starving myself, kept me blind and only able to think obsessively, rigidly, fearfully, like a traumatized animal. Driven by my desperate need to not know and to not feel responsible (as I unconsciously *did* feel) for all I did know and had known all alone from an unbearably precocious age, I had to not know myself as well.

So, after all that, how can a person come to know herself, let alone claim her voice, in relation to such trauma? I would have to say slowly, painfully, strainingly, and, unfortunately, possibly too late to prevent damage to other important aspects of life—like love relationships, raising children, and creative work.

They hospitalized me in April 1951, shortly after my seventeenth birthday. Apparently this was at the urging of my Uncle Worth. At the time I was five feet four inches tall and weighed a little over fifty pounds. Historically that period preceded the drug therapies. Phenothiazines, tranquilizers, anti-depressants, and lithium only came into use in the mid-to-late 1950's. Those years also preceded any systematic understanding of the psychodynamic issues in anorexia nervosa.

Electro-convulsive shock therapy (ECT) was the first thing the doctors tried. It added feelings of mental obliteration to my emaciation.

"Doing O.K.?" the blond lady asked. Bending over the bed, her face came close; her hand gripped my wrist.

I knew her from somewhere: the white coat over her dress, brown eyes, matter-of-fact voice. But I couldn't remember from where. Or why we were together in that white-curtained cubicle. "My head hurts terribly."

"I know," she soothed. "It will for a while…. Try to sleep." Then she disappeared through a slit in the curtains, leaving me with a throbbing head and dense confusion. I did know her. Well, even. The face was familiar. Also the voice. But her name wouldn't come. Trying to remember was sickening because I couldn't. The blankness made me desperate. Finding myself seemed even more urgent than naming the lady. Where was I? How had I got here? What was wrong with my head? And who? WHO? I decided to search outside the curtains.

But standing bombarded me with terrible sickness. Almost falling, I held onto the bed while it and the curtains swam before me. Reaching to soothe my head, I found greasy temples and hair caked with something like salt. What had they done to me?! Still holding onto the high narrow bed, I looked for the opening in the curtains.

Outside there was a narrow corridor stretching out of sight between other white curtains. Following it, tottering, I came on a sudden wide hallway full of people walking fast in both directions. Stepping out among them I kept on, less lost than before because I was following those before me. Until, looking down, I felt embarrassed to find myself barefoot and in only a knee-length gown open down the back. I clung to the crowd through a sliding door into what turned out to be an elevator.

And how my head hurt! My eyes met those of a few other people — a large blue-haired lady with a lot of rouge. A young, thin, curly-headed man. They each looked away instantly. When the elevator stopped, I again went along with the others to a much larger place with more people. But they weren't moving, which threw me into sudden consternation. No longer just hopelessly lost, I couldn't even move.

"Lucy!" a voice cried. "Lucy!" I recognized my name in the sound but not the speaker. And immediately, before I could see, a young woman in blue and white grabbed my arm. "Lucy, what are you doing here?" I let her take me.

My first memory in the hospital is the one I've just described — my confusion after a shock treatment. It's harrowing still, that granulated grease and the lostness that together amounted to total erasure of self. But more horrible still is the memory of the shock being administered. I don't like to recall it; a shudder still runs through me when I do; a wail wants to come from my throat. But I can make myself be specific: I'm stretched out and held in position face up on that high, narrow table. The nurses, preparing for the ritual of horror, mechanically put a pillow under my knees and a rolled up towel under my neck. I always knew time was running out when the doctor jammed the cotton rolls inside my mouth and positioned the Vaseline-lathered pieces of the metal headband on my temples. All were prelude to the moment of plugging me into the black box and blasting my brains to nothing. Again and again and again until the days were inseparable and the terror constant, until the brain, person, protoplasm of me had hopelessly disintegrated.

I've often wondered since why I cooperated with such brutality. Thinking about it still makes me feel weak and ashamed, partly because it reminds me of being controlled by Mommy. But the physical compliance those doctors wrested from me never quelled my fear of dying. I don't know whether I complained in the midst of that continual blasting. Perhaps I was too ravaged to, though it seems equally likely that terror would have been even more obvious in that beaten animal. At any rate I can't remember. The black box blasted too much away. And I do blame the shock rather than the emaciation for that loss because now, long after, I can remember details of being at home when the emaciation was at its worst.

Months later, though, when they were only shocking me twice a month, I did complain and plead and almost refuse. I did so in spite of feeling helpless in my efforts to convey the experience of obliteration to the nurse Christina and the doctors. Because they never did seem to understand:

"In time your memory will come back. . . "

"The headache is only temporary. These pills will help. . . "

"No, your brain has not been destroyed."

They simply could not hear that the shock itself was horrible. . . excruciating. . . devastating. They absolutely had to believe I couldn't feel it. And the worst of this was that the doctors themselves seemed kind. Dr. Horwitz, the one who actually administered the shock, was a hearty, good-humored man in his forties. Dr. Zabrisky, who I suppose now was his supervisor or a consultant, was very old and talked like a supportive grandfather. Still, it was only several months later, when they were shocking me every two weeks or once a month, that they heeded my complaints and started giving me sodium pentothal to put me to sleep beforehand. After that it was a great relief to wake up and know from the terrible headache that the electrocution was behind me for a while and that I had survived again.

However, nothing helped my mental disintegration. Even when I could remember who I was and where, my mind had been blitzed beyond functioning. I could not read or make sense of someone reading to me. I couldn't remember what day it was and found the disorientation unnerving. It was painfully clear that the capacity I'd once had to think and speak and write had vanished. When I verbalized any of this despair, reassurances that these problems were due to the ECT and would pass were little comfort. Despite hoping the doctors and nurses were right, I suspected that my mind had actually disintegrated and that the shock was only delaying their discovery of this. I had no desire to be visited by my parents because I knew that if they saw me, they'd immediately understand that the self and mind that had once been there no longer existed.

Still, some things I felt later were absent then. During the period of the shock treatments I was physically sick and helpless. But "crazy" with all its associations and consequences was not yet known to me. Whereas later, it became my most conscious explanation for things like compulsively peeling my fingers until they bled and not being able to make eye contact with people. The word "crazy" still reminds me of Bea in my early childhood talking about the "loonies at Dix Hill." But for me in the hospital, the meaning of "crazy" gradually changed and expanded from not being able to understand what was the matter with me, to being "locked up with the crazy people," to "if you are crazy, it doesn't matter what you want. They can do whatever they want with you whether you like it or not." Then, still, "crazy" had to do with something wrong with me that I couldn't understand, very similar to not knowing how to stop the selfish greediness that Father had shrieked about. Only years later did this definition expand to: "In the eyes of the world, crazy once is crazy forever."

After several months, when the bulk of the shock was over, I went with the nurse, Christina, back to Silver Hill, a sanitarium in

Connecticut that Christina described as a "treatment facility for people who're mentally ill." I found this hard to comprehend, in part, perhaps, because of the continuing fog from the ECT, but more so because the country club atmosphere of Silver Hill didn't seem like a treatment facility and the people there weren't recognizably sick. Meals were served in a bustling linen-and-silver dining room resembling a country inn. The "patients" seemed to move about freely, taking walks, playing cards, going to "workshop" or competing at tennis and croquet as they pleased. Only because Christina said they were sick did I search their faces and behavior in an effort to label their maladies. Some did look sad, withdrawn, grim in a way that made it easy to guess they were depressed. But it was hard to tell about the rest. The majority seemed to be people who looked and acted perfectly normal and who Christina said were probably alcoholics. There was no one as thin or as young as me. And only a few seemed dazed the way I felt from the ECT.

"Insulin shock" was my main treatment at Silver Hill. This amounted to being given an injection of insulin early each morning and then lying in bed for several hours before eating. In the process I'd grow weak and woozy, confused, and sick feeling; then Christina would bring a tray full of breakfast, the eating of which — at first with hands so trembly that Christina had to help — somehow stopped the perspiring stupor. Confused as I still was from the ECT, this insulin seemed even less understandable. I wondered if I had diabetes and if there was some causal relationship between that and my difficulties with concentrating and remembering. When Christina and Dr. DuBois denied any such connection and said the sweaty, shaking confusion was "expected," I didn't know what to think. More than the treatment itself, I hated the gluttonous, swelling animal it changed me into. Even after breakfast, Christina would urge me to eat throughout each day, because the dizzy weakness could return at any time and, in fact, result in a coma if I didn't quickly drink the bottle of sugary lemon syrup she insisted I carry everywhere.

After collapsing a few times and coming to surrounded by worried people, I learned to drink that lemon syrup at the first twinges of weakness. But by the time my weight had reached the low 80's, I so detested my swollen body that I became more resistant to both eating and drinking the sugar water. Then Dr. DuBois, the doctor at Silver Hill who talked to me a little several times a week, ordered more ECT.

Christina and I rode the train into New York and Presbyterian Hospital for those treatments. The trips were torturous, not only because of dreading the shock, but also because by then I could see and comprehend more horrors than when I'd been in the hospital for continuous shocking. Clinging to Christina's arm as we followed the corridor to the white-curtained cubicle assigned me, I dreaded stumbling across someone having ECT and witnessing the explosion as it sent their body lurching. Christina always promised that wouldn't happen. Still, since I'd seen feet sticking up on the ends of beds in cubicles I knew were used for treatments, I stayed on guard. And one afternoon when we came across a group of strange-looking people sitting together and staring blankly into space, I made myself ask Christina about the way one person's head was bandaged and why the other two had foreheads with weirdly hollowed contours. "What's wrong with them?" I whispered.

"They've had lobotomies," she answered.

"What's that?"

"A kind of surgery. Neurosurgery."

"What do you mean? Neurosurgery?"

"Surgery that involves brain tissue."

"Why do they do it?" I imagined the peopleless bodies falling into a pile of dust.

"It's rarely done . . . a new technique reserved for patients who're in severe distress and can't be helped any other way."

"Distress? . . . What kind of distress?"

"Well, intense, incessant worrying . . . or destructive behaviors that can't be stopped."

"Would they do it to me?"

"Of course not. You're getting better."

However, since I was being shocked again because of not getting better enough, the image of those empty faces became a source of obsessive dread. And that was all the more powerful because of my guilt. Besides being unwilling to eat and gain weight as Christina and Dr. DuBois expected, by then I was terrified by the idea of being "better" and back in the world not only as a high school dropout who could not look people in the eye, but also as a brain-damaged person incapable of further education. This last idea came from repeatedly trying to read books whose words wouldn't take on meaning, so that I could never recall at the end of a paragraph what it was about.

Despite the shock and insulin, Silver Hill with Christina seemed the best I could hope for, even the best I had known. I couldn't talk to Christina, probably as much out of distrust as from having an empty mind, but her being with me so constantly in that non-critical supportive way felt a little like being with a grown-up Bibba. It was only much later that I realized she was with me so I wouldn't lapse into a coma undetected.

Then one morning in the spring of 1952, Christina announced that Dr. DuBois wanted to see me. At his office early that afternoon, she went in first; when she came out, her face seemed exceptionally unexpressive. When I sat opposite Dr. DuBois's quiet, white-coated kindness, he seemed the same as usual. The talking we did for a few minutes several times a week was not what I'd call psychotherapy. My confusion wouldn't have allowed that. Normally, it was just his friendly listening to how I felt and what I was afraid of. But this day he didn't wait for me to speak. In a direct business-like tone I'd never heard before, he said, "Lucy, it happens that today I have to give you some unanticipated and possibly upsetting news...." The hollow-eyed lobotomy patients came to mind. The breath inside me was sucked away. "Your parents have decided to take you to a different hospital. They will be here to pick you up in about an hour."

In the car Mommy and Father were strangers. I sat in the back seat instead of between them in the front as they'd insisted. I mostly couldn't believe what was happening — that after a year they'd suddenly left the other end of the telephone and appeared in person, that Silver Hill and Dr. DuBois, those all-powerful managers of my existence, were now being left behind, and above all that Mommy and Father expected me to ride with them and without Christina. Clutching the seat, I braced against terrors I didn't dare voice or even think about. I studied the backs of their heads for some clue to my fate — Father's driving and occasionally speaking heartily and Mommy's perpetual hat.

"Don't be upset," Mommy soothed, turning to glance at me. "We are doing this for your welfare, Lucy. Everything will be fine."

"And as soon as you get yourself well," Father added, without turning, "you can leave. . . leave and go back to being the wonderful writer you are."

"Where is this hospital?" I asked. "What's its name?" I had told them before on the telephone, told them, in fact, many times about my mind being messed up and unable to think and read let alone write. So the despair his comment triggered felt unspeakable.

"It's in New York State," Mommy replied. "It's called New York Hospital."

"Is it like Silver Hill?"

"We don't know," Father declared abruptly.

And then, after a long silence, "What will they do to me there?"

"We don't know," Father's abruptness bounced back. "Your mother and I are not the doctors. We'll have to do what they say. And so will you. At least they charge less. These 'good' doctors, Lucy, can be pretty money-grubbing."

"Is it a state hospital?" I asked. I'd heard horror stories about those.

"No. But it's not a country club either. It's a long-term treatment facility where they do research and provide cost-effective treatment for patients they're interested in studying."

Then, grasping for a last straw, "Will they give me more shock?"

"I don't know," Mommy answered. Her face was turned so that I could barely glimpse the dimple.

The nurses there were young, Bibba's age, but they were also ominous. They loomed on either side of me, one in a starched white uniform, the other in blue and white. Each held what looked like a wet rolled-up sheet.

The tears that had been unstoppable in the hours since Mommy and Father left me cleared instantly as the nurses closed in. Fear clutched my throat. "What?!" I gasped. "What are you going to do to me?"

I'd asked this same question in the dayroom, when the nurses had first approached. They hadn't had the sheets then, but their coming in two at a time had scared me. "Miss Daniels, please come with us," they'd said simply, curtly, but still comparable to Christina. So I'd been easily persuaded to obey meekly, weakly, half pretending they were her.

But now in this large, gloomy, window-barred room with its bed waiting for the wet sheets, I held back in horror. These nurses had kind faces, but they also looked large and powerful, filling the room as though I were an insect they had to stamp out or experiment with in whatever way they wanted. Peering at them through more tears, I wondered whether they were really kind like their faces or menacing like their size and the sheets. I suspected they were both: kindly performing their assigned torturing, even deadly tasks without comprehension.

"Take off your clothes please."

"Why?"

"For a treatment. The doctor wants you to have a treatment."

My thoughts sprang to rolled cotton in my mouth and being plugged into a black box. "No," I mumbled. "What treatment?"

They moved closer. "The doctor will talk to you about it when he comes . . . Take off your clothes."

Stiffening, I didn't budge. "What is it?" I pleaded. "Is it shock?"

"No." They each grabbed an arm and pushed me toward the bed. "Your doctor ordered it," the starched white one insisted, unbuttoning my blouse and ripping it off. Then she went after my skirt.

When they got to the slip I struggled frantically and tried to slap their hands away. The bed itself looked terrifying. Covered with brown rubber sheets, the wet ones they'd rolled out on it looked like white stripes. I worried about a connection between rubber and electricity.

As they pushed me down on the bed, my nakedness still strained against, but no longer dared to struggle with their strong arms. "Lie down," they commanded. "Lie down, Miss Daniels!" They started wrapping my arms in the icy sheets, slamming me back as I resisted.

Perhaps a shock that is applied to my whole body, I thought. A black box into which my whole body will be inserted and chewed up. A new procedure that will render me worriless but also as personless as those lobotomized ghosts. "Please!" I cried. "Is this another kind of shock?!"

"No," one of them answered, "just tube feeding."

Somehow with those words in combination with the freezing sheets, new tears flooded me. Lying straight as the nurses forced me to, and with arms bound, I yielded helplessly as they ultimately converted me into a mummy, bound so tight that I couldn't stir. So cold that my teeth chattered. More dismal even than the shaking woozy insulin mornings back at Silver Hill. Because after the nurses walked out, leaving me helpless and alone to stare at the ceiling, I knew that Christina would never come back.

In those mental hospitals a patient had no control whatsoever. The staff did to you what they wanted to whenever they decided to do it. With no warning. If you didn't like it, that was too bad. If you protested, you were wrong. As a result I was quietly terrified the whole time I was at Silver Hill and New York Hospital. Thanks to my lifelong identification with the aggressor, I didn't think anyone wanted to hurt me. But I did think those doctors could do something terrible to me by mistake, due to thinking they knew what was best when they didn't.

New York Hospital was a different world from Silver Hill. I'd noted the physical difference driving in — the vastness of the New York Hospital grounds, the somber massiveness of the brick and stone buildings, the barred windows. And even though the view from inside Hall IV's dayroom windows was pretty with green lawns and towering shade trees as well as ivy-covered buildings, other features made it nothing like a country club. All the doors were locked; patients could go nowhere without a nurse. Many ordinary things were not permitted — belts, scarves, eyeglasses, nail scissors, bobby pins, needles, pins, jewelry, matches or anything that came in a glass container. When we went to walk, there had to be a certain number of nurses for so many patients, and patients were repeatedly counted before, during and after each walk and sometimes even while just sitting on the ward. Other things were counted, too, including cigarettes, bowel movements, and menstrual periods. The men in that hospital were in separate wards from the women. I was again the youngest and the thinnest. Since they tube-fed me twice a day, I only saw the other patients at lunch. People looked a lot sicker there than at Silver Hill; some appeared obviously crazy.

Listening to conversations, I learned this was an admission ward and only one of many to which patients were assigned according to their degree of sickness. There were some better wards where people could have belts and eyeglasses and where no treatments like shock and tube feeding were done. Patients on better wards could go out to dinner with a visitor. There was also a "disturbed" ward called Nichols Cottage where people were sent — often suddenly — if they got crazy or hit a nurse or tried to run away. "Nichols" was always uttered with hushed awe.

They took me to Nichols one cold rainy evening because I tried to fight off the wet pack for tube feeding. At my refusal, three nurses came instead of the usual two, and I picked up a chair to ward them off. At that instant it didn't feel like I was the one doing it. Poor little disgustingly submissive Lucy never would disobey like that. And I was even more incredulous when the nurses forgot who I was and took me seriously as well. In a matter of seconds, those same three were fiercely escorting me through an underground passage to what turned out to be Nichols.

There I had no difficulty observing craziness. It showed in everyone. Those in whom it was least obvious were silent, expressionless women who only periodically went berserk and hit people at random or screamed. Any patient who was not in seclusion or in the treatment room was required to stay in the dayroom in constant view of the nurses. Many more things were not allowed — including hard-soled shoes, pencils, and more than one change of clothes. Most ladies wore only grey and white-striped hospital smocks. As a result, everyone looked the same there unless you studied individual faces or the minutiae of strange behavior.

The person who most attracted my attention early on was Althea Bell, who stood in the dayroom like a statue — right hand over her head, left one out in front of her — for hours on end. At first her stance seemed a joke designed to make fun of the nurses and their orders. I expected her to get hit or dragged off to be restrained in wet pack. But nobody else seemed to notice, as if she'd become as much a wall or a door to them as to herself. As she resumed the same position day after day, I grew increasingly curious and afraid of whatever had got inside and controlled her like that. This zombie stiffness seemed a particularly degenerative form of madness that I did not want to contract. Not only could Althea Bell neither speak nor sit down, she also couldn't look at you, or if she happened to, she did so with a penetrating gaze that went right through you. Sometimes a nurse spoon-fed her at meal times. Other days she'd get tube-fed. When a nurse helped her move her arm down, it would go up again as soon as the nurse stepped away. She reminded me of Mommy's pear tree.

There were few conversations on Nichols because everyone was preoccupied with themselves. Therefore, when by chance a patient spoke directly to me, the words seemed especially blessed, like Bibba's visits to the yard. But despite this lack of communication, some unspoken rules and facts were understood by all: give Mrs. White a wide berth, because, as placid as she looked, she could knock you down or try to strangle you with no change in her expression; wrinkled, grey-haired Mrs. Spate was distraught about the petrified baby corroding her insides because the doctors wouldn't surgically remove it; Mrs. Benson wasn't really paralyzed but just couldn't walk or talk or dress herself because of her depression.

Mrs. Delilah Corcoran was a fat, white-haired, 70-year-old cherubic matron who took a particular fancy to me. As the youngest patient on Nichols, I practiced the same silent, nondescript withdrawal as I had everywhere else. And this reticence, combined with my thinness, seemed a magnet for the older woman. Always effusive and frequently excited, she could count on me to listen more receptively than anybody else. She frequently plunked herself down next to me and launched into an intense conversation. The first few times she did this, I was startled and listened intently, partly out of fear and partly in an effort to discern her type of craziness. That wasn't readily apparent, however, and by the time my uneasiness had abated, we were friends. Mrs. Corcoran deplored having to wear tennis shoes and smocks and not having perfume. She was furious at her children for "dumping" her in this "Goddamn slammer," but she also tearfully defended them for not knowing about the "abuse and outrageous insensitivity in this gilded prison." She was most distressed that the doctors kept tube-feeding me and rattled off long lists of delicacies she would ask her daughter to have the cook prepare for me if I'd just eat them. "You know, my dear, you're just the age of my granddaughter, Ann," she said. "Would it suit you to be my protégé here?"

Over time I realized that Mrs. Corcoran's sickness involved being "too happy" and getting enraged when the nurses wouldn't let her celebrate. One student nurse explained this as a reaction to her husband's death a year before.

Except for the students in their blue uniforms, the nurses on Nichols were prison guards who focused on preventing trouble. Unlike the younger students who could be both friendly and kind, the older nurses were cold and no more communicative than the patients. Tuffman, the head nurse, was a muscular Amazon feared by everyone. Without her uniform (as occurred in a few crises) she looked like a man. And in uniform, her skirt often seemed incongruous. Her manner was brusque and deliberate; her voice deep, resonant, and unexcited. Tuffman could flatten a berserk patient against the wall with one sweeping gesture or pick up a passively resistant one single-handed and cart her to the treatment room. Her modicum of words was weighty and respected by patients and staff alike. If Tuffman declared, "Anyone who leaves the dayroom will be secluded," only the psychotic ones in need of isolation would disobey.

For me there was some comfort in Tuffman's substantialness. I never admitted this to Mrs. Corcoran (in fact, one of the advantages of the old lady's friendship was that I was never expected to say anything). I'm not sure how other patients felt. Maybe there were more there than I realized who welcomed her power. Or maybe, because of not being psychotic, I was more afraid than the others of the violence.

In the course of a day (or even at night in the large, cot-lined dormitory where we all slept) it wasn't unusual for the quiet to be suddenly rent by blood-curdling screams, followed by loud pounding, cursing and physical struggling. Sometimes, too, there would be the blast of the police whistle the nurses used to summon help. This noise would eventually fade off into echoes of shoving and the sound of resisting, shuffling feet. And we all knew, the whites of our eyes meeting in the dark, that the sharp, finalized snaps of "No more! Stop that now!" meant that the nurses had won and were dragging the conquered patient back to seclusion or the tubs.

I knew the treatment room well because that was where they tube-fed me. On Nichols I never dared to resist. But they always acted as if, given a chance, I'd vomit up the feedings. Accordingly, they kept me in pack four hours at a stretch morning and evening. The fact that I'd never been a vomiter seemed irrelevant and made me feel that my lack of disobedience was just another example of my lifelong sickening goodness. So for eight hours a day I'd lie there in the wet sheets and stare up at the acoustical tile.

The treatment room was shiny and well lit by both fluorescent ceiling tubes and expansive windows through which the sunny or dark sky was always visible. The atmosphere was crisply professional with everything about it as ultra modern and mechanically efficient as its chrome and polished tile. In actuality, that room consisted of two giant bathrooms joined together by an open space where the nurses could observe both.

I was always in the room with six treatment beds where people were restrained in wetpacks strapped down with more taut sheets. The other room contained four big bathtubs with canvas covers into which people were tied with just their heads showing. Sometimes no one else was in pack. Sometimes two or three were. Usually there were at least two people in the tubs. Most had been distraught and screaming; there they'd stay restrained for many hours.

I can well remember how one morning, as the room reeled with its usual raw craziness, I was preoccupied with Mrs. Corcoran. She had been dancing in the dayroom before they brought me to treatment. Tuffman had said two different times, "Sit down, Mrs. Corcoran. You're headed for trouble." She'd obeyed both times, but I knew, lying there waiting, that she was probably at it again. Any minute they might drag her in singing at the top of her lungs and with her fat old body naked, three of them yanking and shoving her, three like it always took.

Staccato heels in the hall outside. Jangling keys fumbling with the lock announced the doctor. As he entered with Tuffman and they mumbled together, relocking the door, I could tell his voice was one I hadn't heard before.

By the time he stood over me, yellow hair shining, blue eyes looking everywhere but at my face, Tuffman said, "Miss Daniels, this is Dr. Hughes." The student nurse brought the tray with the pitcher of feeding, mineral oil, and iced tubes.

He looked at it too long and then clumsily tried to get it in position. I thought about Mommy's enemas and then tried to forget them while bracing to help make it easier.

As the cold hard rubber tube entered my nose and found its way down the back of my throat, I felt a flood of relief. I knew I was the only regular participant in that scene. The nurses changed shifts. The doctors alternated rounds. Sometimes, like this one, they appeared brand new. So that if anyone was to know how to get the tube down — thick or thin and with a minimum of pain — it had to be me. Me, no longer resisting or crying. Me, blandly docile, even though I despised myself for acquiescing. Even though I so detested the fat forced on me by the liquid poured through the funnel that I sometimes plotted suicide.

"Get me out of here," a lady I didn't know yelled. "The Chinese will force you to let me out!"

The new doctor left without saying good-bye. At the door I heard him ask Tuffman about the new lady.

Back in the dayroom, I felt so fat that there seemed no way out but to die.

"Just tell them you'll eat," Mrs. Corcoran kept saying. She was still on a tear, singing and dancing in the corridor a few minutes before, until the aide on duty had yelled at her again to stay in the dayroom. Waltzing and singing and drowning out the television for everyone in the room until a nurse came in and commanded sharply, "That's enough, Mrs. Corcoran! Have a seat."

I was sitting on the floor beside the window, looking at my hands, measuring the circumference of my upper arm with thumb and middle finger, pressing for hipbones in frantic grasps for reassurance. None of which worked. My silent tears attracted Mrs. Corcoran.

"I've already told them," I said as her hippopotamus body plopped down beside me. "Tuffman says the tube feeding order can't be changed till my doctor comes back from vacation." Looking at the old lady's red, sweaty face with tangled hair wisping all around, I recalled Celeste in the Babar books. Grand in both size and manner, Mrs. Corcoran did not mind being fat. But if she had and they'd wanted her to get in wet sheets, she'd have said, "No," and have fought so fiercely that it would have taken six instead of three nurses to put her in. It only took two for me.

Sitting there with her pudgy hand kindly patting my knee as her wild blue eyes tried to incite me to riot, she lectured in her most grandmotherly tone, "Listen to me, Lucy. You are too fine and sensitive a girl to let these things get to you. Clearly, you are not fat. But fat is not the worst inhumanity. Mind control is. Depriving people of their thoughts. They tell me not to sing. Because my singing disturbs their order. Right now I'm not singing because I'm talking to you. But when I want to sing, I will." Her fat head rolled back and she started up, "Should o-old acquaintance be-e forgot a-and days of auld lang syne —"

"Mrs. Corcoran!"

Without so much as a nod to the nurse, she turned angrily back to me, saying, "Lucy, you are too talented a person to be confined here. The inhumanity is not fat. It's incarceration. Of the spirit, not the body. And, Lucy, your spirit is young. You are a child! A BABY! The most criminal incarceration of all. You must not submit!"

I could see her growing more agitated with each word. Rolling back and forth on the floor, pulling at the buttons on her dress. To me, nineteen was not a baby. It was old, almost dead, because of the ruins it incorporated. Too many years in hospitals. Too old to graduate from high school. Too old and wasted to go to college or be a debutante. Too empty to have talent or sensitivity. Inwardly dead and petrified. Still I loved Mrs. Corcoran for believing the sensitivity was there. I prayed she'd behave so they wouldn't hurt her. "Tell me some more, Mrs. Corcoran," I urged. "Talk to me instead of singing."

"Doing what the guards require is the same as imprisoning your-self," she declared in a louder voice. Then, "Do. . . re. . . me. . . fa. . . " She stood up with her voice surging higher and louder. "It's not the fat," she announced still more loudly, pirouetting on her toes. "It's the lack of caviar! Sol. . . la. . . ti. . . "

"Mrs. Corcoran, that is enough!"

"Put your dress on this minute!"

"Sol. . . la. . . ti. . . Soul! To your soul and mine, honey!" She was dancing fast now. Flouncing about in just her slip. Flinging her nylon underpants in the aide's face.

"Mrs. Corcoran!"

"Your soul and mine!" she squealed.

The whistle shrieked. And the others came rushing forth. In white aprons and blue-striped blouses, little white caps bobbing. "Mrs. Corcoran! Mrs. Corcoran!" they recited in a soothing chorus. But their bodies lurched; their polished white shoes stomped fiercely; their arms twisted and struggled against her flabby fat ones, bumping her bare bouncing bosoms, her elephant thighs. I was amazed that a seventy-year-old grandmother could fight like that. I wondered whether they would kill her!

And then her screams were for me: "Lucy, help me! Save me from these murderers! He-l-p!" Blood-curdling, desperate, dying shrieks.

Terrified and guilty, I nevertheless did not intervene while the five starched uniforms dragged her to seclusion.

When we went to bed, Mrs. Corcoran was still not back. Her empty cot glowered at me from across the darkened dormitory. With all thirteen of the other cots occupied, the neatness of her bodiless one taunted me — even though I knew my fears of the old lady dying had not come true. Twice in the evening I had asked a student nurse to walk down the seclusion corridor with me so that I could look in the window of Mrs. Corcoran's door. One time she'd been sleeping on the mattress; the other she was dancing and singing again, naked. But I longed to see her calm enough to return to her bed.

As usual, the fat aide sat in the doorway with the hall light pouring over her blue uniform at an angle that emphasized its contrast with the white blanket spread over her knees. Due to my belief that one possible means of starving fat was to burn it off by not sleeping, I kept myself alert by focusing on things like the aide. And that night, sitting there with silver flashlight ready (like a pistol) in her lap, she seemed like a policeman guarding our room full of craziness.

One of my nightly fat-fighting rituals involved threading through a roster of the ward's insanity. The list always worked around the room to end with Anne Walker, who daily wrung her hands and talked to voices that had caused her to slit her throat, but never let her talk to anyone real. And I imagined, looking over to the next bed with the loose long hair hiding the ugly scar, that her problem might not be too different from how Mommy had never wanted me to need Bibba or Bea. Christina had once told me about hearing voices in a manner similar to the way she talked about lobotomies. She'd said that people who heard voices were psychotic or out of touch with reality, which, I knew, meant crazy.

It was far into the night, with the aide snoring, before my thoughts got to Dr. Wall, the big brooding official head of the hospital. He had come that afternoon and taken me alone into the conference room for five minutes or so. His echoing voice, along with my own scared surprise, had brought back a feeling from years before when Father returned from a trip and his strange deep voice had made baby Adelaide scream in terror.

"How are you doing here?" he'd asked, like the mâitre d' of a restaurant.

And I, not understanding why he wanted to talk to me, had seized the opportunity, a la Mrs. Corcoran, to say, "I don't want to be tube-fed. I told Miss Tuffman I'd eat, and she said I can't till Dr. Willard gets back from vacation."

Not a muscle flicked in his round bland face. "That's true," he said. "Dr. Willard is in charge of your treatment. Talk with him when he gets back."

Though further discouraged, I wasn't surprised by that answer and, in fact, felt vaguely reassured — that he, too, said nothing could be changed with Dr. Willard away. Thus he hadn't come, as I'd feared, to tell me something awful like, "Miss Daniels, we have decided to give you a lobotomy." In the few minutes he spent with me, Dr. Wall had said something else that seemed even more surprising and undecipherable: "Miss Daniels, when are you going to commit yourself to life?"

When I couldn't answer, he stood up and took me back to the dayroom.

chapter eleven

LIFER

After a few months the doctors did let me eat instead of being tube-fed. And that allowed me to move from the acute ward to Hall VIII, where no treatments requiring restraints were given. Besides the great relief at no longer having my body controlled and fed against its will, this move also initiated a whole new kind of existence. The other patients on Hall VIII were not bizarre, which meant to me by then that their craziness didn't show. This made for a placid, structured, sealed-away life, strikingly lacking in the noise and violence I'd become inured to. On Hall VIII there were no variations in the weekday routine which included Occupational Therapy, Recreational Therapy, meals, and a fixed bedtime. There, too, people were pretty unsociable and everyone was at least ten years older than I.

Looking back now with a psychologist's eyes, that relatively non-descript ward also seems the first step in a peculiar buried-alive journey to recovery. My main companion on that trek was the same straining-to-decipher timidity that had been with me at camp and in my early days at George School. On Hall VIII, however, social ease was unnecessary and supervision was required even with simple everyday tasks. Sometimes this felt like the mothering assistance with growing up I had missed out on earlier. I particularly remember that shaving legs and underarms felt like a rite of passage.

"Miss Daniels, do you want it wet or dry?" The aide's black face and homely manner resembled Leanna's. The lady in front of me had said she didn't want either. For her, leg shaving was too much trouble. It was also one thing they'd let you refuse. Not O.T. or gym or breakfast or baths or even shampoos. But leg shaving, yes. We were all lined up with heads wrapped in towels. This was just my third week on Hall VIII. The week before I'd refused and the week before that I'd done it dry, which was the only way I'd known before. Every time brought to mind Bibba's using that depilatory during the war and Mommy's gasp of "disgustingly common." Liz had always done it dry. I'd watched her and obsessed for a long time before trying it myself.

"Wet or dry?" the razorkeeper asked again.

"Why do people do it wet?"

"Some says it's easier that way...Some uses soap. What do you like?"

"I don't know. I've never done it wet."

The aide handed me the dry razor and motioned for me to sit on the bench beside her. Razors were regarded as very dangerous — more so than scarves, belts or knitting needles. That was why they had extra staff on Sunday mornings to watch us use them.

That was the way on Hall VIII, constant watching. Much more than on Nichols where, with the first thing they didn't like, they'd put you in the tubs or seclusion. On Hall VIII they watched instead and allowed some things, like shaving, simply because they watched. They weighed us every Wednesday morning; they came around with a book every evening to record BM's and periods. Knitting was only allowed under supervision, and they collected it and counted the plastic needles every night. Smoking was permitted only after meals and only in the dayroom or on walks with a nurse who provided the matches. In the dining room, the nurses' eyes hawked not only me but my plate when it was carried out. I eavesdropped on their comments and developed a strategy of eating all the least fattening food on my plate and leaving the rest, and drinking six glasses of water before each weighing. Despite the relief at no longer being tube-fed, I'd abandoned hope of losing weight; my aim by then was simply to fend off further fattening distortion of body from tube feedings. But the new mode caused more guilt. With tube feeding, there had been no decision, just condemned submission, whereas with eating there were constant doubts: How much was required to ward off Nichols and tube feedings? How much went beyond that and surrendered myself?

So I watched the nurses as they watched me.

Another solace I discovered on Hall VIII was that I could read again. It didn't come from trying. I'd abandoned that way back at Silver Hill because the pain of struggling and failing had been too great. But reading some bits from magazines on the dayroom table, I discovered that I could not only read but remember what I'd read. And that set a sweet quiet hunger going in me. When the library cart came, I checked out a book of short stories and was relieved to a point close to exhilaration at the possibility of my mind coming back. Gradually this led to the choice of particular books and even to some pleasant hours of reading on my bed like I remembered doing before George School.

Nor was I the only person who seemed relatively at peace on Hall VIII. After living there for several weeks, I began to notice that a few patients had therapists who came to see them once or twice a week. This made them seem special; it also made me wonder if their problems were less hopeless than mine. I saw a young doctor every two weeks or so, but only for fifteen or twenty minutes. This doctor changed every six months. He was sort of like a clerk-traffic cop who wrote orders for things like aspirin or the urine collections they seemed to do a lot of, or permission to be excused from gym.

With the discovery that a few ladies had someone to really talk to while I did not, my sense of abandonment loomed larger than ever before. I became newly and acutely aware of how other people had visitors much more often than I. A resigned loneliness emerged that made the hospital seem a realization of the dread of being lost I'd felt going to camp. I did know where I was and had no wish to be anywhere else, because I wouldn't have known how to manage. At the same time, I felt forgotten.

"How do you like it here?" the mousy woman asked. Mrs. Squire. ("I don't know a Mrs. Squire," I'd said to the nurse. "It must be a mistake." Then after re-studying the list, she'd explained, "Your sister.") Oh, yes, Bibba! But in a navy blue suit? Acting proper and distracted?

"You're looking good," the new mousy Bibba continued. "Not as thin as I'd expected."

"No, I'm fat. They tube-fed me so that I gained a lot of weight. I hate it."

"How much do you weigh?"

"102."

"Oh, Lucy, that's not much. I'm shorter and weigh a lot more. I can't resist the food I cook for the boys. . . . Did you know I have two little boys?"

"No."

"I thought Mommy might have told you."

Stunned and worried about my brain again, I strained to consider why it didn't recall the developments leading to that moment. But it wasn't the little boys who upset me. It was the woman. The navy suit instead of torn shorts. Short hair neatly curling instead of long and dirty. Taut contained face. Evasive brown eyes. The diamond ring on her manicured hand.

Afterwards I lay on my bed and studied the yellow walls of the room I shared with Betty Cook. Comparing this Bibba and the other one, this Lucy and the one in the yard. Bibba's visit had reminded me of something I couldn't bear to remember — that there still was a world outside the hospital, a world that was changing and to which I would never return. Not that I really wanted to. I was too afraid and too empty, a lump with neither feelings nor brains. But it made me terribly sad.

The day before, Dr. Wall had popped in to see me again. Why? I wondered. And my new awareness of a few people getting therapy piqued my curiosity further. Besides being the head of the hospital, Dr. Wall differed from the young order-writing doctors by not asking anything about my eating or my tendency to stay off to myself. His visits seemed mostly social, perhaps because he'd known Father at the University of North Carolina and wanted to be friendly. He never stayed more than five minutes at intervals of about two months. But the one question he asked every visit increased my sense of lostness: "Now, Miss Daniels, when are you going to commit yourself to life?" Always near the end, leaving me feeling vaguely ashamed and worried.

Lying on the bed, I rethought Dr. Wall and his visit. I was some better — enough to count calories, enough to read a book, *The Pearl*, and Edna St. Vincent Millay's poems. But I knew that that wasn't enough to manage on the outside. And I knew that Dr. Wall and the others knew it, too, and expected me to stay at New York Hospital forever. I went on to wonder if that was the reason Bibba had come to visit. But this proper, nervous Bibba further confused me.

I automatically compared her to Mrs. Corcoran. The old lady didn't know I would have to stay at New York Hospital forever. But she was still on Nichols. I'd seen her only once at O.T., wild-eyed and hugging me effusively in that way that made me feel stingy. But mostly, I'd heard that she was still in the tubs and seclusion. Simply because she had to condemn incarceration of the spirit. Though I was relieved to be separated from the sickest ones on Nichols, remembering Mrs. Corcoran made me sad. I prayed she'd be able to keep her clothes on long enough to come to Hall VIII, too, and I repeatedly looked for her in the line of Nichols patients (wearing tennis shoes and with sweaters tied over their heads) walking through the fall weather to O.T. Her elephant shape should have stood out. But I never saw it.

Five or six months after the move to Hall VIII, they transferred me to Hall VI, again with neither warning nor reason. At the time I never understood that either. The only logic I can apply now, nearly fifty years later, is that Hall VI was a warehousing ward. There, at nearly 19, I was not only the thinnest patient, but the youngest by at least thirty years.

The air on Hall VI was kept parched and suffocating for the old ladies' sake. I had become so used to it myself after a couple of months that I would never have noticed the heat that April day except for the contrast with the cool freshness of our walk home from O.T. Dumping my knitting and sweater on my bed, I went to use the toilet before lunch. Somebody had preceded me into the next stall, but I didn't see who. She was just leaving, letting the door slam behind her, when I noticed the blood. A splash of it glaring up at me from the crotch of my underpants. Its electric vividness sent a wave of horror through the hair on my arms. My mouth went dry. Though my mind knew there was no need to worry, that this was just the normality of my period coming back, my body was alarmed.

After getting a pad from the nurse, I tried to think while securing it to my underpants. Tears clouded my eyes; the goose pimples still lined my arms; but not a single image came into my mind. Maybe I realized only then how not having periods for more than three years had soothed me.

After lunch I sat alone in the corridor some distance from the day-room, trying to read. But the ladies' conversations and my own turbulent feelings interfered. "Normal," my logic kept prompting. But I still dreaded menstruating. When the student nurse came round that night with her ledger to ask about B.M.'s and periods, I'd have to say "yes" to both. And I hated that. I wondered if she'd be shocked or confused — to look back at thirty-six months of blank squares and now to check "yes" for period. Too distressed to read, I tried to focus on the cross-stitch project I'd designed and brought home from O.T. It was really a knitting project with cross stitch applied to make a decorative blanket. But the skin on the cuticles of my thumbs intervened. Pulling at their roughness, I was driven by a kind of frenzy followed by cooling that could quiet my body. I didn't so much know this as feel it. Although I'd peeled the skin on my fingers for years by then, I'd never decided to do it. It had simply happened automatically; an urge from inside compelled me to pick at whatever rough skin I could find or to create some if there wasn't any. I knew well but never could have articulated the satisfaction I got from pulling the skin away to leave smoothness, with a numb disregard for pain or blood. As I determinedly, absent-mindedly but purposefully pulled the hardened skin away, blood did trickle forth. It hurt, but, still worse, it felt shameful. When I couldn't stop the bleeding, I went to the nurse's station and asked for a Band Aid.

"What is the problem?" Mrs. Groethe asked.

"I pulled the skin off."

"But why?"

"I don't know. I just pulled the skin off." Though ashamed that I couldn't tell her why, it would have been still more embarrassing if I had known and could tell her. That particular nurse, Mrs. Groethe, frequently wore a concerned, puzzled expression and asked questions that others didn't bother with. I'd never heard answers to her questions, nor was she the kind of person who spouted interpretations or gave instructions. But I did feel a kind of ongoing imperative from her that craziness was to be understood. Today, having struggled for decades to understand that skin peeling habit and why it shifted from fingers to left heel some years ago, I wonder if Mrs. Groethe's theories were like my own — that the peeling was an unconscious struggle to break free of a mold, to feel more alive through the pain and blood. Whatever her theories, Mrs. Groethe never voiced them.

On Hall VI there were very few visitors. Some of those old ladies had no family at all. Even those who had children or cousins who came only rarely for short Sunday afternoon calls complained about the intrusion on their privacy and routine. In a way, this lack of visitors was comforting for me, too; it bolstered the sense that Hall VI was all there was, that feelings in relation to some world beyond were pointless. On the other hand, since I, too, seldom had or expected visitors, when Mommy or Father did come, it was usually upsetting.

I knew about most visits weeks in advance. Mommy or Father or both would come every three or four months. If they were in New York long enough, they might come on two visiting days in the same week. But with no contact except letters in the months in between, it was hard to relate to them in the two to five o'clock slot we were given to visit. Father came more often than Mommy because he came to New York on business, and he sometimes visited for only one of the three hours permitted. The shortness or the infrequency of visits was not the cause of pain, however. The misfit between us was. I don't know how they felt; maybe they went home feeling satisfied. But during our visits sadness often overwhelmed me, while afterward my isolation loomed with new grimness.

One cold Saturday, not expecting company, I was working in the alcove on my blanket for O.T. I'd adopted this as my sitting place because there I could be alone without the nurse pestering me about staying in my room too much. That day I was also re-reading and memorizing bits from the collection of Edna St. Vincent Millay's poetry Mommy and Father had given me for Christmas. Given my interest in Millay (whose work Father had introduced me to), the hospital librarian had begun urging me to do a presentation on her and her poetry for some of the patients. This urging pleased and frightened me. My own interest had propelled me to think and read books on the subject (including a biography and a collection of letters), which was the most reading I'd done since George School. "Sharing myself" in this presentation would also require writing, which I hadn't attempted in years. I could even picture Father being proud of my doing it.

Thinking about all this that day, as I also recited,

"We were very tired, we were very merry —
We had gone back and forth all night on the ferry . . ."

the skin on my thumbs wanted peeling. Rough uneven dried spots that I picked and then picked further.

"I had a little Sorrow,
Born of a little Sin,
I found a room all damp with gloom
And shut us all within . . . "

Slowly, persistently, steadily, one skin shred and then another until there was blood that wouldn't stop.

And I was at the nurses' station getting Band Aids when a visitor was let in, who turned out to be Father. Startled, I probably looked a little scared stepping back. Because Father seemed uneasy as he hugged me and said, "Hello, beautiful! . . . How are you?"

"All right."

In the alcove he found another chair to sit in, with his coat draped across the back. "I didn't know I could come till the last minute," he said. "There's a newspaper meeting in New York, and I wasn't sure I'd be able to get away." He was pink-faced from the cold and hearty in manner like when I'd gone into Philly to meet him for a weekend when I was at George School. His blue eyes did not look sad.

"Dr. Wall told me you've been reading a lot of Edna St. Vincent Millay."

"I have. I love her." I picked at the Band Aids. My eyes did not want to meet his.

"We have to go around to another place to smoke, don't we?"

"Yes. Do you want to?"

"In a minute. . . Dr. Wall said the librarian had told him you know so much about Millay that she wants you to do a talk for the other patients."

"Yes. I don't know if I will. . . . . I don't know if I can." Something about his asking made my throat ache and my eyes water.

"You should. It's a great opportunity to see how well you can do."

"Maybe. The librarian tries to be kind. I'm sure the patients would be, too."

"Do you know that Edna St. Vincent Millay was an idol of Babs'?"

"Maybe." The ache had eased, and I could look him pretty much in the face, as he played with his unlit cigarette. "I'm not sure, but I think you may have told me once."

Father put the cigarette down on my open book and rummaged to pull something out of his coat pocket: three slender worn-looking books. Then, placing these on his knees, he reached over to take both my hands in his. His urgent, heartfelt grip clearly meant to convey a special message. In the midst of it I could see tears in his eyes. "I brought you these books," he said softly. "Because of how Babs loved Edna St. Vincent Millay, too."

As he handed them to me, I had no doubt about the importance of those worn little volumes. I had the sense that Babs had loved them because they were worn and contained poems about ordinary people with down-to-earth feelings. When I opened the top one and saw the smudged inscription on its front page: "Elizabeth Ann Bridgers," I could picture Father and Babs as the couple on the ferry, sitting close together, laughing and talking like people in love. That made me feel sad and guilty and loving all at once. But all I said was "Thank you" as I picked at the Band Aids.

Father's sadness shifted to merriment as he said, "Don't do that," and began reciting:

"Safe upon solid rock the ugly houses stand:
Come and see my shining palace built upon the sand!"

After that we walked around to the lounge so he could smoke.

As my mind reclaimed itself, it increasingly denounced me for being a high school dropout. At the feeling level, that in itself was reason enough to stay locked up forever. Nor did I regard my deficits as simply the result of an aborted education. Rather, my lack of a diploma seemed only an inspector's testimony to the ruin of my intelligence, and there was no school in that hospital to challenge such convictions. Therefore, when I agreed to take the correspondence course in creative writing that Mommy and Father discovered and urged me to pursue, it was with very mixed feelings. I didn't feel up to it, but I did not want my fear to keep me from trying what had once seemed the most valuable thing in life. If I failed, I would know the truth even if Mommy and Father wouldn't believe it.

The assignments began with the basics. There was a paperback textbook that you read a little from and then did the assignments at the end of the chapter. Some of the answers you wrote were just "exercises." After that you were supposed to complete the assignments and mail them off to your teacher in a brown envelope. I can't remember my teacher's name. In some ways, because I never met him, he was not a real person. Rather, I'd say, he was like a voice coming out of a typewriter and connected to (or separated from) me by a long string of brown envelopes.

Mommy sent me a large supply of envelopes and typing paper. One day when Father came to visit, he brought an Olivetti portable typewriter with two extra ribbons. Even though I preferred to write by hand, the teacher wanted typed copy. So, besides studying writing, I brushed up on the typing I'd learned in high school. I finished the first assignments easily. Then going on to the more demanding tasks, I found the lapse of time provided by the brown envelopes getting back and forth comforting. But even as I progressed from three-sentence descriptions to one-paragraph essays to recorded conversations to a two-page account of meeting an old friend to a short story, I never felt confident about being able to do the next task. I always dreaded the return packet with the teacher's comments. But the writing, the exercises the course encouraged, and even the feedback helped to fill the emptiness of my days.

"Go tell the nurse," withered Mrs. Weiss droned that afternoon. "Go tell her you need some aspirin." She was talking to Mrs. Spencer who, thin and gnarled, perched as usual on the edge of her straight chair, all the while staring vacantly and whining. As far as I could tell, Mrs. Spencer never said anything. But after a silence, Mrs. Weiss always resumed, "Go tell the nurse," as if in response to something.

Since I couldn't read with them talking, I decided to do what the correspondence writing course stressed: "Learn by writing down the conversations around you."

"Go tell the nurse," Mrs. Weiss continued.

Mrs. Spencer moaned.

Writing this down, I found myself listening for the next sentence instead of trying to shut it out.

Mrs. Spencer moaned louder.

Mrs. Weiss's nagging became more irritated. "You better watch out. First thing you know they'll transfer you to Gero. That's why. . . you look at me, I'm always busy, no matter how sick, how full of gas, how achy, how neglected by my children. I keep on crocheting. I never stop."

"Gero" caught my attention. We had to walk past there when we went to O.T. through the underground tunnel on rainy days. It looked sterile and reeked of urine. The women there were flat and grey like cardboard cutouts. They mostly did not speak, though a few gibbered, and one was always calling out, "Save me! I've been kidnapped." I wondered what made anyone get quivering and urine-soaked like that, why a person did get transferred to Gero.

I dutifully wrote down Mrs. Weiss's words.

Perhaps it was the writing course. Or perhaps, being able to read and think again. Or the increased sense of isolation in the alcove where I felt more comfortable separated from the old ladies. Regardless, I began to long more than ever for some means of feeling less cut off from people. Nobody on Hall VI had a therapist. But whenever Dr. Jane O'Neill, a tall, big-boned friendly-seeming psychiatrist came on rounds, I found myself thinking afterward about how it would be to have her for mine. One night when she came through, stopping as usual to speak to each old lady in turn, I got up my nerve to ask.

"Good evening, Lucy."

"Dr. O'Neill, could I speak to you a minute?"

"Surely." She walked with me — her slow, overgrown-horse gait emanating a calm confidence — to a spot beyond the nurse where we could speak in private.

"Dr. O'Neill," my voice faltered. I tried but couldn't really look her in the face. "I've noticed that some people have therapy. . . Not here, but on Hall VIII, I think I saw you come to see some people regularly, maybe two times a week."

She didn't speak. Her serious face fringed with fuzzy brown hair did not change, nor did the angle of her stooped shoulders as she waited for me to finish.

"Well, I've been thinking it could be good for me to see somebody like that. I'm wondering if you would be my therapist."

Even then, she didn't speak right off. She stood up straighter, with her face still serious like she was thinking about it. "Lucy. . . I'm flattered by your request, and I wish I could give you an answer right now. But this isn't something I can decide myself. Concerns like this have to go through staff conference. What I'll do, if you like, is take your request to our next meeting and let you know."

"Okay. Thank you." Walking back to my chair, I wished I hadn't asked.

In 1954, the February before I turned twenty, both Mommy and Father came to see me. They wanted me to reply to the Raleigh Terpsichorean Club's invitation to participate in their debutante ball.

"You did receive an invitation to be a debutante, didn't you?" Mommy asked, sitting in the chair beside my room's writing table. I could see her trying to not be nervous.

"Yes."

"Did you reply?" Her dimple was starting.

"No. I didn't know how to or what I should say."

"It's an honor that they invited you. . . Your response should be gracious." Her coolness triggered the tic.

"Who are they?" I pressed. "What should I say?"

"Just thank them," Father put in with warm practicality. "Tell them you'd like to be a debutante but can't because you'll be away from

North Carolina at the time."

"But don't they know where I am?"

"No."

"I'm embarrassed."

"There's no need to be embarrassed," Mommy assured. "Just write a nice note, saying you're grateful but can't attend. I've brought some formal notepaper for you to use."

"Don't be too proper," Father joked. "They probably aren't up to it!"

After they left, I did write the note. But in doing so, I wondered what the Terpsichorean Club would think. Would they realize my letter was from a mental patient with a life sentence?

The alcove remained my sanctuary, even though the nurses nagged me to go socialize with other patients. Alone in the alcove I could read and think about things like the uselessness of writing to the Terpsichorean Club. I also came to understand — with a kind of stunning and overwhelming sense of reality — that that empty alcove was representative of my life forever.

That moment of realization is still accessible to me — like peering inside the glistening, frozen clarity of a snowflake. I was making a rug then, a small cross-stitched rug with elves on it. As I pushed the green wool into the eye of the blunt tapestry needle, it suddenly occurred to me that despite my having designed it, there was no reason whatsoever to make this rug. Bibba's children, whom I'd never seen, would be too old before I finished it. Then, pulling the wool long and knotting it, the next thought stopped me: I would never be able to have children. In fact, I would never be able to leave the hospital. I would grow old here and become just another lonely old lady without ever being loved or marrying. I felt sad thinking that and lonely, but not unsafe.

chapter twelve

INCHING OUT

It was late in March. Cold, raining, blustery outside, so that we had to go to the dentist through the underground tunnel. Just me and a student nurse. And, to my surprise, there was Mrs. Spate with a nurse, waiting for another Nichols patient. "Remember me, Lucy?" she asked.

"Yes. Mrs. Spate."

"What hall are you on?"

"Six. How are you?" I asked.

"Some better. . . They gave me shock but they still won't operate. I'm trying not to worry about it because I want to move to Hall VIII. And there may be some new medicine that will dissolve a dead fetus."

"How is Mrs. Corcoran?"

Her worried grey face grew suddenly smooth; her eyes bulged. "You didn't hear about Mrs. Corcoran?" she exclaimed.

"No. What about her?"

"She died. At Christmas time. Had a heart attack and died. Not sick a minute. No suffering like they keep me going through. Just in the seclusion room. Lay down and died."

The shock of those words lasted for years.

A week or so later, again on rounds, Dr. O'Neill came to the alcove to tell me that my request for her to be my therapist had been turned down. "I'm sorry," she said with pleasant blandness. "But I wanted to tell you myself."

"Thank you."

Despite feeling unworthy of therapy, I was able to hold my tears back until after she'd loped off down the hall with the nurse. But even then crying seemed foolish. Before that night I hadn't had a therapist. Now Dr. O'Neill had told me I couldn't have a therapist. No change. So crying didn't make sense. Yet, in spite of all they'd done to help me, I couldn't hold it back.

The tears wouldn't stop, not even in the restaurant. Sitting across from Father, I felt his eyes watch me cry, while my own eyes studied the white plate in front of me. The leave book allowed five hours, and I'd wept for almost the whole time. I'd saved the calories from two days for this meal, and still the tears came.

"This man at the correspondence school, Frederick, I think his name is, wrote to thank me for enrolling you. Said you were moving right along with the assignments."

"Yes."

"How is the criticism you get back?"

"Okay. I'm not as good as you think."

"Well, you have to get back in the swing. You've only been at it six months."

I had nothing to say. The tears kept on.

"You know you probably have excellent material to write about here. You could try every day to write a sketch about someone in the hospital."

My thoughts jumped to Gero.

"You should avail yourself of these opportunities."

"That's what the writing book says too. The first assignments were listening to conversations and writing them down."

"And you do that?" He was sprinkling salt on the steak the waiter had set before him.

"Some. But later assignments have to do with making up conversations." I cut a bite of the roast beef I'd hoarded calories for.

"I hope you do it every day," Father said from above the napkin tied under his chin. There seemed to be tears in his eyes as he added, "You know you are my boy. You have the gift. If you can overcome this illness and write, Lucy, you have the ability to do anything in the world you want."

Tears flooded my eyes.

But he continued as if blind, "Not like poor Adelaide. She is driving us crazy. Expelled from the third school. She just can't leave the boys alone. Or whiskey. And you know how stupid and strait-laced these teachers are. They don't use any common sense, don't ever realize that making a rule is just asking Adelaide to break it. In and out of bed with anybody I'm sure. Your mother is outdone. I'm just afraid she'll turn up pregnant and have to marry some idiot. You see she doesn't have much else. She lacks your ability, your sensitivity. Let's face it, she is a pagan, a flat-footed, warm, but tediously dull earth woman."

"Live life to the hilt!" was what I heard. Adelaide ran giggling, squealing, screaming into his arms. Grabbing her, holding her tight, he cried, "Oh-h-h, I'm going to roast you, little pig, with an apple in your mouth!" Adelaide shrieked, laughing and crying. "Go tell the nurse," Mrs. Weiss said. "It's no use," Mrs. Spencer whined.

Conversations without end. With me forever the removed listener.

Only a few days later the charge nurse told me my doctor was going to change again. Dr. Espy, the latest one writing my orders, would be going to Paine Whitney full-time. The new one would be Dr. Burdick.

This both surprised and unnerved me. Dr. Burdick was the portly white-haired head of the women's side. She didn't normally have patients, and I thought she was probably very strict when she did.

Later that evening she came by in the white coat that made her look like a baker and spoke to me. "Good evening, Miss Daniels. Has the nurse told you that I'm going to be your doctor?"

"Yes."

"Good. I'll be by later this week to see you."

Despite my concerns about Dr. Burdick, I wondered if this could mean I was going to have therapy. Mrs. Weiss, who'd heard her speak to me, called me over to the couch where she was crocheting and said, "I heard Dr. Burdick say she was going to be your doctor."

"Yes," I nodded pleasantly.

"Well," she continued in a very private tone, peering at me over her glasses, "I hope you know you're very fortunate and highly honored."

I listened politely.

"Dr. Burdick's been my doctor for seventeen years. It's a very secure feeling. You, her patient, and only you have her loyalty and attention."

"Does she give you therapy?" I asked shyly.

Mrs. Weiss hooked a couple of crochet stitches before she answered. Then, again peering at me over her glasses, she almost whispered, "I really couldn't say. Thanks be to God, I've never been a person who needed therapy."

When Dr. Burdick did come, she seemed no different than Dr. Espy or the others. But in the conference room, leafing through my chart, she stopped and focused her penetrating green eyes on me before saying, "You do not belong here. We need to do whatever is necessary to get you out to where you do belong."

I was so stunned that I could neither feel nor think. Probably several minutes went by before I caught the next remark:

"Ninety-four pounds is simply too little for someone your height to weigh. I will expect you to raise it to 100 as soon as possible."

Since Nichols I had lost weight, but this was the first time anyone had challenged that. My private understanding of this was that they were being tolerant because I was not openly dieting. I also suspected that they knew the tube feedings had made me gain more weight than was necessary. Now, in response to Dr. Burdick, I asked, "What if I can't bear to? What if 100 feels like too much?"

"I expect you to raise it to 100 and maintain it. If it turns out that you can't, we'll have to tube feed you."

More strict than I'd feared. After that I devoted my ingenuity to finding some way to co-exist with Dr. Burdick.

"Yes, Mrs. Thomas heard it from the night nurse. . . new medicines that make the voices go away." Mrs. Weiss's crochet hook continued its lacy pattern in expectant silence. Then, when there was no response from Mrs. Spencer, she resumed, "I'm thankful not to need them myself. I'm glad I never have heard voices or seen things. But those poor wild souls on Nichols. . ."

Perhaps Mrs. Spencer mumbled. But even squinting at them up the corridor, I couldn't tell what she said.

"Who?" Mrs. Weiss said. "Well, not you. You're too old. Besides, they're for voices. Do you hear voices?"

No answer.

"Randall did say some people can't take them. There have been a few bad reactions. Some got sick, and I believe a few even died."

I was just listening to this conversation, not writing it down. I'd heard about the miracle medicines other places too. They were changing the O.T. schedule to fit in an extra class for the people who had always before been in tubs and in seclusion but now would be uncrazy enough to knit and make baskets.

"Miss Higgins is worried about their letting all those sick ones come up here. But I don't think they will. . . Besides, if they weren't acting crazy why would it matter? But Miss Higgins says the medicines only take the voices away, can't change the person. . . We'll have to see, but it is worrisome, isn't it?"

Listening to them had distracted me from planning my story about a young black man fighting for rights his father didn't think black people should have. The idea had come to me from reading in *The New York Times* about the Supreme Court's decision to end the segregation of public schools. That story had made me think about the black people in Raleigh who had always been so kind to us children: Leanna and her schoolteacher daughter, Mamie, and Spurgeon, Grandfather's longtime faithful driver and companion. I'd begun to imagine how Spurgeon's children might react to this new law and how that might clash with Spurgeon's devotion to Grandfather and later *The News and Observer* and the Daniels family. I decided to call the young black man Caleb Blake. This story would be longer than the others I'd written and that in itself felt helpful. The correspondence course was finished. Keeping myself writing would be easier if I had a project that continued over time.

Leaving the hospital was constantly on my mind in those days. Leaving it and never leaving it. With dread either way. The talk about the new medicines figured into both sets of fears. Those medicines with their unpronounceable snake-like names were supposed to be miraculous for people like Mrs. Corcoran—could save them all manner of torture and distress by making them calm enough to go home. But what about a person like me? A person whose true empty inadequacy was no longer hidden by intellectual over-achieving? I knew no medicine could correct that. But I wasn't at all sure that the hospital doctors wouldn't try them. For years they had periodically collected my urine. "For research," the nurses always explained. Asked what kind of research or why with me and not with other people, they pleaded ignorance in a convincing, uninvolved way. But I'd never been able to dismiss the worries about those collections leading to some gruesome conclusion that I couldn't even imagine. And I had similar fears of the medicines. Besides being dangerous for some, I'd heard that they made most people fat.

Mixed in with all this was what Dr. Burdick had said: "You do not belong here. We need to do whatever is necessary to get you out." What came to mind whenever I did try to picture "not in the hospital" was Bibba's childhood magic of making people "disappear into thin air." Today I'd call such thoughts concern about not existing. But then they were central to my ruminations about the catastrophe of having to choose between medicated fat and returning to a world where I couldn't survive.

Working on my story about Caleb Blake became a respite. In it Caleb was telling his little brother Saul about the new law to give blacks equal rights. Saul sat on the front steps looking earnestly up at him and trying hard to understand. One problem was that Pa didn't say the same things about the law as Caleb did. Pa talked about life being much better for black people now than when he was growing up, mostly because of the help of white people, like the Atkinses and the Gibsons. He said the new law wasn't necessary because things were gradually getting more equal anyway and gradual was the only way for change to work. But Caleb called the white people "oppressors" and said that the new law wouldn't help unless blacks fought to have the rights it promised.

In the conference room with Dr. Wall I still tried to figure out the reason for his visits. Besides friendly kindness, could it be my youth or the "research"?

That particular afternoon he began as usual: "Well, Miss Daniels, how're things going?" But then, after hearing my downcast "All right, I guess," he pulled some folded typewritten papers from his jacket pocket. "I understand you've had a birthday," he said, perhaps in response to my uneasy squint.

"Yes."

"Twenty-one, is that right?"

"Yes."

"That's a real important one, Lucy. . . Makes me want to ask you again when you're going to commit yourself to life?"

I looked down as his brown eyes focused on me. "I don't know."

"Well, today I've brought a contract we need you to sign." He pushed one of the papers across the desk.

"Why?" I asked, looking at it but unable to make any sense of the bewildering legal language.

"Every patient has a contract," he answered blandly, his affable face flat as stone.

"But I don't understand," I protested. "Why haven't I ever signed one before?"

"Because you've been a minor. When you came here, you were seventeen and your parents signed the admission papers. . . Now that you're twenty-one, you need to sign your own contract."

Studying the maze of words on the stapled pages, my mind couldn't take them in. Partly because of the legalese; more because of my dread of what I might agree to without knowing it. The best I could do was deny the dread and please the good doctor by doing as he asked. The two lines that most stood out were, "I am a voluntary patient" and, much further down, "I have been advised of my rights and know that I am free to leave at any time so long as I give the hospital thirty days prior notice." There was no mention of research. What rights? I thought, but felt too dumb to ask.

After I'd signed both copies, Dr. Wall smiled and took his glasses off again, saying, "Fine. Thank you. Now we have that all taken care of."

Out in the corridor again, Mrs. Weiss was saying to Mrs. Spencer, "Don't worry. I tell you they will not let the crazy ones come up here. They know we need our peace and quiet. . . It's understood that we're old and need our rest and that since we have no place to go, we need to be here, like they say, 'indefinitely'."

Mrs. Spencer sighed and whimpered. I imagined her pleading, "Are you sure?"

It alarmed me to acknowledge how like Mrs. Spencer I felt. How like her and yet how distressingly different. Because of being younger. And because my contract read "thirty days."

Dr. Burdick had her appointments during rounds. But she was persistently demanding in each of our five-minute sessions. Besides requiring me to reach and maintain 100 pounds, she spoke repeatedly about setting a course for life outside the hospital. After our first meeting, it didn't occur to me to argue or plead; rather, my focus, again, was on self-preservation through simulated compliance. By gaining three pounds and drinking eight glasses of water before each weighing; by finding some way in the hospital to prepare for outside.

What developed out of this was the discovery of a New York City tutoring school — something I could do at the hospital to be ready for life after the hospital. Tutors there could help me prepare to go back to school. What school I might aim for — college or high school — seemed unclear. So was where I'd live if I did go to school again — New York or Raleigh or someplace else. I enrolled at the school by mail, which was relatively unthreatening. But to attend it I had to move to an open ward. Dr. Burdick wrote the order for that ward, Brown Villa, the Saturday before the Wednesday I was scheduled to go into the city for my first tutoring sessions.

My worst fear that April morning was of getting lost. My second worst was of looking foolish. I'd written down how to go — by train to Grand Central, by bus from there, then by foot two blocks over to Third Avenue and up another block. Though I rehearsed this continually inside my head, it felt as meaningless as some math formula. So did the money in my pocketbook. Not having been out on my own in four years, I was especially worried about looking foolish in relation to money. And my dread of getting lost on a train re-emerged with new urgency.

That experience was a kaleidoscopic terror-spin with only a few stark moments clear enough to recall. One of those was arriving early, a possibility I'd overlooked. My sense of awkwardness increased the minute I stepped off the bus and realized that I'd reached the school 45 minutes ahead of time. To calm myself I walked slowly to the building, checked the sign beside the elevator to be sure the school was there, and took another walk. But I was shaking inside by then and felt like everyone passing me could see the terror on my face. I took refuge in a coffee shop where the anxiety inside me almost felt like hunger; I'd learned by then that hunger could be appeased by caffeine. However, that morning I most wanted the coffee to hide me while time passed.

"What can I get you, Miss?" the young man behind the counter asked.

"A cup of coffee, please."

"Large or small?"

"Small." Looking around furtively for the price, I couldn't bear for him to discover that I'd never bought a cup of coffee before. But I didn't see a sign.

He brought a steaming paper cup. "Cream or sugar?"

"No." I could feel his blue eyes puzzling over me. I couldn't really see his eyes, because I couldn't look at him. But I knew my craziness was obvious.

"Here or to go?"

Sitting there seemed as awful as walking to the front and out. I hesitated, about to dissolve in tears. "Here." I prayed he would tell me the price. But he didn't, just stood there looking at me. "How much is it?" I finally asked after a deep breath.

"Seventeen cents."

There were only a few pennies in my change purse. And as I pulled the wallet out of my new pocketbook, I realized that, horror of horrors, I only had five dollar bills. He took the one I handed him without a word and went to the cash register. I still couldn't look at his face to judge the response.

"Your change is four eighty-three," he said counting it into my hand. But when I was putting the dollars into my billfold, the eighty-three cents fell in a clinking tumble to the counter where some of it rolled and clinked again as it hit the floor. My sense of humiliation could not have been greater if my clothes had fallen off.

The school turned out to be less intimidating than I'd feared. Three teachers — one woman and two men, all middle-aged to old — and a youngish secretary. The front door was frosted glass with the name "The Tutoring School" in large black letters. It gave you the feeling that if you needed a tutor, this was the best place to come. But inside, the rooms were seedy. Waiting in the lobby, I felt desolate. How could a school as dilapidated as this one be up to the huge job of teaching me?

The teachers were nice, though. They did have the confidence I lacked. Also, patience and good sense. I didn't meet the woman teacher; I think she taught people more advanced than I. One man (I can't remember any of their names), who was tall and thin and white-haired, started me on American history and gave me a book to study from. The other, a kindly, dark-haired plumpish man, would teach me English and Latin. He, in particular, kept commenting on how much I already knew. But that only made me feel worse, because I thought he said those things to relieve my nervousness.

Since the school shut down for lunch between English and Latin, I resolved to look for a place where I could eat lunch every week — a place that served salads and had enough chairs that they wouldn't mind me sitting there to read for an hour. I walked and walked and looked and looked, but found nothing like what I needed. Of course, being afraid to ask didn't help. In the end I just went back to the building and sat on the front steps trying to read until school opened again. After Latin, where the teacher was just as encouraging as before, I took my books and, because I was so afraid, took a cab to Grand Central Station and the train to White Plains.

But the fear did not decrease. In fact, the more I thought back over all the inadequacies and humiliations of that day, the more ruined I understood myself to be. I did the assignments but they too felt futile, as though it would take years of similar study for me to ever get to where I could do anything capably. The next week felt worse than the one before. The third week I didn't go back. Even when Dr. Burdick insisted I go the fourth week, I refused. I decided she and the others just didn't understand how inadequate I was.

I can't recall now exactly what happened. Perhaps my weight got below Dr. Burdick's limit. I'm sure I was terribly depressed and hopeless about ever being able to live in New York or anywhere out-side the hospital. Anyway, I got moved back to a closed ward for a few weeks — one of the better ones where you could have eyeglasses and go out on passes with visitors. While there, I'm sure with the help of Dr. Burdick, I decided to get a job instead of going to school. In my own head a job seemed safer than school because certain jobs wouldn't reveal my ruined mind.

In July 1955, I moved to Open Ward again and got a job in the billing department of *Reader's Digest* in Pleasantville, New York. Besides its being a job where my perceived intellectual and writing deficits wouldn't show, all I had to do to get there was catch a bus at the bottom of the hospital's hill that went directly to the *Reader's Digest* office every morning and back again in the late afternoon. That job turned out to be one of the most helpful experiences since George School.

Not long after starting there, I renewed my effort to work regularly at writing. I'd stopped in the third or fourth chapter of the novel about Caleb Blake. With an order from Dr. Burdick allowing me to get up and write at 5:00 a.m., writing every day before going to work became a habit that felt good. I had no expectations for this beyond its keeping me in the writing mode. But doing that had come to feel as necessary to my sense of well-being as not eating too many calories. By late September, Caleb's story was nearing completion, but I no longer liked its planned ending. Too staid, too boring, too much like what Father would have called the Casper Milquetoast in me. For a week I went to work troubled about this, but I also could-n't think of another ending. The conflict between father and son had been out in the open for more than five chapters. Yet how could it work out? How would a father so adamantly and spiritually opposed to the things his son was doing act to protect his other children and the family name?

Only in mid-October did the brainstorm come that answered this question. I was riding the bus home from work. Excitement flared up in me; early the next morning I began to write the ending. By the end of the next week I'd completed the last chapter. Then I put that notebook in the box with all my other writing and took out a new one to start a story about children riding on a train with their alcoholic mother.

Too afraid to live in New York and not knowing anyone either there or in White Plains, I decided in the end to return to Raleigh.

"It probably will seem easier there to get around to work or to school," Dr. Burdick said as solemnly as she said everything else.

"And at least in Raleigh there'll be Mommy and Father if there are things I don't know how to do."

"That's true. But you really need to be as independent of them as you can. You'll need to have a doctor there you can talk to and a job or school." Her bland face did not stir, but her eyes opened a little wider than usual as they seemed to rivet me. "I've told your parents it's very important that you not live with them. You need to be on your own now."

That was the third week in October. When I gave notice at work, my supervisor was surprised and disappointed. She'd been planning to promote me.

Recalling this now, I've dreamed:

I had to go through the underground tunnel to O.T. It seemed long, maybe endless. I was alone. . . feeling my way through the dark to find Cleves and save her from what had happened to Adelaide. The only light was from single overhead bulbs hanging far apart. My mission felt urgent. The air was musty. I felt a little sliding cabinet door in the wall, like the movies portray confessional doors, just big enough to speak through without being seen. To my knock, a man's voice replied, "Speak." But when I tried, I couldn't, and suddenly remembered that they had given me medicine that makes voices go away. "Speak!" the man's voice yelled again. But I still couldn't. . . . Then I was wandering like a waif. . . wandering and wandering in some place like a desert. . . but with high grass blowing in a light wind. I had no idea why I was there or where I was going.

chapter thirteen

LEFT FOR DEAD

The telephone rang three times.

"Please answer the phone, Lucy," Mommy called.

Alone in the library, I struggled with myself, feeling ashamed, stupid, weak, crazy, hateful, but still unable to pick up the receiver.

The phone rang twice more.

"Goddamn it!" Father bellowed. "I'll get it." Then after a few minutes, hollering down the stairs louder than before, "Lucy, I'm sick and tired of your shit! . . . A lunatic who can't even answer the phone won't go far in this world!"

I knew he was right. I should do it. Like I should ride the bus downtown and shouldn't run upstairs to my room every time the doorbell rang. I felt awful about being a "sniveling ninny" as Father called it. But the fear of being recognized by people outside the door or on the other end of the phone was stronger than that of being a failed but invisible weakling.

Already then — in mid-December 1955, home from the hospital less than three weeks — those struggles were continuous. Why people frightened me I couldn't understand. I longed to find someone who could accept me. I even missed the old ladies on Hall VI because I'd at least belonged there and been able to listen to their conversations without having to speak. Saying the right words or speaking with an appropriate voice was somehow central to my idea of being "normal." I dreaded being rejected for sounding weak or crazy. And, in fact, that fear was always consummated, because in every human interchange I believed that the other person pitied or despised me for being a mental patient.

The hospital had given us a list of four things I needed to do within two months: move to my own apartment, find a psychiatrist, take the high school equivalency exam, and start school or work. I was terrified by all of it, but seeing a psychiatrist and studying for the high school equivalency were least intimidating. I could study alone without having to speak to anybody. Nor was there much cause for indecision about the doctor; I couldn't drive and there were only two psychiatrists in Raleigh. One was Wilmer Betts, whom I'd known before the war as Bibba's boyfriend and had seen talking to Mommy as a resident at Duke during my treatment there. The other was a much older doctor who mainly worked at Dorothea Dix State Hospital. I chose him, thinking Wilmer would be too much like a friend. But one session with the older doctor convinced me otherwise. Despite his professional status, he was pinch-faced and had an office that was stiff and sterile, with two straight chairs and an examining table that reminded me of ECT.

So I ended up seeing Wilmer, whose office in Cameron Village I'd be able to walk to from the apartment we'd picked out. His waiting room and office were comfortable and homey-looking. I'd have preferred someone who was older and more powerful. His ears did stick out like Father said, and I had some fears he'd think of me as just Bibba's little sister or Mommy and Father's little girl. Still, seeing him was relieving, and since he was a psychiatrist, I figured he could stand my weirdness.

Wilmer didn't talk much, but he acted like everything I mentioned was important. It surprised me to hear him say, "Of course," when I told him I felt weird and afraid of people. He said he agreed with the doctors at the hospital that I needed to have my own apartment. He was more like a school teacher or a minister than a psychiatrist. I suspected Father was right about his being "second rate" and not really able to help me, but his ability to tolerate my weakness was a comfort. When I told him I was afraid I'd fail the high school equivalency exam, he said, "Well if you do, you can take it again."

The day the letter arrived about my passing the GED, Mommy and

Father said I needed to sit right down and fill out an application to the university. That was the day before I was supposed to move to the apartment. I was incredulous about having passed but also desperate to get through to Mommy and Father that there had been some kind of mistake and that passing it didn't mean I could do college work.

"Stop sniveling, Lucy!" Father snapped. "You don't have to do college work right now. You just need to apply!"

So I did, even down to answering the questions about: "Have you ever been treated by a psychiatrist?" "When and why?" Father said it would look "smarter" to put my new address on it. So I did that, too. And the day after the moving people transported the furniture from the basement to my apartment, Mommy drove me to get a snapshot made so we could glue it to the application and mail it off.

I can still feel sick recalling this. Even today, thinking it through with the hard-earned wisdom of a full life. And talking to Dr. Howie about it decades later, I did decide that I'd been "left for dead" by those doctors in the hospital. I was less emaciated and knew that I had to eat a certain amount in order to keep my body from being further mutilated, but otherwise, I was no better off after the hospital than before. Just older and less capable, more ashamed and afraid from all that time being locked up. Like some war casualty beyond helping. Only, like Dr. Howie has reminded me, it was worse, because I wasn't dead. I knew and felt what was happening to me.

That Raleigh apartment — in a building with three others at the corner of Woodburn Road and Smallwood Drive — was the best thing the hospital ordered because it came to feel like mine. It was one block from a bus stop. It was on the second floor, and light streamed through its living room window; the bedroom and kitchenette had small windows as well. Though I felt terribly alone there, if someone called or came to visit I knew it was me they wanted, not Mommy and Father. The first and only visitors for many weeks were my neighbors on the same floor, Ron and Beverly Shavlik. Ron was a basketball star on the N. C. State team, and he and Beverly were newly married. I felt surprised and honored by their friendliness.

The apartment had hardwood floors and white walls that I gradually found pictures to decorate. Its furniture was predominantly discards from home supplemented by purchases from J. C. Penney. By saving S & H green stamps, I was able to buy a record player that could play both 45's and a stack of 78's. But probably what most helped make the apartment my home was that the bulk of its furnishings had memories attached. The single bed was the one I'd slept in in Washington. The desk where I worked on my Olivetti typewriter was the substantial but battered ten-drawer desk that had been Bibba's when she was reading me the Oz books. The dining table and matching wooden bench were those discarded from the breakfast room with the post-war renovations. They and the round table I used for the record player looked "smarter" when I painted them black.

But I felt fat all the time then and spent whole days in the apartment alone, wanting to binge and occasionally doing it. When I did, I got so depressed that I sometimes called Wilmer for an extra visit. Eating like that made me want to die. The best means of warding it off was to not eat all day until night. But that was hard, because I was trying to write again and writing made me ravenous. And lonely. Sometimes I pretended I was back in the hospital with the old ladies from Hall VI just in the other room. I wished I still knew Eleanor and Liz.

My time in the apartment was only temporary, however — until the fourth item on the list could be worked out. But going to work or to the university became the most formidable undertaking of my life. I knew I needed to in order to look at all like a normal person, but I knew just as certainly that I wasn't prepared to do what was required. Father said I could go to the university as a special student in creative writing. I felt a little more capable of that, even though the university's being in Chapel Hill — thirty miles away when I couldn't drive — meant I'd have to move there and give up Wilmer. With a job in Raleigh, I could keep seeing Wilmer, but I'd also have to see other people in town who knew I was an ex-mental patient.

The first development in that decision was the university's response to my application. One night when I went to my parents' for dinner Mommy read the letter aloud while Father and I listened.

It ended, "In order to determine whether you can be admitted to the university, you and your parents will need to meet with Dr. Houston. Please call for an appointment."

"Stupid fools!" Father cursed. "Arrogant show-offs!"

"Jonathan!" Mommy tried to quiet him.

And it worked momentarily. Slightly more restrained, he continued, "It just pisses me off how because of a little honesty these officious M.D.'s make it hard for Lucy. No doubt that when they talk to her and see her George School record they'll take her in with open arms. But first they have to strut their M.D. superiority!" He took another sip of Bourbon before adding more angrily, "As if anorexia nervosa had anything to do with academic ability! Diplomaed imbeciles!"

"Jonathan!" Mommy corrected. "We'll have to do it this time." Her dimple was ticking.

Not one doctor but four. For once I felt skinny and grotesquely small between Mommy and Father with that battery of four looking back from across the table. A sickening sense of being studied rather than helped. Then, one of the doctors took me into another room, leaving Mommy and Father with the others.

He was older than Father. His head was bald, and he had bushy grey eyebrows that bunched together angrily over his rimless glasses. I felt like a bug under a microscope as he declared, "You've had considerable hospitalization," and then asked, seeming to lecture, "What understanding of yourself and your illness did you gain in the process?"

I was dumbfounded. I'd been told that no one understood anorexia nervosa. Haltingly I mumbled something I'd once heard Mommy say: "Anorexia nervosa remains a mystery. Its most frequent victims are gifted adolescent girls from upper-class families."

"But what about your anorexia?" Dr. Shands probed. "Why have you been unable to eat?"

I didn't know what to tell him. I didn't know which answers to his questions would be right. I didn't even know if there were right answers or if I seemed stupid trying to give some that didn't exist. Still, I struggled to. Having the doctors' permission was essential. I also needed their approval to feel less humiliated.

But the ordeal was much more comprehensive than any of us had expected. Back in the room with Mommy and Father, I understood even more keenly that these were not just more kind doctors who wanted to make me well. The other three had apparently grilled Mommy and Father in my absence. I could see that in Mommy's haggard face with its slow dimple and in Father's silence. After a few more questions, all four of them went out and left us alone.

"Sons of bitches!" Father muttered. "Ideological lunatics!"

"Jonathan!" Mommy whispered back.

"None of this is any of their Goddamn business. The university is public. It has to do with education and intellect. 'Unconscious conflicts' is baloney and off the subject."

When they returned, Dr. Shands again did the talking, ending with, "Therefore, it's our consensus that a prerequisite for Lucy to enroll at the university under any circumstances must be that she enter psychoanalysis."

Watching Mommy and Father, my heart sank at how shocked they appeared. Even Mommy's dimple had stopped.

Dr. Shands continued, "Despite the radical treatment Lucy has received, there has been no serious psychotherapy. And in order for her to succeed — at the university or anywhere — it is our opinion that self-understanding is essential. Psychoanalysis is the treatment of choice in this case."

I said nothing. I was praying so hard that they wouldn't ask me to speak that I didn't even notice how we got out of there.

Driving home, Father raved. "Psychoanalysis is the treatment of choice!" he yelled across me at Mommy.

She shook her head in silence, but her dimple was going.

"As if anyone knew that about anorexia!" he raged on. "Do you know what they mean by psychoanalysis?! Do you?!"

"Not exactly," Mommy sighed.

"Paying thousands of dollars for years of talking daily to an idiot like Houston! Forking up thousands of dollars to some degreed fool who tries to convert human emotions into science."

"Jonathan!" Mommy soothed, still ticking.

I said nothing and stared straight ahead at the cars swishing past. We all pretended I hadn't heard a word.

I become perplexed as well as sick at heart recalling that interview. It's always been so. What has changed over time are the proportions. In 1956, the sick-at-heart feeling nearly drowned out the puzzlement. Today the puzzlement is large and nagging. Piecing together that single interview, which seemingly barred me from the university, with those long, bleak, terrifying years in hospitals, with the wasted person I felt myself to be afterward, with the woman, mother, grandmother I am today, how is all this to be understood?

Writing a memoir — as opposed to a novel — requires answers. The truth makes a story and a life real. In the present, psychoanalysis has taught me to believe that the truth is in me — in my dreams, feelings and thoughts observed curiously. Many a time I've looked into the bathroom mirror as if to see the truth there — in the width of my lips stretched thin to smile, in the blue of my deep-set eyes with the right one still straggling. But the answers to these questions have to be sought elsewhere: Why did they give me such radical treatment in those hospitals? And why no real psychotherapy? Also, was I committed? If I hadn't been so afraid, could I have left? Why after the hospital, with those doctors at UNC urging psychoanalysis, was I limited to seeing Wilmer once a week?

Early on especially I would have liked answers to relieve my guilt about the price our family had paid for my illness. When Father complained about the high fees of psychiatrists or the expense of my hospitalization, it made me feel like a hopelessly bad person. Not only had I cost a lot, but despite the money spent, my fat fear was as present as ever. Because of distress over this, I once talked to Bibba about it. That was years ago; Father was still alive; maybe Mommy was. But it was after I started seeing Dr. Howie, because I can remember his commenting on it. Bibba and I went to dinner alone as we used to when she came to Raleigh. And I asked her what she knew about the cost of my treatment.

"What makes you worry now?" she asked in that flat, serious manner of hers.

"Because Father still talks about it, calling psychiatrists 'highway robbers.' In analysis I'm trying to understand things — especially what is my responsibility and what isn't. And I've always felt guilty about the money they spent on my anorexia."

"Well, I don't think there's any reason for guilt about that," Bibba replied earnestly. "I don't think they spent any money to speak of after Silver Hill." She went on to explain that the mother of her high school roommate, an administrator at New York Hospital at the time, had told her that the doctors were afraid I'd die if I went home. Thus, they had pressed Mommy and Father to commit me and had believed that my less expensive care as a ward of the state would persuade them.

That fell on me like a ton of bricks, but because I was in analysis, I also made myself go ask Father, who by then was in his mid-70's.

"Don't be such a puritanical nitpicker!" he chided. "Who in hell can remember what happened in those days?"

At that time I wasn't up to further questioning. And even now, clinical reading about anorexia nervosa provides only present-day assistance. All it reveals about the past is confusion characterized by a mixture of psychological breakthroughs and almost determined blindness to them. Clinicians rarely mention the use of electrocon-vulsive shock therapy or insulin comas. Some strongly advise against forced feeding and hospitalization except to relieve emergencies. Some advise against removing patients from home, insisting that the parents need treatment as well with a different therapist, because working out psychological separation from parents is the major task. However, one history of anorexia nervosa (*Holy Anorexia* by Rudolph M. Bell, 1985), which covers the period from the Middle Ages to the present, shows how frequently the same mistakes of trying to control these patients and focus on their physical rather than emotional problems have been repeated, despite evidence that uncontrolling psychological treatment is essential and more effective. Since 10% of such patients die, these mistakes are both understandable and devastating. They also leave additional problems that have to be overcome before the internal dilemma of anorexia can be addressed.

With the possibility of my going to the university eliminated in early February 1956 by Father's unwillingness for me to have psy-choanalysis, the next plan was for me to work in the newsroom of the *Raleigh Times*, the afternoon daily *The News and Observer* had bought a couple of years earlier. I dreaded doing that. But after Father talked to the managing editor Pat Kelly, and editor Mark Ethridge (neither of whom I'd ever met), I called Mark like Father told me to. I felt pitiful and useless! But all Mark said was, "Hi, Lucy. I was glad to hear from your dad that you're back in Raleigh." And then, hearing me recite the reason for the call: "Well, why don't you come down around three tomorrow and talk with Pat and me."

Mommy's response to this was that she would give me a ride and that I must be sure to wear a hat.

"A hat?" I grimaced.

"Certainly," she replied. "It's very important to look your best for the initial interview."

"Your mother's right," Father said. "You need to make a good impression. The better your appearance, the better they'll treat you. A hat looks proper, as well as titillating."

I did not own a hat, but before I went back to the apartment that night, Mommy helped me try on several of hers and finally sent me home with a grey one with feathers and a veil. I kept trying to think that out. If there was any place I did not want to look weird, it was the newspaper. But the more I thought about it, the more I realized I didn't know what was appropriate. I ended up wearing the hat because I was afraid not to.

As soon as I got there, though, I knew it was a mistake. When I asked a group of reporters for Pat Kelly or Mark Ethridge, they looked me up and down. All those people, including Mark and Pat, had rolled-up sleeves like they'd been working hard. I'd heard about Mark from Father: a hardworking young editor they'd brought in from the *Louisville Courier Journal* to make the *Times* seem independent of *The News and Observer*. He was friendly and had a kind smile that made me want him to like me. Pat I'd never heard much about. He was younger than Mark, but slicker, with dark eyes and a five o'clock shadow. As managing editor, he'd have more to do with me than Mark would. When I asked Pat what I'd be doing, he said, "We always need more help with obits and church notices. We'll start you there and see what happens."

I left a few minutes later having agreed to return a week from

Monday at 6:30 in the morning.

"What are you afraid of in this instance?" Wilmer Betts asked.

"The people and the work." The words come out of me easily there as long as I didn't look at him. I'd learned that, and even though I wanted to look, if I had something to say I didn't. To prevent my eyes from skittering off in the helpless way that made me feel crazy. "They'll all know," I continued. "They'll be sorry for me and kind because I'm sick and weird."

He didn't say anything, and I couldn't see his face to guess about his thoughts. Mine went to the hat and my fear that I had schizophrenia. I hadn't told him about either. Because there were some things I couldn't tell anyone. I felt terribly grateful for Wilmer even though Father made fun of him as a "Poor Pitiful Pete" and defended him as "cheaper than the others." I could talk to him about loneliness and shame and about hating to feel weird and pitied by people. I could talk to him about my badness and binging and wanting to die. But not about psychoanalysis or schizophrenia. Father had told me that Wilmer was not a psychoanalyst and that the doctors at the hospital said psychoanalysis would be bad for me. Somewhere, too, maybe even from those university doctors who'd said I ought to have it, I'd learned you had to be un-crazy to have psychoanalysis, that it wasn't for "schizophrenics," which was what Miss Higgins on Hall VI had called all mentally sick people.

I wished I could talk to Wilmer about all that, but I did not want him to tell me I was schizophrenic. So instead I labored in silence to diagnose myself. I did not hear voices; I had never heard voices. But I'd been locked up for five years, and most people locked up for years were schizophrenics. God only knew why I didn't eat and worried about fat and couldn't look at people. Or why I'd worn Mommy's hat to the interview when anyone with sense wouldn't have.

"How come you stopped talking?" Wilmer asked.

"I was just thinking."

"About?"

"Still about the people and the work." What Wilmer and I do here, I went on to myself, is pretend I'm not crazy. Unhappy, isolated, different, unable to "commit myself to life," but not crazy. Because we maintained this pretense, I could call him up when I wanted to die and have an extra visit in which he said, "What you're doing right now is extremely difficult. And your way of dealing with hard things is through food — by eating or not eating, so it makes sense that in this transition from hospital to Raleigh the eating is worse." In the rules of our relationship, I could count on him not to say, "That's right. Your craziness is food. Some people hear voices. Others count calories to keep the voices from being heard." Still we both knew the truth, I felt, and I had to help Wilmer not say it by not asking.

"Again, you stopped talking," he reminded me.

"I don't know anything to say."

"You were talking about your anxiety over working at the newspaper."

"Yeah. But I already said it. . . that the people will pity me for being an ex-mental patient. And. . . well, they have to hire me, and suppose I can't do the work?"

Wilmer didn't answer right off. Probably he didn't know what to say. So he asked, "Why couldn't you do the work?"

"Because. . . " I didn't know how to answer him. Like with Mommy, I didn't want him to know that my brain had been irreparably damaged. Finally I said, "Because I never finished high school. . . because I haven't been to college."

"You know," Wilmer responded more quickly. "It seems to me lots of writers never went to college. Faulkner or somebody even said college can ruin a person who wants to write."

He was trying to make eye contact with me. But my eyes clung to the trash basket rim while I struggled to figure out whether he was encouraging me because he still believed I was a "gifted, sensitive person" or because he'd finally realized I was mentally deficient and needed to do whatever I could.

The Saturday before starting work I bought a brown suit with flecks of blue that the saleslady said highlighted my eyes. Also, a pretty blue shirt to accent it. The suit's loose jacket and boxy skirt were the latest style, but they especially appealed to me as concealers of fat.

That evening I dressed in it for supper at Mommy and Father's. Scrutinizing my reflection in the dresser mirror while waiting for

Father to pick me up, I wondered how he would say I looked. "Sexy?" . . . "Woman of the world?". . . . "Self-centered greasy-grind?" I never could guess for sure. And his opinion mattered a lot, because he was real. Whatever he felt, however he saw me, even if exceedingly critical, felt like he really knew me for myself. I'd cut my hair short at his suggestion.

In the car Father kissed me but didn't notice the suit. "That was a smart idea getting your hair cut," he said, driving along. I thought about the picture of Babs I'd seen at the Bridgers's. Flapper haircut. "It changes your skinniness to sophisticated sexy." Then, stopping for a red light, he glanced over and added, "You know you could be a mysterious temptress. . . a seductive femme fatale."

I didn't know what to say. In spite of uneasy excitement, I just smiled politely.

At the house, Mommy was in the kitchen because Leanna had stopped working through dinner. "Hello, beautiful," she said, giving me a kiss and looking me over severely, worried like always. "How are you?" And then with a surprised, almost insulted simper, "Is that new?"

"Yes. I bought it this afternoon. To wear to work."

"It's lovely," she said. "Looks so smart with your hair. There's lettuce for salad in the refrigerator. Leanna has chicken broiled plain the way you like it in the oven."

"Lucy," Father interrupted absently as he poured Bourbon into the glasses for him and Mommy, "the novel you gave me to read is good. . . I think we should send it off."

That knocked the breath out of me. Pressured since before leaving the hospital to let him see my writing, I'd finally given him the novel about Caleb Blake after the university doctors' interview. But that was weeks earlier, so I'd assumed he'd forgotten or didn't want to tell me it wasn't good. Besides, with all my other worries, writing didn't matter much. "Really?" I gasped.

"Yeah." He handed Mommy her drink, and I followed them into the library. "Come," he said. "Let's talk about it."

Father settled into his red leather armchair, and I sat in the corner of the sofa I remembered hiding in as a little girl. Mommy sat in her usual straight chair. "I am so delighted," he began and then went on to say a lot more that I had trouble listening to. His sentences seemed to roar like ocean waves before giving way to blurred silence. The words sounded powerful and exciting, but also confusing and unreal. "Yes," he exulted in a way that I could grasp, almost like coming up for air. "It seems to me to be a stirring, steadily moving, powerful little book. The characters are strong. The language. . . You know about people, Lucy. So your people come alive, credible and human."

Inside my head I brooded over whether he really thought all this or was just desperately seizing on another way to make me worth something.

He drank silently for a few minutes, staring straight ahead as if in a dream. Then he whispered with intensity, "I'm very proud of you, Lucy."

"So am I," Mommy echoed, beaming over her drink.

My body and my mind were at odds in response to this praise. I knew that I should not only feel proud but happy that what I'd written was so pleasing to them. But the hair on my arms was standing up as though in response to something horrifying. As I pondered this, they were ready for refills and I became the bartender. "Lucy, come take care of an old man. . . Put a little sweetener in your mother's glass."

When I returned with their refilled glasses, Mommy said, "Thank you, Lucy. You are so wonderful."

Taking his drink, Father added, "Sweet slave, give an old man a kiss."

I did so and retreated to the sofa corner, still giddy and feeling (for some crazy reason I couldn't understand) sickeningly agitated. I remained there even after Mommy went back to the kitchen.

Father was silent, gazing at the books on the wall opposite him. But then he turned to peer at me. "You know, Lucy, it's very strange. Have I ever told you that you look like Babs?"

"Babs? How could I?" My heart was beating fast; my face was hot. What's wrong? I thought. Why am I worried? Because that day I had not eaten too many calories.

"I don't know," he said wistfully. "But you do. It may be something about your new hair style. The way it sets off the curve of your jaw, the little bump in your nose." He took more slow swallows, twisting his glass in between.

Still feeling hot and blurry, I kept looking at him despite the fear that drove my body back into the shadowed sofa. Even at that distance, I could see his eyes were wet.

"She was also very gifted," he whispered. "And at writing. Probably more practical than you. Not as beautiful as your mother, but warm, sunny, sensuous. And you are strangely. . . wonderfully like her."

The sofa's shadows bulged, blanketing my fevered fuzziness. Mommy's voice calling, "Dinner's ready," was a relief.

In the kitchen, however, everything was incredibly reversed.

"Why do you wear that suit?!" Father chided. "It makes you look like an Hungarian refugee."

"I just bought it today, to wear to work at the paper."

"Well, for God's sake, take it back! It makes you look like an emaciated concentration camp survivor!" He shook his head disgustedly as he poured another drink. "A Goddamn toothpick stuck through a raisin!"

"Jonathan!" Mommy scolded. Then, with her injured pleading tone, "Can't you say something helpful?"

"But, it's the damn truth! She'd do better not dressing like a refugee!"

"Well, I think it looks very smart." Mommy's dimple raced as she deliberately turned to the roast before speaking. "Lucy," she said, testing it, "Your father is just old-fashioned. It's the style he's critical of. Not you. He really loves you very much."

Three weeks into it, I was relieved to see that I could do the work. I answered the phone, "*Raleigh Times* Newsroom, Lucy Daniels speaking." While the others raced toward deadline, I went to get morning coffee for them. I pasted up the radio and television schedules, working hard and studiously to keep the others from looking at or talking to me. If somebody called with a public service announcement or to give more details to the story some reporter was writing, I took the call like Pat told me to and often felt surprised to have so little difficulty. Even the part that scared me most — taking obits over the phone, or worse still, a story at deadline — I did terribly slowly, but without anybody complaining. Each time, though, I'd feel so pitiful afterwards that I'd long to die.

That particular noon, after taking the deadline copy to Pat, I sneaked into the ladies' room to cry, again flooded with disgust from seeing my own inadequacy.

Blowing my nose, I heard the outside door open and high heels click into the other cubicle. In the midst of her peeing, the other woman said, "Lucy, want to go to lunch with us?"

Studying the brown pumps, I thought, Bette Elliot? I didn't want to go. I wanted to disappear after first edition, go home "sick" and cry in peace. Furthermore, I didn't really know Bette Elliot. I hadn't spoken to her more than twice. Wilmer had said, "Maybe you'll be able to find some friends at the paper." Still, I didn't want to have to do the work of being with them and feeling weird. I didn't want them to see me eat.

"A bunch of us are going to the pharmacy."

Wilmer would say, "Go."

"Sure. . . Thank you."

And at the pharmacy with seven of us scrunched together around two little tables pushed end-to-end, I did feel so weird and inadequate that I could hardly keep sitting there. It wasn't their fault. They were kind to include me. I strained to act as if I did belong. When I ordered soda water and took out my foil-wrapped diet bread and lettuce sandwich, I did my best to act casual the way Father always told me to. Some of them had sandwiches from home, too, but they ordered cokes or milkshakes. It was so late that we were the only people still eating. They laughed and talked together like in the newsroom, except that they weren't preoccupied with getting out copy. I was quiet, like a foreigner who didn't know the words, relieved when they didn't speak to me, pleased but scared when they did.

In the apartment I was still trying to be a writer. At least, that was what I called it. Partly accurately, but also to put a better front on the loneliness that engulfed me from 4:30 every afternoon until I could go back to work the next morning at six. Sometimes the words did come with ease, making me briefly hopeful. But usually the paper was so relentlessly blank that I felt deficient by 5:30 and despondent later. Then the eating would expand from a gnawing worry into a menacing monster.

That afternoon, after trying to stave off the hunger with a cup of black coffee, I had to pay the higher price of eating some lettuce and then a piece of diet bread. Which led to two, three, four pieces. I made myself stop and face the gaping paper. But before I could get a word down, I again felt so at hunger's mercy that I had to go back to the kitchen. With ice milk in the freezer and broiled chicken in the refrigerator, I managed to hold them at bay with another cup of coffee. But I felt like an animal, ravenous to eat everything in sight. "Why shouldn't I have some ice milk?" I finally surrendered. "My life is so awful, and I'm so alone. Why not?" Then I filled a bowl with ice milk. At that point eating no longer mattered. However much or little I ate after that, I'd be desperate until I slept. So I closed my mind to the screaming accusations.

And spooning up the vanilla cream, I tried to press back everything else by writing. Getting into the story, I was briefly hopeful. Until it occurred to me how much depended on my becoming a writer — to conceal my lack of education, to give me value so that other people wouldn't see me merely as a former mental patient. Then the writing seemed as worthless as I was. It was much worse at home than in the newsroom, where what I did had to be used whether it was good enough or not. Alone in the apartment I could no longer deny that the reality I needed to escape was that of never having been as good as Mommy said, and never having had the guts to be less, and that all the money spent on hospitals hadn't helped because the damage of my cowardliness was clearly uncorrectable.

chapter fourteen

BEST SELLER

That March evening I felt relieved to be at my parents' house and spared of another night of fighting off the food alone. Lulled by the tinkle of ice cubes and the cozy glow of the lamplight, I was also eager to hear more about what Father had said on the phone when he invited me to supper: "Bernice Baumgarten [his literary agent] likes your novel very much. She thinks she'll have no problem selling it."

In the library, though I still didn't believe it, there really was a letter. Father spread it out under the lamp. Mommy and I listened as he read aloud:

"I am delighted with Lucy's novel. Far and above any interest I would have in its having been written by your daughter. It is a remarkably impactful, poignant, beautifully wise and forceful little book. Regardless of age, this writer is for the reader wonderfully seasoned by a blend of irony and compassion."

The ice cubes clinked louder as he paused. I had no trouble listening because I did not know the person or the book this letter was about. Mommy's face looked haughty in its stillness, as if poised to attack any shortcoming she might detect. Looking at her, I thought she was foolish to take this so personally. Father went on:

"I want you to know that this praise of Lucy's novel is not simply my opinion. Carol Brandt [her associate] has also read it, and this letter incorporates her views as well as my own.

"The one reservation Carol and I have is that this novel is likely to be both widely acclaimed and controversial given that its hero is a black male in pursuit of twentieth-century equality. In light of Lucy's illness, we assume you must consider the likely impact of stress of this kind."

"Well, I've always known it," Mommy said, her diamond pin glistening benevolently. "What?" I asked.

"How remarkable you are. . . I am certainly relieved to have these others recognize it."

"What does she mean by 'controversial'?"

Father took another sip. "Describing Negroes as human and worthy of respect is controversial today," he said. "Your father's daughter!"

"What should I do?"

"We'll call them tomorrow. . . See what publishers they have in mind. Also the money."

"What about the 'controversialness'?"

"Don't you want it published?"

"Oh, yes. But —"

"Then there may be controversy."

"My darling, I am so proud of you," Mommy said.

My eyes jumped to the Oriental rug. I was still unprepared for her talking like that. "You will call Mrs. Baumgarten with me?" I said to Father.

"Bernice Baumgarten," he corrected.

I studied the blue scrolls in the rug's pattern. The ice cubes tinkled. Then Mommy asked, "Well, how's the paper?"

"Okay, I think."

"What do they have you doing this week?"

"The same as last week. Obits and TV schedules."

From the corner of my eye I could see her dimple start. "Are they planning to send you on a feature story soon?"

"I don't know. In a way I hope not. Because I don't know how."

Her dimple sped up. I knew she was feeling "mortified" that her "most gifted" child felt inferior. She sipped her drink to keep from talking.

I recounted the rug's blue scrolls.

"Poppycock!" Mommy finally snapped. "Lucy, of course you know how to do a feature story!" I could hear her sucking breath in between her teeth. "When you put yourself down like that, you invite them to overlook who you are. You have more sensitivity and sense than anybody down there! You can do anything you put your mind to — feature story or otherwise!"

Tears sprang to my eyes. "Listen, Mommy," I pleaded without looking up. "I don't know how to do it. I never did it before. The other people are college graduates, and I didn't finish high school. Besides, I feel weird. I'm even afraid to talk on the phone."

"Lucy, stop that sniveling! You are as capable as anyone down there, college or no college!"

"What's college got to do with it?" Father put in. "Some of the world's most brilliant and productive people never went to college. . . Shakespeare. Thomas Edison. William Faulkner."

"But everyone in the newsroom has."

"And that's all they do with it!" Mommy snapped. "Besides, your score on the high school equivalency was extraordinary."

"But most of what I learned in school has left my head."

"Poppycock!"

My tears started again. So did Mommy's dimple before she got up, silent, to head for the kitchen.

Father motioned for me to come sit on his lap. As I did, he kissed my ear with lips heavy with bourbon. "You know, Lucy," he said, smoothing back the hair around my ears, "Your mother's right about your sense and sensitivity. Bernice Baumgarten's saying the same thing." Tracing each cheek with his finger, he took hold of my chin with one hand and turned my face so that he could kiss my nose. "You are more gifted than most people ever dream of being." Then, mischievously squeezing my thigh, he added, "And good looking legs besides! . . . All of which shows in your novel." He grinned, shook his head, and drank deeply. Then he offered me a sip.

As usual, I refused, but I also silently berated myself for being so prissy. Adelaide always giggled as she drank deep and kissed him back. Mary Cleves did, too. Sitting there, I could feel myself become unnerved. A mixture of excitement and fear, at once inviting, threatening, and totally incomprehensible. Weak. Numb. Encapsulated. I shivered as he abruptly gripped my thigh again and, playfully tweaked my nose, saying, "You need to have some fun, my sweet!" Then, jiggling his knees mightily beneath me, "Fun! Excitement!

Mischief! 'All work and no play makes Jack a dull boy,' you know."

I said nothing. What I felt was dead.

Suddenly his face went sad. And still. His eyes seemed to look across hills before he continued. "Of course, too, you are my boy. . . my writer! Who needs most of all to learn to live life to the hilt!" He raised his glass in a toast. Then, stopping the jiggling to squeeze me, he planted another whiskey-wet kiss on my neck. "You are my boy," he sighed. "My wonderful wise, witty, bewitching, libidinous boy!"

When the news that I'd sold my novel got out, the newsroom made a big deal of it. People at the paper had tried to be friendly and kind all along, but this gave them something real and upbeat to relate to me about. Yet even with the book, though my response was as friendly and appreciative as shyness permitted, I inwardly resembled a porcupine whose automatic reaction to attention from others was to fire needles of shame and guilt into myself. This resulted in my having to take on new tasks and friendships while feeling further damaged. Feature stories, for instance. And reporter Helen Tucker and women's editor Bette Elliot asking me to join their "just us girls" lunches.

When I did, those conversations were quite different from the ones at the pharmacy. Helen and Bette exchanged newsroom gossip and listened sympathetically to each other's problems — Helen's with dating, Bette's with raising two children alone. After asking about my novel and writing, they moved to questions about guys and dating. Hearing I had no boyfriend, they began talking through the list of available men they knew — at the paper and elsewhere. In time, men became a standard topic among us. It was from Helen and Bette that I first heard about Tom Inman — an experienced photographer who'd recently returned from two years in the service. He was too young for Helen and "too brash and red-necked for you," Bette told me.

Mommy's voice ground on with relentless clarity, marching my eyes across the print. But there were knots in my stomach and my thoughts refused to stay on the subject. I just kept looking down dutifully, catching what I could and praying Mommy wouldn't guess how little that was. I was excited. When I'd called to tell them about the galleys for my novel arriving, I'd been breathless and exultant and reminded of how the same corrugated bundles periodically came for Father.

But there in the library, as we proofread together, I was bored. And worn out with Mommy. My ears kept wincing in response to her haughty enunciation. My eyelids continually faltered. Until she snapped, "Don't go to sleep!"

"I'm not."

"You look like you are. Lucy, this is serious business. You don't want to look like a fool in print, do you?"

"No." But Mommy's voice did make me sleepy. "Maybe I could read to you."

"It goes more slowly that way. You saw the note: 'Return as soon as possible.' You can't afford unnecessary delays. They can result in delayed reviews."

I felt tired enough to let them print the book any way they wanted. I felt as though I didn't know what was correct from what was wrong. And that Mommy was the only person who did know. "You keep reading," I said. "It does go better that way."

But my mind departed. For the newsroom. To Pat and Mark talking about my story on the Budapest couple trying to settle in Raleigh despite not knowing any English. Pat says almost nothing from under his celluloid eye-shade. Mark says, "I hear we have a novelist on the staff." And when I complain of being incompetent, he adds, "It may take you some time, but it seems likely you'll find your way." Pat and Mark seemed to be satisfied with what I wrote, sometimes even complimentary after cutting it. At the pharmacy people said, "Oh, you're Lucy Daniels. I know your stories." And I felt incredibly important.

"Lucy!" Mommy snapped. "Wake up! Can't you understand how important this is?"

"Yes, m'am."

"Or are you sick?"

"No." Just sleepy, I thought. With knots in my stomach that twisted and tightened. But better than hungry.

"Let's continue then."

"Yes, m'am."

Today I would say I was furious at Mommy then for taking me and my accomplishment over and driving us to suit her agenda. Also, afraid because of my anger. But then I was just sleepy and had a knot in my stomach that got so hard and so constant I could hardly eat. Whereupon Mommy and Father soon told Wilmer they thought I needed to go back to the hospital.

In my session he said, "Your mother and father are worried about your loss of appetite. Have they talked to you about it?"

"Yes. They think I need to go back to the hospital."

"What do you think?" he asked.

"I don't know. I feel real inadequate. Maybe in the hospital I wouldn't feel as afraid."

"But you've felt inadequate before. Why would you go back to the hospital now?"

"Because I'm having trouble eating. . . Because Mommy and Father say Dr. Burdick thinks I should." My eyes did manage to flitter up and momentarily collide with his.

"How would it be with you if I call Dr. Burdick?"

"Fine."

"You know there could be other ways besides hospitalization to deal with a knot in your stomach or not eating or even weight loss."

I didn't know what he meant, and I didn't want to know. The snake-named medicines came to mind. Also, questions about outpatient ECT or other things with doctors I didn't know. "But I know what the hospital is like."

"Well, since it's less than four weeks till your book gets published — which might make anybody tense — let's wait until I've talked to Dr. Burdick."

"Okay."

As it turned out, despite Wilmer and Dr. Burdick's agreement that the hospital wasn't necessary, I did go back for evaluation to quell Mommy's and Father's fears. I clung to Wilmer's last words the whole time I was gone:

"When you come back. . . and I don't think it would take longer than a week. . . you and I will go on working as we have." His ears had seemed to stick out more than ever. I found them comforting.

To my relief that return to the hospital did turn out pretty much as Wilmer had predicted. They put me on Hall V with the better patients and the most freedom of the locked wards. Some of the nurses knew me from before, and Dr. Wall and Dr. Burdick came by to see me briefly a couple of times. I'd received a copy of my book, *Caleb, My Son*, just before leaving home and showed it to everybody. Dr. Wall and Dr. Burdick seemed to think I should be proud of both the book and all I was doing in Raleigh. When I left after a week, the knot in my stomach was smaller and felt like just another part of the stress of being a writer who would be on the *Today Show*. Taking the train home alone reminded me of telling Grandfather good-bye when I went to George School.

And in Raleigh, my apartment and Wilmer and the *Times* newsroom were all expecting me. Also, Mommy and Father with their directives about the final preparations for the swirl of New York publicity around *Caleb*'s publication. In fact, in the newsroom I was sort of queen for a day, because they'd decided my book was so sensational that they needed to have a front page story about me with a picture. Pat wrote it.

Lippincott, my publisher, had kept us posted about the interest in the book shown by early reviewers. *Caleb* was already in its fourth printing before the big day. And other radio and television shows had requested me as a guest. Thrilling! But also overwhelming and intimidating. Looking back, I can say, "Of course! Less than ten months out of the hospital, I was about to become horribly conspicuous after having spent my life locked up and invisible." But such conscious clarity wasn't available to me then.

To compensate, I bought a navy blue silk dress with a blue and white polka-dotted tie and navy heels. Also, a couple of other dresses that would look "smart" in New York but still be usable for dress-up in Raleigh. Mommy offered to go with me, and I was much relieved to have her, despite the sense I always had with her of being a pet on a leash. Riding the train together, I recalled the first trip to George School. I wished I were strong enough not to need her, but the best I could do was tell her I wanted to go to the shows and other places with the public relations person and without her. She agreed that would look "smarter."

Looking back with the capacity for ambiguity that psychoanalysis and life have taught me to appreciate, I regard *Caleb*'s publication and success as traumatic good fortune. The whirlwind of recognition — book review of the day in both *The New York Herald Tribune* and *The New York Times*, interview with Dave Garroway on the *Today Show*, luncheon with critics and publisher at the 21 Club, radio talk shows — was exciting and, blessedly, something I was able to face with unanticipated poise.

But it also evoked a new fear that I couldn't articulate. Suddenly becoming so conspicuous after having been invisible made me dread death by appropriation. Probably I sensed that fear first on the *Today Show* on hearing the voice I barely recognized as my own answering Garroway, "Yes, an incredible day! I can hardly believe it. I wonder if my life can ever be the same after this."

"Certainly seems unlikely," Garroway said. "Today, September 9, 1956, is a red-letter day for Lucy Daniels, a day that will leave her forever after an acclaimed novelist."

Something inside me lurched as he spoke. I both liked it and I didn't. It made me feel overlooked and forgotten. Lucy, the anorexic, the cub reporter, the lonely girl in her apartment, all felt abandoned. The best comfort against that was the statement from the book's jacket that the politically savvy publishers had put into my mouth: "This is just a book about people, plain people like some I've known. It is not allied with any particular cause or point of view." Those words reminded me that I was like Caleb Blake, and that the book was about the black people who once had taken care of me. They gave me hope that this talented 22-year-old best-selling novelist would not obliterate the girl who'd written the novel inside a mental hospital. And that the real me would not be erased by either the phony, polished, public genius Mommy raved about or the clever, down-to-earth mischievous boy Father claimed.

Recalling *Caleb*'s publication now has brought sinister dreams in recent nights:

This woman was making everybody live inside the walls. In hiding. There was something sinister about it. Not that we were rushing to hide from someone. Rather, this was a way of life, living inside the walls, a way that must be strictly maintained. I went obediently to where she placed me behind metal meshwork like the covering on a stereo speaker. Then I peed in a way that formed a puddle going from inside to out.

At the dining room table again. Me at age four. "Pass your plate!" Father bellowed. When I did, he was standing there waving the carving knife and fork. But his face — his head — was gone.

"You'll have to get this one, Lucy," Pat yelled at me across the newsroom. "Three alarm fire at the Hilton. Meet Tom Inman out front and phone me something by 1:30. Tom drives a blue Chevy."

"Brash and hard-shelled," I thought on the elevator, trying to picture the photographer Bette had described as "A red-necked kid Korea turned into a hardened go-getter."

"Hello, Lucy," he said, pushing open the door on the passenger's side. "I'm Tom Inman. . . Haven't had a chance to meet you yet."

"Hi." I felt empty. "No. Somehow you've not been in the newsroom when I was. But I've heard people talk about you coming back from Korea."

Settled on the front seat, I noticed two jagged scars on his face — one on the left cheek just below his eye, the other across his forehead. Surprising that no one had mentioned them.

"Yeah. I've been back a few weeks. But it's a big change after two years in the army." He abruptly transferred his attention to the traffic in front of us and, driving fast and determinedly, fumed at the cars that got in his way. "As I get it," he continued, eyes fixed ahead, "This will have to be a quickie. . . Pat wants a shot for the front of the second edition. I'll have to have some back in the soup in 25 minutes."

"When I was leaving, Pat said the fire had already spread from the gas station to the Hilton's kitchen."

"Yeah. And since there was an explosion, the gas station will be one shot. Kitchen, too, probably. But, with a lot of legislators staying there, I need to look around for some V.I.P.'s too."

His eyes glancing at me were ice blue. His hands gripping the steering wheel were rough as though he were used to working outdoors. "Brash and hard-shelled," Bette had said. I searched for it.

"What do you want to do?" he asked, continuing to look ahead. "Ride back with me or stay and phone in your copy?" It was only eight blocks; I thought I could walk back.

We were approaching a place where the police and fire trucks had closed off the street. I was scared to death to be covering such a big story. I wished I'd told Pat I couldn't. Though I knew he'd have said, "You'll have to anyway. There's nobody else to send." It crossed my mind to stay in the car and let Tom's pictures do the job. Pictures were the most important part of fire stories anyway.

"Let's see," I made myself say. "Let me meet you back here in twenty minutes, if I don't see you before. If I'm not here when you need to leave, go without me."

Over time our just-us-girls lunches flowed together, becoming more personal and reminding me of talks with Liz and Eleanor. Bette and Helen were both envious of my success with *Caleb*. But they also made it their business to advise me about men — how most of them were problematic and how you shouldn't take anybody's friendliness as reason to like him.

Pat's use of me to fill in at deadline cut into those lunches. And the fact that the deadline stories often paired me with Tom Inman was a point that Helen and Bette both pounced on.

"No, it's nothing," I said. "Just the shift he works in photo."

But Bette laughed. "You are so innocent, Lucy! You can bet your bottom dollar, chance has nothing to do with it!"

"No," Helen added. "Unless it's something spectacular, none of the photographers like having to run out and print up on deadline. And Tom, even more than the others, doesn't take pictures he doesn't want to take."

"Yeah," Bette agreed. "Tom can only be taking your pictures because he wants to."

"Why would that be?"

"Well, you are a Daniels," Helen quipped. "And now you're a best-selling novelist. Tom probably figures it can help his ass to cover stories with you."

Her words jolted me with the sick feeling that trying to be realistic always caused me in those days.

Even with Bette and Helen I was still predominantly a Daniels. They did not speak of me being an ex-mental patient, but as much as they gossiped about other people, they probably knew and classified me that way, too. As different as those two qualities — Daniels and anorexic — seemed, they appeared to combine with "writer" to give me a significance unrelated to myself. I could not have stated this then, but now I'd call it "the feeling of being turned into a valuable oddity," one of those relics people bid for at auctions and take home to decorate a shelf. As the all-too-conspicuous author of a best-selling novel, I was even more starved then to "belong" with someone than I was for food.

Despite the possibility of Tom's liking me and the success I was as a feature writer, fiction writing in the apartment only grew more difficult. Hunger started the minute I sat down with pen and pad. In fact, continuing to write despite the hunger triggered so many eating binges that I came to see writing and eating as forces that opposed each other. Eating had to be controlled to make writing possible. But that was difficult — first, at times, because I had nothing to say, and second, because obeying the correspondence school's advice that "even bad writing is better than none at all," I often discovered that the adage was wrong. What I put down was dull, fake, pretentious, sweet, empty, wooden. It made me believe that *Caleb, My Son* had been a fluke.

Yet other people's expectations continued. A man from Chicago called to ask me to speak. In an article for *The New York World-Telegram and Sun* about being the writer-father of a best-selling author, Father expressed both pride and pain that after having had to spend the first half of his life in Grandfather's shadow, he might have to spend the second half in mine. At the courthouse, people said, "Oh, you're the one who wrote the best seller! What are you writing now?" I always tried to smile. "I haven't decided," I'd say, and get to work as quickly as I could on the list of marriages and divorces for the newspaper. Recognition like that should have made me feel better, but instead, my reaction was excruciating, making me feel crazy.

If someone had asked me then if I was depressed, I'd have denied it. I was just inadequate and ashamed of being inadequate. The fluke of the novel was a spotlight that magnified this. At that time, too, I was still cut off from the reality of my inner feelings. So trying to think about this situation only reinforced my sense of craziness and my belief that other people saw me as weird. Writing was only a sort of "cover" for this, something that, if successful, could hide my ruin from others.

When *Time* magazine wanted a black and white photo of me, Tom Inman called my parents' house to ask if I was there and if he could come take the picture. That was the first time he and I had ever collaborated on anything that wasn't a story for the paper. He had me pose sitting and standing in more than one location; he took three or four shots of each pose. "I'd like to give them more than one good picture," Tom said in the process. "If I can give them what they want as fast as they need it, I hear they pay stringers well." As I posed, I thought about how enterprising he was and felt envious.

Afterward Father offered him a drink, and they talked newspaper talk while I listened from the couch. When Tom finished his drink, he thanked Father again and said he needed to go print up his pictures to be able to get some on the 11:30 bus to *Time* that night. On the way out he said, "Lucy, would you like to have supper some night?"

"Certainly," I replied, goose-pimpling inside and thinking about talking to Bette and Helen.

"For God's sake, Lucy, what will it take for you to stop holding back?! Best-selling novelist, experienced feature writer! You should jump at a chance like the Chicago speech!"

Again I'd gone to my parents' house for dinner, and they were talking over their drinks. "Well, I just can't," I said. "I'm too afraid. I talked to Wilmer about it."

"What in hell does he know about it?! Goddamn weak-voiced shrink!"

"He knows about my fear."

"That's beside the point! What does he know about being a successful writer?!"

"I haven't asked him. But he does know how I'd feel trying to speak in Chicago. He does know about how afraid I am."

"That's the problem!" Father sneered. "Stupid mealy-mouthed shrink just going along with your whining! Of course, you're afraid! But why focus on it?!"

"I can't help it."

"You don't try. And it doesn't sound to me like Wilmer's any help. With just a little effort, Lucy, you could be an alluring, sensual woman all the boys were crazy over. Pretty, bright, good sense of humor. Now, a best-selling novelist! But instead you hide in your apartment eating lettuce!" He stopped to drink, eyeing me expectantly.

From the sofa's shadow, I said nothing.

Mommy sat stiff in her chair with lips pinched and disdainful eyes fixed on me. The room reeked with scorn for my weakness. But then, with eyes fading from hatred to sadness, Father said, "Lucy, come sit on an old man's lap."

And, like always, I did, relieved that he still loved me.

"I'm sorry it's so hard for you to embrace life," he sighed, stroking my shoulder. "I want you to be able to run out into the world — wonderful, sensitive, witty soul that you are — and give yourself to it and let everybody know who you are."

I sat still, relieved, tingling. I hoped he wouldn't mention the Chicago speech again.

"You're your Father's child, Lucy," Mommy crooned, beaming at us. "He's so proud of you."

Still no idea of what to say.

"My boy," Father soothed, outlining the contour of my cheek with his hand. "Lucy, you are my boy . . . No other man can be so fortunate as to have a lovely daughter who, in fact, has the mind of a man."

Staring straight ahead, I felt goose pimples prickle my upper arms and thighs.

"Lucy, when you do embrace life," Father said, squeezing my thigh, "you'll never be afraid again. . . I'd give anything to be your age with the world before me!"

The next challenge was Father's suggesting I apply for a Guggenheim Fellowship. He'd received one for his novel, which had not been any- where near as successful as *Caleb,* and he liked the idea of our being father and daughter fellows. Once I'd been reassured that the Guggenheim people wouldn't care about education or want to interview me personally, my resistance eased. Since they would only judge the quality of my writing and the plan for the project for which I wanted funding, there didn't seem to be much to lose. I wrote for an application.

Tom and I had supper together quite a few times. I wouldn't go so far as to call those dates, however. Whether planned ahead or not, they tended to be merely breaks in Tom's taking pictures and developing prints. He'd call and say, "How about if I pick you up in thirty minutes and we get something to eat at Finch's?" I nearly always said, "Sure," whether his call was something we'd discussed in advance or just out of the blue. It made me feel excited and valuable for a man to want to spend time with me. But those are the most confusing feelings of all to look back at now. At first they were a mixture of excitement and pleasure. Later they became something stronger, like infatuation, and still later, something bordering on love. In all stages, however, there was a large component of relief and gratitude that I, as a person, could be valued by someone.

It was not a reliable relationship, though. Or rather, it was dependably unreliable. Even when we'd made a plan in advance, I never knew when or whether he would call. And that made for a frequent teetering between fear of rejection and relief; also, it led to a stronger sense of happiness when things seemed more secure. I barely mentioned those suppers to Bette and Helen, who rolled their eyes and acted like I was being naive not to see them as important. I didn't mention Tom at all to Mommy and Father.

Looking back at the two of us now, from the perspective of having children older than we were then, I am filled with compassion and respect I wouldn't have understood at the time. Feeling ruined and doing all I could to live with and not reveal that state to others, I was much more aware (even then) of my problems and insecurities than Tom was of his. But he, no less than I, had grown up in family circumstances that I now regard as devastating. And probably that fact more than any other drew us together. Practice as a psychologist has shown me that what attracts people to each other is having similar problems with different solutions. Both Tom and I had grown up under conditions of abuse and severe emotional deprivation. But his family was poor, which inspired in me fantasies of real, salt-of-the-earth caring; my family had wealth and prominence, which I suspect seemed substantial and respectable to him. We were both ambitious, lacked the education needed for our endeavors, and were willing to work hard to make ourselves better.

Tom was the youngest of eight children in an eastern North Carolina tobacco farm family. His older brother's club feet and surgeries had saved Tom from being pampered as his deprived mother's baby. But his father's alcoholism had made all their lives tortured both before and after he was struck and killed by a drunk driver one night when he himself was walking drunk along the highway. Tom, at eleven, had received that news near midnight as he and an older brother tended the fires in their tobacco barn.

The remainder of his childhood had been characterized by hard work in and out of school, trying to stay out of his lonely mother's clutches, and living with some of his older married siblings in an effort to do this. Photography, which he'd taken up with a Kodak Brownie at an early age, had been his ticket out. When a picture he'd snapped of a motorcycle plowing amok through a crowd was not only bought by *Life* magazine but awarded a prize, he'd had what he needed to go to Raleigh, at eighteen, and get a job as photographer with *The News and Observer*. He'd been successful enough there, before being drafted during the Korean War, to resume his job when he returned in 1956 at age twenty-three.

As Tom and I began spending weekend as well as evening time together, I could hardly believe in my good fortune. To have a boyfriend, rather than just talking to Helen and Bette about it, made me feel blessedly acceptable and normal. I identified with Tom's combination of imperfection and ambitious industry. His lack of a college education and desire to get one with the G.I. Bill impressed and inspired me without stirring feelings of inferiority. I allowed my food worries and lack of confidence to show with him more than with any other person I knew. He seemed to take them for granted as facts of life about me, realities that were just part of who I was. And that felt closer to "belonging" than anything I'd experienced since George School.

Photography was as important to Tom as writing was to me. At that point in his life he wanted to become a photojournalist like those who worked for *Life* magazine. In short, you could say, he wanted to tell stories with pictures like I wanted to with words. Working as a newspaper photographer was a way for him not only to earn a living, but also to have experiences to help him grow in that story-telling direction. Our suppers at Finch's were filled with talk about this.

"The other night I got this neat shot of the train coming into town. I didn't know it was as good as it was at the time. Now I have to get the other shots I need." When his face was animated, the scars barely showed. Freckles and blue eyes gave it a boyish down-to-earth quality that made me feel mistaken about the hardness I sometimes worried over.

"How many more shots does the story need?" I asked, taking a bite of the fried shrimp I liked there.

"The story would only have three — the train coming into town, a bustle of people at sunset, then its disappearing into the dark. But getting the right ones is the problem."

"How do you get them?"

"Go down there and set the tripod up and wait. Then shoot like crazy when the train comes through. It can take hours. And not till I get to the darkroom do I know what I've got."

"So you could work all evening and discover later that none of it's any good?"

"Yeah."

"How does that make you feel?"

"Tired. Sometimes pissed off."

How sensible and hardworking that sounded to me. Practical and self-accepting instead of neurotic and whiny. "I admire the way you keep working at it without getting discouraged."

"Oh, I get discouraged," he grinned, knocking catsup onto his fries. "I just don't give up. Mad don't hurt you, but giving up does."

Thinking about my writing, excitement flickered in me about how good we could be for each other — Tom working on his pictures, me on my stories — each with the other for example and support. It occurred to me, too, that anger might be less formidable than despair.

Indeed, even the hardness I sometimes detected in Tom seemed an offshoot of the "street smarts" he had that I needed. And there were several other opposites that made us fit well together — his sociableness and my shyness, my boring dependability and his unpredictability, my fears and his fearlessness.

Looking back, though, our insecurities and mutual need to find self-worth through another person seem glaringly obvious. I didn't recognize that as a problem at the time. I doubt I could have said self-esteem was something I lacked or hoped to gain. Perhaps, in fact, many people in love do the same — forget themselves in pursuit of the other. But forty-odd years later, from the perspective of having devoted time and pain to finding and being true to myself, it's dismaying to realize how little each of us was able to value ourselves then.

The April 1957 letter granting me a Guggenheim Fellowship was short and to the point: $3,000 to assist in the execution of my project. It was also exhilarating in a quiet, substantive, weighty way. Like a college diploma after all, a college diploma for my self, without the four years of greasy-grind work to get through. It seemed to recognize not only *Caleb, My Son*, but me as a writer, by approving the new novel outlined in my application. And in that way it gave me a future as well as a past.

I decided to go to New York for a few days alone — to talk with my agents, Bernice Baumgarten and Carol Brandt; to take Father's advice and pay my respects to Henry Allen Moe, executive director of the John Simon Guggenheim Foundation; and even more important, to celebrate and press myself to claim the status of writer. I telephoned to make a three-night reservation at the Tuscany Hotel and booked a berth on the train going up and back, which made me feel even more excited and capable than I had before. Then I discovered that a green tweed suit I'd been admiring for months in a local shop had been reduced 50%. I bought it with the delicious sense of its being the perfect outfit for my trip. Wearing that suit, I'd look neat, stylish, and too sophisticated for anyone to imagine me scared or crazy. A true intellectual! Finally, I also called a young woman I'd known at the hospital and asked her to meet me for

PHOTO ESSAY

Father (Jonathan Daniels) holding Lucy in her christening dress in late spring, 1934.

Lucy, age 3, alone in the yard after her second eye surgery.

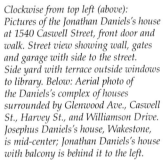

Clockwise from top left (above):
Pictures of the Jonathan Daniels's house
at 1540 Caswell Street, front door and
walk. Street view showing wall, gates
and garage with side to the street.
Side yard with terrace outside windows
to library. Below: Aerial photo of
the Daniels's complex of houses
surrounded by Glenwood Ave., Caswell
St., Harvey St., and Williamson Drive.
Josephus Daniels's house, Wakestone,
is mid-center; Jonathan Daniels's house
with balcony is behind it to the left.

Above: Bibba with Lucy, age 3, in 1937. Both are dressed for a play (at Bibba's school) in which Lucy was a jester.

Left: Father (Jonathan Daniels) and Babs (Elizabeth Ann Bridgers) holding infant Bibba, 1926.

Bottom left (l to r): Bibba, Adelaide, Lucy, and Patsy in 1939.

Bottom right (l to r back row): Bibba, Father, and Mommy. (l to r front row): Adelaide and Lucy on Mommy's treasured balcony in 1937.

Top: Family at Grandfather's in 1938.
Back row (l to r): Evalina Daniels, Josephus Daniels, Jr., Bibba (Elizabeth Daniels), Jonathan Daniels, Josephus Daniels, Sr., Lucy Cathcart Daniels, Ruth Daniels, Frank Daniels, Sr.
Front row (l to r): Patsy Daniels, Lucy, Nanny (Adelaide Worth Bagley Daniels), Frank Daniels, Jr., Edgar Foster Daniels, Adelaide Worth Daniels leaning against Nanny.

Top left: Flora.

Above: Lucy holding Mary Cleves in 1939.

Top: Family in Washington, 1943 (l to r): Lucy, Mommy, Bibba, Mary Cleves, Adelaide, and Father.

Bottom: Extended family at Daniels Day on Roanoke Island in 1946.
In the middle (back row l to r): Jonathan Daniels (Father), Lucy Daniels (Mommy),
Lucy (in checkered dress), Dr. Worth Daniels, Frank Daniels, Jr.,
In front (l to r): Grandfather (Josephus Daniels), Adelaide, Mary Cleves, Worth Daniels, Jr.

A

new

star!

31

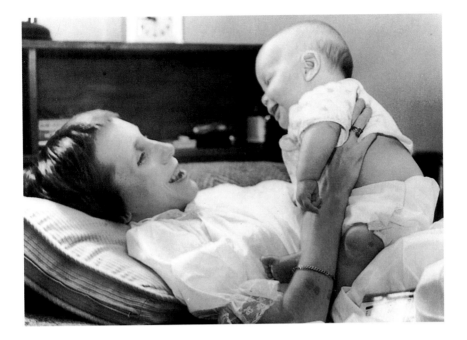

Opposite page: Newspaper ad runner for <u>Caleb, My Son</u>, 1956.

Above: Lucy holding her first baby, Patrick, in 1959.

Left: Lucy's photo on the back of <u>High On A Hill</u>, spring, 1961.

Above: Sisters in summer, 1961 (l to r): Mary Cleves, Adelaide, Lucy, Bibba.

Left: Rear of Shamrock Drive house.

Below: Front of Shamrock Drive house.

Above: Patrick, Lucy, and Jonathan with Lucy in October 1965.

Left: Lucy and Patrick with Lucy at North Carolina State Fair in October 1965.

Above: Inman family photo circa 1968-69 (l to r): Lucy, Ben, Tom, Lucy, Jonathan, Patrick.

Above: Family photo in fall, 1976 (l to r): Lucy, Lucy, Patrick, Ben, Jonathan.

lunch in New York.

Several days after the letter and a couple of nights before Tom put me on the train for New York, he asked me to marry him. And that seemed far more incredible than the Guggenheim. That I, just turned twenty-three and less than eighteen months out of the hospital, could actually appeal to a man enough that he'd want to marry me! I wasn't sure whether I loved Tom enough. Certainly, then, issues of self must have clearly outweighed my capacity to love anyone, and one aspect of those was whether I, as someone still severely limited by anorexia nervosa, could be a good wife. I talked seriously with Tom about my eating problems. But he didn't care. And that added to my sense of belonging, as well as suggesting hope for a future in which we could work together to make our lives better. I told Tom that I'd have to think about it during my time away.

Today I recall very little of that trip. The mood mainly. It was predominantly upbeat, making many things that could have been frightening relatively easy. And the tweed suit helped as expected. I did go to Brandt and Brandt to speak with Bernice Baumgarten and Carol Brandt, whom I'd only seen before at the time of *Caleb*'s publication. It was a successful visit. They'd sold the publication rights for *Caleb* to publishers in Finland, Denmark, and England, and were dealing with a publisher in Spain. Henry Allen Moe, by contrast, whom I also visited at the Guggenheim Foundation, was a tall, heavy-set man with neat, dark goatee and balding head. He was cordial and respectful without seeming to consider it remarkable that I'd been awarded a Guggenheim.

But the moment that still comes back most clearly after all this time is my lunch with a young woman who had also recently been discharged from New York Hospital. I didn't know her well; she was five or six years older than I and fairly undirected. Now I can recall neither her name nor her face. I've not seen or heard from her since. But I do remember what she said toward the end of our lunch in that tearoom: "I have the feeling you're headed for all kinds of new things. Also, that it'll be a long time before I see you again."

Back in Raleigh, marriage seemed another challenge I should press myself to take on. With no capacity to consider my own needs, the combination of Tom's seeming to accept me as I was and my own incredible accomplishments of the past eighteen months made me believe I could be a good-enough wife. Putting it simply, as lonely as I was, I felt I could love anyone who really wanted to be with me. So, being good enough for Tom seemed both sufficient and essential. Moving toward the wedding set for July 2, I felt wonderfully in love and the luckiest person alive.

At the time of our first visit to his family's farm in May 1957, I idealized both the difficult step I knew I was about to take and the good people I expected to help me with it.

"Don't be too concerned with how they act," Tom tried to prepare me as we drove toward Whiteville that afternoon. "They're sure to feel inferior and intimidated by your wealth and accomplishment."

And while I assured him that however they treated me would be all right, inside myself I was still thinking: "good, warm, simple, close to nature, kind-hearted, decent." Red-and-white-checkered tablecloths, homegrown vegetables and homemade bread, layer cakes baked with Leanna's 1-2-3-4 recipe — these were my expectations as we drove into the yard of his mother's small, weatherbeaten frame house.

In fact, however, the Inmans were distant or garrulous, busy or bashfully vigilant. At supper the vegetables were store-bought and canned; so were the biscuits. The one too-small roasted chicken and a mix cake with canned icing were washed down with sweetened iced tea and crude joking. The fare quickly tarnished my conception of poor, and the family made Tom seem vulnerable and reticent by comparison. Also, more oppressed.

Naturally, the most important family member for me was Mrs. Inman, whose image seemed identical with the grey bleakness of her little house: she was a hunched, grey-haired woman with no make-up on her pinched, wrinkled face. Her sullen grey eyes peered out of the darkness as she told me it was nice that I could come, and that Tom didn't tell them much about his life in Raleigh. "So it's always a treat if he blesses us with a visit," she said. Her handshake was the limpest I'd ever felt.

Undoubtedly this description is more critical of them than I was able to be at the time. But even then I felt much greater compassion for Tom after meeting his family, compassion made more poignant by the abrupt loss of my illusions about "poor." That night as I tried to relax listening to snoring sounds from other rooms in that small grim, creaking house, I felt lucky. And drifting into sleep, I realized that there was even something lovable about the scars on Tom's face, and that I'd never asked him how they got there.

The speed with which our relationship was moving did not seem a problem. At the time experience had taught me that all good things happened quickly and, perhaps, that taking time was akin (in feeling) to being weak and confined with crazy people. My parents, who considered not marrying the worst of failures, had been delighted since the very earliest rumors about Tom and me being an item. Probably I was the daughter they most feared would shame them as an old maid. Long before my anorexia Father had chided me, "Boys don't make passes at girls who wear glasses." Probably, too, Mommy and Father felt embarrassed about my illness and were relieved to have someone take me off their hands. At any rate, they were wholeheartedly in favor of a speedy marriage. Mommy moved in on planning the wedding in the same way that she had read the galleys for *Caleb*. The celebration itself seemed to be hers, while any worries about whether I was doing the right thing were left to me. I'm sure I talked to Wilmer about it, but I don't recall any particular help he gave me.

Doubts about marrying Tom — and I had doubts about anything I tried to do in those days — were most eased by being with him. Tom acted certain that being married to me was how he wanted to spend the rest of his life. Nor, despite all I had told him (and Father had told him as well) did he have any reservations about my capacity to succeed at doing the things we talked about doing together — pursuing careers in writing and photojournalism, having children, sharing old age together. Before the wedding he added earning a degree in journalism at University of North Carolina to this list. And best of all, none of this made me feel inferior. With the exception of my fears about childbirth, I felt in agreement with and capable of all the things Tom wanted.

Because of Tom, I no longer felt that I needed to be a writer. I still spent afternoons in my apartment stringing words together, but without the life and death urgency that once had accompanied writing. In fact, Tom probably would have liked me better if I hadn't tried to write. He was praising and encouraging; but when writing worried me, he'd say, "Don't fret, Sport. This is one man who loves you. I couldn't care less about the writing unless it makes you happy." And I believed Tom meant it. With him I discovered I had a previously unrecognized asset — that of being "unpretentious." He saw my writing much as I saw his photography, not as the brilliant production of a child prodigy from whom future masterpieces should be inevitable, but as a craft to be developed through personal ingenuity and work. But he had little patience for weekend writing that conflicted with his free time, or my worrying about writing when I was away from it. "Goddamn it, Lucy, give yourself a break! Whoever wrote one best-seller right after the other? What makes you so important that you have to seriously try to do that?" And as irritated as his voice was, his practical words and down-playing of performance had a calming effect.

Tom's own ambitions centered on sufficiently re-establishing himself as a photographer so that he could afford to go to the university full-time on the G.I. Bill and still work nights or weekends at the paper. That pragmatic, hardworking life view was one I felt increasingly confident would complement my own determined perspective.

But sex was also important to Tom, and with him my sexuality felt a greater deficit than not having gone to college. I tried to hide my uneasiness, yet was thrilled that he found me sexy after all. "I want you, Sport," he had a way of announcing out of the blue. "I need you!" And those words would set me tingling, excited, wanting him, too. But as soon as he kissed me or tried to touch me, my body would die. And not just Tom, but anything that brought sex to mind automatically made me afraid, numb, inadequate. It seemed as though all those years of not having periods had permanently damaged me. After we are married, I had thought, when that's no longer a barrier, Tom may discover that sexually I was ruined. Ruined? Withered? Empty? I strained to decipher the truth and prayed that my fears were just ignorance.

> Bye-bye, love,
> Bye-bye, happiness,
> Hello, loneliness,

I think I'm - a going to cr - y.

That was our song. We played it everywhere. The song of the year of our wedding. On the car radio, in TV commercials, whistled on the street, on the Everly Brothers record that Tom gave me and we listened to together.

> There goes my baby with someone new.
> She sure looks happy; I sure am blue.
> She was my baby till he stepped in,
> Good-bye to romance that might have been.

We'd smile at each other, listening. I liked the way the lilting tune contrasted with the sad words.

Naturally it was on the radio as we drove away from our wedding. Tom grinned at me from behind the steering wheel. "I do love you, Sport," he said.

"I love you, too."

"It wasn't as bad as I expected."

"Mommy's reception?"

"No. My family. They don't know how to act at occasions like this."

"The only one I really talked to was your mother. She looked anxious but not like she didn't know how to act."

"She's scared of alcoholic beverages."

I was thinking about sex and that there was no longer any way out. In fact, I was sensibly prepared. With diaphragm and jelly in my suitcase. With the repeated embarrassing efforts in the gynecologist's office to learn to place it inside my vagina. But in myself, I was woefully unprepared. Whenever I put my hand inside to feel the rubber circle in place, I felt reassured about my sexual adequacy. But sitting there beside Tom in the car, all the reassurance slipped away. He kissed the top of my head and reached his hand over to squeeze mine. I felt cold, empty, my insides sinking away. Again, here you are, I lectured myself, still the cold, selfish intellectual, who can neither feel nor be herself.

chapter fifteen

CONSEQUENCES

The seventeen years Tom and I spent together would not have surprised any psychologist or even any emotionally aware human being who knew our family histories. As they teach in undergraduate statistics class, the best predictor of the future is the past. Our strengths remained constant and growing; so did our weaknesses. Moreover, the parts of ourselves that we could not bear to know swelled large with our ignorance. We were able to work hard enough to accomplish the external goals we set and to shine in the eyes of the world for doing so, while never sacrificing our internal deadness. I remained starved (more emotionally than physically), lonely, guilt-ridden, and feeling inadequate; Tom remained hard-driving, aloof, angry, and rigidly certain. While we each strained against hated ties to our mothers, the unbearable, ignored bonds with our fathers became our tyrants. By its very nature, the unconscious left to itself takes over and pillages on schedule, like a rampaging ghost. We were no exception.

Nevertheless, especially because we were too deprived to expect any better, those years felt rewarding as well — in terms of both happiness and growth. Tom was more successful professionally than most of his brothers. Our marriage allowed me to strive for and achieve fulfillment I'd believed myself utterly barred from when I was in the hospital. Despite being short on money, our combined energy, hope, and capacity to appreciate together the rewards of our separate efforts, made the earliest years the best. Also, then, the things we couldn't bear to know were just beginning to take their toll.

In recounting here the milestones of our life together, the need to chronicle my own emotional journey has been the guide for selection.

Because of *The News and Observer*'s nepotism rule, I had to stop working at *The Times* after marrying Tom. While that in itself made me lonelier, it turned out to be insignificant because within six months we moved to Chapel Hill so Tom could go to college on the G.I. Bill. There, as he labored to graduate Phi Beta Kappa in three years while working nearly full-time as reporter and photographer, the loneliness I struggled with was mitigated only by a few new friends and work on my novel. My not knowing how to drive, our living in a tiny house on the outskirts of town, and Tom's always needing the car all exacerbated this. Nor was Wilmer as easily available for help. Since both Tom and my parents considered that being married meant paying your own way, and since with Tom's salary and my Guggenheim we still couldn't afford a psychiatrist, I only saw Wilmer when I was too desperate not to. It's clear looking back that this situation only increased my sense of being "unhelpable." But since in all our eyes, perhaps, I could only be "perfect" or "messed up," help was also irrelevant or demeaning. I had no concept in those days that psychotherapy was a process in which I could grow and find release from unconscious torment.

During our second year of marriage, when I woke in the dark to see Tom still studying in the lamplight, I found him more formidable and less reachable than ever. Making my loneliness ache! The card table he worked at was in the corner of the bedroom to conserve fuel. Tom worried over every dime. So he believed he saved a lot by heating only the bedroom at night and studying there while I slept. In those days we talked a lot about money: my guilt about not going to work to earn some; his fear that if we didn't guard every penny, he wouldn't be able to finish school. But those talks never brought any real relief because I felt uncertain about what work I could do and because Tom was adamant about getting through school on just the G.I. Bill and what he could earn. When I talked about needing to learn to drive and get a part-time job to help us and my loneliness, he was always discouraging. "I need the car. Besides you are working.

You're writing a book on a Guggenheim," he'd say. So the talking would cease, leaving my guilt and his fear as nagging barriers between us. And when all his other work made it necessary for him to study far into the night, I never protested his choice of the bedroom as a workplace. I preferred having him there to study than not at all.

Turning over to watch him, I nursed coziness by pulling the blankets tight under my chin. Even after a year, being married only changed the loneliness without relieving its intensity. Part of trying to be cozy was to keep from saying anything that would make Tom mad and more distant. I believed my needs and my whininess did that. If I could have been as self-sufficient as Tom seemed, we'd have been all right. At times I tried to be; at other times I'd persuade myself that he needed me more than he showed, too. Then I'd reach out with a kiss in the midst of his reading or a hug before he drove off somewhere. But if he didn't take it well, if he seemed irritated instead of warmed, I could feel devastated. At other times, like that night, I'd just stay conflicted about my needs so that anger and depression see-sawed inside me: aching, smarting; aching, smarting. "Tom, please come to bed," I said finally.

No answer.

"Tom?" I insisted.

"What?"

"You have to sleep sometime. Please come now and sleep with me."

"I can't. I have to finish this."

"Please, Tom," I begged.

"No!" and then he added, "Lucy, I've told you I have to do this. I don't see why you can't understand."

I didn't answer. I didn't know what to say. But I kept thinking about how much Tom was like the rest of the Inmans — calloused and closed. Maybe even mean at times. He maintained a wall that wouldn't let me near and that responded to my reaching out with anger that slapped me back. Maybe because they all felt inferior and didn't want anyone close enough to see. But I also told myself that the others didn't matter and that Tom had done more for me than any other person. By just accepting me, by letting me be good enough for him. When I thought of how grateful I was for that, the love feelings would swell strong inside. Now they persuaded me to plead again: "Please, Tom. Just for a little while."

That made him angry. When he looked up and turned to face me, the scars were bristling scarlet. "You know, Lucy," he said, "life is not as easy as you would like. Some people have to work. Can't you stop being such a nagging bitch and take care of yourself for a change?!"

Tears welled up. "I can," I said when I'd caught my breath, "but I worry that you don't love me any more."

Tom didn't answer. He focused on his book again so that all I could see was his profile with the scarred cheek toward me. And I knew he was right. If it weren't for my greediness, he'd be studying in peace. After all, he was the one who went to school and worked at the paper, while I spent my days writing a would-be novel for a $3,000 Guggenheim we'd long since spent.

Tom was away so much then that I felt ignored and clingy when he was there. In the long days alone, I'd had some food binges. I'd stopped telling Tom about those because he was too busy and I thought they disgusted him. And that was a change, since in the beginning he'd seemed to understand and didn't regard me as weird. But living with the anorexia made him mad. When he couldn't help or make me stop worrying about getting fat, he took it as his personal failure. And whenever Tom failed at anything, he had to drive off in the car and stay to himself. He'd yell at me and then leave. Like it had once been with Father. Still I couldn't figure out what it was about me that caused this.

Probably, I knew, the real reason he didn't come to bed was his disappointment about me not having orgasms. That distressed me, the same way as waking up to a new day and remembering the hospital and the lack of a college education. The only difference was that the orgasm problem was immediate and more mystifying. Something I hadn't been able to think about ahead and hide or correct, because I hadn't even known women could have orgasms until Tom told me. Since then their absence had become physical proof of my inadequacy, in a form that Tom might not be able to overlook.

I'd warned him. Not about the orgasms, but about the anorexia, and about always having felt inferior to Adelaide's "pagan sensuality." He'd acted like the anorexia was nothing and answered the part about Adelaide by saying, "Who wants a pagan?" Still, it made him angry when I didn't climax.

His face that night made me think of how it looked when he came. Also the sounds. One minute holding me tight; the next limp and sleepy on top of me. It discouraged me that as hard as I worked at it, I couldn't be that way too. I'd watched; I'd tried to copy; I'd made resolutions to give myself over to him physically and to let the feelings come as they would. But nothing worked. And even though I could have intercourse and like it, when once the very idea had terrified me, I remained a failure. Proving how right Father had been all along, that I really was sexually lacking. What a woman needed to be complete sexually, I didn't have. Even though the periods had come back. Even though I did excite Tom. Even though my body had got to where it easily, even happily received him, I was still no good. Dead. Deformed. Perhaps sterile.

In time I closed my eyes so that if he looked again, my being awake wouldn't piss him off. But inside the closed lids, his blue eyes stabbed and his voice sneered, "What's wrong with you? Doesn't anything excite you?!"

Scars in the lamplight again. Over his thick turtleneck. My nose outside the blankets measured the chill and sniffed his coffee. The sky outside was black; midnight or dawn, all the same. And the coffee had the same stale smell either way, because it was used to combat fatigue rather than rejuvenate.

A young woman Babs had been. In a blue dress. Totally unsuspecting. By the time of my learning about her, she'd been invisible a while — able to see and hear the people she loved but unable to speak or be touched by them. A blue silk dress with lace. A dead baby.

Under the blankets my hands explored the bulging melon of my belly. With curiosity. Wonder. Pride. Disbelief that could grow into dread. Babies and the swollen bellies that presaged them were simple, ordinary, known facts of life. To everybody but me. I'd been told about the baby boy that could not live and about the beautiful woman in the blue dress. But the part in between had always been deleted. From Bibba's first saying, "She died having a baby." Because there had been no bearable way to give it meaning. Forgetting had been required for living. Even that night, as my hands traced the hard roundness of my body, the forgotten fantasy demanded acknowledgement: the image of a body like my own, broken open and mutilated. That night the image bludgeoned me into sweating horror. Until I remembered that pregnancy could not be happening to me. It had happened. . . to Babs; to Mommy; to Bibba; to Adelaide. But never to Lucy.

The gynecologist once had said as much. Not to me, but to Mommy. "He says most girls with problems like Lucy's are unable to conceive," she'd told Father. "So there's no need to worry about the size of the birth canal." Still, that same gynecologist had given me the diaphragm. And I'd tried to use it right. The failure had not been caused by my fingers' early difficulty learning the contours of my vagina, but by my not being able to bear the hurt of Tom's ignoring me after having myself ready.

It did seem that somehow between the feel of the vagina ledge with the circle of rubber positioned behind it and the feeling there in the bed of my swollen belly, there must have been a time when I was a full woman. At the hospital, Dr. Wall had said, "Lucy, when are you going to commit yourself to life?" Now? I thought under the covers. But I was surprised to see that proof of it while I still lacked the courage. Surprised? No, horrified. If I was a woman, a last margin of safety had been lost. A sexual woman, a live woman could become a dead woman. Looking back with a sad smile that knew the truth she couldn't speak.

"Listen, Sport," Tom had said. "Thousands. . . probably millions of women have babies every day. What's so different about you?"

Despite trying to comfort me, his voice and face had remained impersonal. And I had no answer beyond what he already knew, what I'd repeatedly told both him and the obstetrician: "I'm afraid I'll die having this baby." But he was too stubborn or determinedly sensible to really hear me. Like the obstetrician, who'd been so focused on fear of pain that my fear of death was literally inconceivable to him. The doctor, as much as Tom, had gaped back at me like I was deranged. And not because of the anorexia, either, which he classified as a strength because it had kept me thin. "Sport, stop making yourself sick with worry," Tom said. "Some things really do take care of themselves!"

Finally he came to lie beside me. On his back, stretching his long body to wring the weariness out, he put his hand on my belly to feel a kick. The two things I most feared were not on the doctor's list. Nor Tom's. One was unspeakable; the other voiced, but unbearable: explosion of flesh leaving a mutilated cavern of blood and viscera, ruptured, torn, ravaged. Yielding up a deformed monster with flailing limbs and rubbery blobby face that continually sucked, but could not cry. A monster that bludgeoned with silence after it had destroyed everything that had been before. Bloody specter that itself could never be erased, that even blackened by death remained a shrunken, scorched reminder of a mouth.

But in the end, the reality of Patrick's birth was worse than my fears. Terrified of both fat and pregnancy, I finally went to see Wilmer, who recommended an obstetrician at Duke, Dr. Creadick. But in the sixth month, when my feet began to swell and toxemia was the diagnosis, Dr. Creadick's warmth and sensibleness were not enough. First, he put me on a more stringent diet even though, in his eyes, I was still too thin. In the eighth month he prescribed medication and bedrest. Though the toxemia diagnosis was frightening, the doctors' concern also made me less panicky. In recent years I've realized that toxemia was probably not as real to me as my fantasy of a baby breaking its way out of a woman's body. Perhaps, too, the toxemia was a physical representation of that fear.

In the last few weeks, the medication to keep my blood pressure under control made it impossible to read or knit or even walk to the toilet unattended. Poor Tom had to cope with all that as well as work and school, and he really did it very well. Instead of worrying, he acted, reassured me with his own confidence, and tried to provide practical comforts. Getting through crises had always been one of his strengths. Situations that required dealing with feelings were those he couldn't handle.

In the midst of a December snowstorm, in about the eighth month,

Dr. Creadick decided I needed to be hospitalized. But when they induced labor one week later, my worst fears were surpassed. With premature separation from the placenta a short while into the procedure, the doctors and nurses around me became visibly distressed. I feared I really was dying. Lots of oxygen and no anesthesia. In time Dr. Creadick began reassuring me that I was "as good as any peasant woman" who managed to deliver her baby alone in the fields. And finally late that night they showed me a red, five-pound boy before carting me off, with my bladder still catheterized and intravenous tubes in place.

But the relief of that moment was short-lived. The next morning, after they'd inspected my tubes and long before Tom had made his way back, the pediatrician came in to tell me that the baby had breathed in a fair amount of fluid and had pneumonia. As he put it, "His condition is serious but not critical. His survival seems probable at this time but not certain. If he does survive, there may be brain damage."

A whole new nightmare that I hadn't prepared for. I did ask about the brain damage. He said that none had been detected yet, but that it probably couldn't be ruled out for one to three years. Straining, I managed to hold back my tears until he left.

Now I can't remember whether I was crying or between tears when Father arrived. There was snow on his overcoat as he pulled it off. His face and hands were cold when he kissed me. When he stepped back again, I noticed tears in his eyes. Then his focus met mine and he said softly, "Did you know that this is the day Babs died?"

chapter sixteen

BOOKS VS. BABIES

That was decades ago. The struggling baby I wept over is now married and a college graduate. Given his father's middle name so he would be his namesake without the burden of being a junior, Patrick has still had a difficult life. But not because of brain damage. Rather, in part because of his birth position in our family, and in part because of the hard courses his brightness and his unconscious lead him to take.

Several months after his birth I underwent kidney-function tests to determine whether I'd need to avoid future pregnancy. The negative results, along with Patrick's normal and even precocious development, helped me focus on a daily life of mothering and trying to write a novel. But I was most reminded of "really" being a writer by a call from *Coronet Magazine* in November 1959. As the sophisticated New York editor put it, *Caleb* made me "the natural" to write about how the white people of Prince Edward County, Virginia, had closed down their public schools to avoid having to integrate them. The Whites had also established a private school, leaving the Blacks with no schools at all. "We want a story that depicts the warring of these two factions while emphasizing the human point of view, and we think the author of *Caleb, My Son* is just the person to do it."

Tom and Patrick drove me there after Tom's exams in January 1960. And in Farmville, the reality was far less intimidating than my expectations. Farmville had only one hotel. In the whole county, the total number of school children including Blacks and Whites, was fewer than 3500. But the small numbers also contributed to the intensity of the problem. Not only did Blacks and Whites not talk to each other, both tried to conceal their fears about this. There definitely was a story.

My two most vivid memories from those few days are scarier now than they were then. After interviewing the white mayor and a black minister, I was escorted into an office in the Black church to interview a behind-the-scenes local NAACP coordinator. He was a quiet, middle-aged man in a wheelchair. As I entered, I couldn't see whether there was something wrong with his legs or some other problem because a blanket draped his lap and lower body.

"Hello, Mr. Wicker," I introduced myself. "I'm Lucy Daniels, the writer from *Coronet Magazine*." As we shook hands, I thought of Grandfather's black caretaker Spurgeon; I'd been very fond of him all my life, but we had never shaken hands. My sense of inadequacy eased a bit. The black face looking back was kind, solemn and unrevealing. When I asked him to help me understand Prince Edward's story, we gradually settled into a more collaborative conversation.

"You have to be particular," he said. "You can't talk open in these times. What I tell you could cause the bank to repossess my farm. It's happened. Worse than that's happened."

I wrote this down. But then his voice was still and his impassive face looking back at me seemed to go blank. "Like what?" I asked quietly.

"You have to be particular," he said.

"I understand," I replied, feeling my own shyness gain ground. "Would you rather I didn't quote you?"

"How would I know?"

"No way, I guess. All I can do is promise you. . . You could tell me things I could use in the story without even mentioning that I interviewed you. Some others have."

The expression on his face did not change. "Okay," he said. Then after a moment, "You see this?"

And there on his lap, beneath the blanket which he'd folded back, lay a shiny pistol. "I didn' know," he referred to it. "When they told me you were coming, I didn' know what the real reason was. I didn't know which side was doin' it. . . You have to be particular."

My other vivid Farmville memory is of a home visit after dark.

It was pitch-black when I arrived. Just like the slick, black, outspoken NAACP minister had directed. Tom and Patrick left me there with a plan to be back in two hours to pick me up. They waited while I approached the shuttered, utterly abandoned-looking house and knocked. "Who is it?" a voice asked from inside.

"Lucy Daniels." (I'd decided to keep this as my writing name to keep future recognition as simple as possible.)

The door opened just a crack, revealing the barest sliver of a gray light. "Yes, please come in." Then the door opened. "Reverend Griffin came by. Mama's expecting you."

Inside, the living room was surprisingly bright, lit by a kerosene stove and oil lamps. Gathered together there, besides the teenaged girl who'd let me in, were Mama and her five younger children, two boys aged nine and eleven, and three smaller girls. They all watched Mama with bead-black eyes while her own dark eyes darted to meet mine and then moved away again. She was supposed to give me an interview. Reverend Griffin had said she would. But she couldn't.

"Do you worry about your children's education?"

"I couldn't say."

"Do you think the public schools will reopen?"

"I couldn't say."

The only thing she would say was, "Being uneducated is like being heathen." Which echoed Lester Andrews, the white-businessman chairman of the then-functionless public school board. He'd said, "Two things have been overlooked — the children and education."

Only later when I was safely back in Chapel Hill writing that piece for *Coronet* did I realize how scary the time in Prince Edward had been and how much kinship I felt with the locked-out Blacks there.

In August 1960, Tom graduated from UNC, and we moved to Indianapolis for his job as a reporter for *The Indianapolis Times*. That same year I published a short story in *The Virginia Quarterly* and "Blackout in Prince Edward" in *Coronet*. But Lippincott rejected my Guggenheim novel (for which it had the right of first refusal) in a period when our efforts toward a second pregnancy were also failing. I now recall 1960 when I need encouragement during difficult times. Because no sooner had we settled into our new home than

I discovered I was pregnant, and editor Bob Gutwillig called from McGraw-Hill to buy my novel.

Even from the start, that year in Indianapolis went quickly. Patrick was so active that in order to have time to work at writing, I hired a housekeeper three mornings a week. Tom's salary and the advance for my book now made this possible. Furthermore, even though far from home, Indianapolis was much less lonely than Chapel Hill. Some of our acquaintances there whom we'd met through acquaintances in Raleigh, turned out to be friends. Some of Tom's fellow reporters were friendly as well. Tom was home little more than he had been in Chapel Hill, but we both had a greater sense of buoyancy than perhaps at any other time in our history together. Even my worries about having toxemia with the second pregnancy didn't materialize.

I went to the hospital twice for my daughter Lucy (the fifth girl to bear that name in a chain extending back to my great-grandmother). Coming home after nearly twenty-four hours of false labor, we found the galleys for my new book, *High On A Hill*, on the back steps. And no sooner had I started reading them, than Mommy and Father arrived from Raleigh to babysit Patrick when it was time for me to go back to the hospital for real. Their coming was a total surprise. Mommy was eager to help with the galleys. Perhaps Father was already, then, wanting to talk with Tom about returning to Raleigh. But probably the most compelling reason for their visit was their fear that this delivery would repeat the previous horror story.

It didn't. About 3:30 the next morning labor started up again in earnest. Tom drove me to the hospital. Even then I was consciously associating Lucy's birth with the first successful U.S. space rocket flight a few weeks earlier. No toxemia. Wide awake because of how fast she was coming. No need to get prepped because that had been done a day earlier. A violent thunderstorm raged outside. Lightning flashed across the opaque windows of the delivery room. A crashing blast of thunder preceded the baby's first piercing cries by seconds. It was thrilling to be told she was a girl and then to hold her all wrapped up, but not yet washed.

However, this victorious delivery also thrust our young family into turmoil. When I arrived home from the hospital, Father had left, but

Mommy was there hellbent on reading the galleys for *High On A Hill*. And 29-month-old Patrick was irate over both baby and book. I tried all imaginable ways to juggle these three. But nothing worked and Mommy became exasperated.

"Baloney!" she snapped at me. "You've just got to let him cry until you can get this done. If he can't leave you and the baby alone, he may need a good spanking!" Sometimes she too wrestled with Pat's tearful demands. Then, when he was finally in bed, she let me know how poorly she thought I was managing things.

That time though — God knows why! — my response was different than with *Caleb*. Anger filled my mouth with confidence: "I think you need to go home. You can't help me by being here, because the way things are is too upsetting for you. I have two babies that need everything I have right now. And I'm not going to strain myself to read galleys when they do."

Her dimple was going strong as she replied steely-eyed, "Of course, the children need caring for. That's why we have the nurse. But not taking care of the galleys and yourself will only make you worried later."

Mommy left the next morning. Haughty and wounded, but civil. And our life settled into a grueling routine of feeding, diaper changing, soothing Patrick, and too little sleep. I now can't recall what I did about those galleys. I hope I didn't, but I may have sent them back without reading them at all.

After three or four weeks, this otherwise cooing and easy-going baby was colicky from 4:30 to 10:00 p.m. every day. Since these hours coincided with Tom's time home from work and the hours when Pat expected attention from his father and bedtime stories from me, our life together became unbearable. Pat asked many times why we had to keep this baby. And Tom, who was angry that these were the conditions he came home to, spent more and more time on assignments. As disaster stalked us, Tom sometimes got drunk as well.

Comparing myself then and now, I see an important difference. Now I am very tuned in to both my body and my inner feelings. A change in either prompts me to try to understand what's happened and what this change means I need to consider in myself, as well as what I need to focus on in terms of relations with others. But in those days I had no capacity to recognize unconscious motivations or to deal with my painful feelings compassionately. Whatever the problems in our world, I habitually blamed myself. Perhaps the main change with a husband and children, was that my self-blame could no longer be managed through starvation of felt "fatness." I still felt fat and worried about food. But our life problems were bigger and my failings uncorrectable.

It was in this context — personal and familial — that we returned to Raleigh for Tom to prepare for leadership at *The News and Observer*. There he was first assigned to the graveyard shift on the copy desk from 5:00 p.m. to 2:00 a.m. Besides compounding my loneliness, that meant trying to keep two small children quiet during the day while he was sleeping. I still tried to write, getting up early in the morning, sneaking off when the kids napped. But it didn't work. Furthermore, *High On A Hill*'s publication right after we moved proved disappointing. The reviews in *The New York Times* and various other national and North Carolina papers were generally good, speaking of me as a young star whose course bore following. I was asked to speak a few places. But *High On A Hill* was not a best seller, and there were no plans for a trip to New York. My respect for myself as a writer sank, but this sense of failure mattered less because of all the other things I had to cope with.

It's amazing, looking back, to see how I felt utterly helpless and yet assumed all the responsibility. Tom had no time to deal with things like Pat's pushing another child off the top of the slide at preschool. I did deal with it, but felt personally to blame for Pat's transgression. And those dynamics held sway through the other complexities of our life as well. If the bank account was overdrawn or Father was impatient with something Tom did at the office, it still came back to me in one way or another. Nor was this just Tom being negligent and hard on me. Both Tom and I held me responsible for whatever hardship beset us.

Toward the end of that first year back in Raleigh, Tom began to drive a company car and to go to Rotary Club on Mondays. There was also talk of my needing to join the Junior League to help him socially. When he got promoted from the graveyard shift, we bought a lot in

Brookhaven, a subdivision well outside the city limits, and prepared to build a house with four bedrooms. Both its distance from town and having an extra car helped me develop into a comfortable driver.

But, the tension that I later realized had always been substantial in Raleigh, increased to a painfully unbelievable level with Tom at the newspaper and my parents' involvement. Mommy latched onto Patrick in a way that made him angrier and more entitled whenever he returned from a visit. Raleigh confronted Tom with the two things that, I'd now say, had always threatened him most — authority figures and the possibility of closeness with me. Up to then he'd worked so hard that we'd never had much time together. But off the graveyard shift and coming home for supper each night, his attitude was hostile and he avoided me by spending time reading or with Patrick. After being alone with the children all day, I frequently resented that. And despite making a concerted effort not to nag or take his aloofness personally, I did both at times. I also badgered him about his silent brooding. Usually he wouldn't say what was troubling him, but when he did, it frequently had to do with conflicts at the paper or with his thoughts about needing to learn things like quail and deer hunting to feel more confident as a man. In those days, too, troubled by his spending so much time away, I would sometimes ask point blank if he still loved me.

After only two months in the new house, discovering that I was pregnant forced us to finish the extra bedroom. By then, I enjoyed pregnancy — a state in which I felt pleased and whole as a woman as I rarely did otherwise. Different from my childhood expectations, in pregnancy I felt sensuous and more vital than at any other time. By then, too, life was easier because we'd hired a black woman, Juanita Lucas, to help me three days a week. And Lucy's easy delivery had ended my fears of toxemia. Perhaps, too, in pregnancy, having a baby inside made me less doubtful of Tom's love.

Tom was covering a political rally down east the night in July 1963, when Jonathan was born. When my water broke at about five o'clock in the afternoon, I was in the kitchen with twenty-six-month-old Lucy.

Blanching and growing wide-eyed, she gasped, "Mother! Don't wee-wee on the floor! Sit down and have a cup o' coffee!"

Calling the paper was little help except that the people on the desk promised to give Tom the message when he phoned in his copy. Mommy stayed with the children until Juanita could be located, and Father drove me to Duke.

The labor room was like the continuation of a nightmare. The pains came faster and harder than I'd remembered, and I was worried sick about Pat and Lucy alone with Juanita, let alone Mommy. Especially my image of Lucy chewing her peanut butter sandwich while solemnly asking, "Are you sure your hole's big enough?" Worries about them; despair about Tom. The nurses just couldn't get it through their heads that Tom wasn't coming, that he couldn't even be reached. And their questions kept reminding me of how much I was to blame. Could I have tried harder to find him? Did the way I was make him stay away?

"Good morning, Sport," his voice cheered over the telephone the next morning. "Looks like you went ahead and took care of things all by yourself. I'm proud of you." Maybe I didn't answer. There wasn't much for me to say. But it seemed like he went right on: "Things are really popping down here. Local politicians warring in a big way."

In spite of knowing better, I couldn't keep from asking, "When are you coming home?" My voice sounded timid, though, the way that always made Tom mad when I was trying hardest not to.

"I'm not sure," he said, probably trying hard right then not to get angry. "Since there's no longer any pressure there, I think I'll wait and come when there is need. . . I can give you some numbers — "

The tears again. I blurted out, crying and all, "Tom, I don't want to take numbers. I want you to come home now."

"What for?!" he growled like when he sometimes called me a nag.

I told myself not to. I knew better. But scared as I was, I guess I felt as if we were already in it. "Tom," I pleaded. The whine came back, and the shaking in my throat. "Tom, we just had a baby. I need you at home. Patrick and Lucy need you."

"Aw, Lucy, . . . don't give me that sentimental shit! You're O.K. The baby's O.K. Juanita's glad to keep the kids. Pryor is definitely going to the Senate. And his backers in this campaign make this the story of the year. For me to leave here now would mean walking out on the chance of a lifetime."

My nose was stopped up and the receiver was slippery with my tears. Desperate, the wrong words just fell out of my mouth. "Please, Tom. I need you."

"Do you realize what an insatiable baby you're being?" he yelled. "How whiny and selfish?. . . But, we'll have it your way. I'll be there tomorrow. I just hope you understand that I'm coming because of you and your demands, not because I think it's necessary!"

chapter seventeen

ACTING OUT

Depression dogged me after every baby. But in those days I didn't know to call it that. For me then, "depression" was still the paralysis I'd seen possess Mrs. Benson on Nichols, a stupor that made her unable to speak, walk or feed herself even though the brown eyes in her expressionless face beseeched the world. Consequently, the leaden but agitated sense of shame, guilt, and ignorance with which I labored to care for each new baby along with the other small children seemed no more than the real "me" showing. Furthermore, when life was difficult in those pre-therapy days, I blamed my own inadequacies—lack of college education, years in a mental institution, deficiencies in feelings and sexuality Father had always cited. How could such a loser be an effective housewife, let alone a mother!? The same refusal to give up that had been my post-hospital key to survival remained the only prop I could muster as a young mother. But guilt over failing my dear innocent children made this tenacity less effective.

Indeed, my sense of responsibility and desperate need to make things better blocked both insight and common sense. Straining to live and face my fears resulted in what I now call "acting out," acting on unconscious feelings without recognizing the fact. I was oblivious to the repeated pattern of pregnancy leading to more babies that I felt inadequate to mother. As a castrated woman (unconsciously controlled by Father's declarations that I lacked both feelings and sexuality), I was driven by my unconscious to overcome the very condition it confined me to. Furthermore, this acting out worked.

During pregnancy I did feel alive and sensual; afterward I loved my wonderful children. But the needs of these children made my own insufficiencies loom larger than ever. And that, of course, is why acting out gets repeated—to relieve the pressure of repressed unacceptable feelings/capacities which, once acted out, result in an even more oppressive inner state, requiring additional release in order to keep the original trauma out of one's awareness.

At the same time, having babies was not something I did thought-lessly or irresponsibly. I rarely acted without thought, sometimes years of thought. But, regardless of the issues involved, that thought was seldom productive. It could go on and on without reaching a satisfying conclusion. And when I did act, I was often only able to do so by ceasing to think.

Because we had health insurance and because I remembered that Wilmer had been able to support the mess of me after the hospital, I resumed seeing him weekly after Jonathan's birth. He was still kind and supportive, but I found his help limited, because this time he mostly just praised me for doing as well as I was. Although fat feelings and food still tormented me, I talked to him most about my terrible failings as a person. He seemed to regard this as an improve-ment. But since he couldn't recognize the severity of my deficiencies, I often felt talking to him was useless. I did it, though, straining to make him see my problems. And maybe as a part of trying to get help for the mess of me, I didn't tell him about the nights Tom didn't come home till morning, smelling of alcohol.

One unexpected benefit of building our house in Brookhaven was having Helen and Murphy Evans as back-door neighbors. When we moved in, they had three children — Helen Hughes, Gin, and Murphy — close to the ages of Lucy and Pat. Their fourth child, Thomas, was born two weeks after Jonathan. Helen became my clos-est friend during those child-bearing years. We took turns watching each others' kids; we carpooled to nursery schools; we spelled each other when a child had to go to the emergency room. Eventually, I even told Helen that I'd been hospitalized with anorexia. I still remember how comforted I felt by her saying, "I'm so sorry!" and then seeming to forget it. Murphy's family was widely respected in

North Carolina for the family business devoted to farming and farm equipment they ran in Scotland County. This provided a commonality with Tom's and my experience with *The News and Observer*. Helen's brother was the writer Tom Wolfe, which may have made her find me easily familiar. But to the extent that I thought about it and read Tom Wolfe's books, that association idealized Helen and made her a little intimidating for me. A good friend, nonetheless. For years Helen was to remain a rarity in my life—a person who had seen my deficiencies and not condemned them.

This mixture—Helen's example and acceptance, my own sense of guilty despair and Wilmer's inability to see or help repair the mess of me—coalesced over time into another solution I now also recognize as "acting out." At the time it appeared as a brainstorm, a realization that there was one thing I could do that might help improve my life. I could give up writing altogether! Doing so would end Tom's complaints when I stole an hour here or there to try to write. It would make me less resentful of the time the children required as well as help my feelings of inadequacy over not being a successful writer. Furthermore, it would free me to fully embrace womanhood and motherhood with a friend like Helen. I even considered the psychological advantages of standing up to Mommy and Father by refusing to remain the stand-in "boy" who gave them glory by straining to write when I couldn't. Yet another booster for this resolution was the emphasis on daily reality which had been my main comforter ever since the hospital. Even though I felt I really wasn't a writer, I most certainly was a mother. As I'd been saying to myself for years when severe depression made me doubt my capability as a wife and parent, "Give yourself credit. You're doing very well for a person who spent five years in a mental hospital." So I gave up writing. I gave it up, I realized much later, just as I'd given up eating sixteen years earlier.

This decision produced tremendous relief initially and repeated surges of confidence later when I responded to invitations to speak by announcing that I was no longer a writer. Those moments were increasingly and painfully overshadowed, however, by deepening depression. My lack of formal education loomed large, and my parents and Tom's dismissal of my worries about that no longer helped. In the

Junior League, which I'd joined reluctantly to "do my part" in helping Tom become a community personage, I felt shy and inferior. Reviewing children's books for the newspaper and reading to or playing with the children were insufficient solace.

So in the three years between the births of Jonathan and Benjamin, I never stopped being depressed. Even that last pregnancy, which again pleased me, did not provide the pickup the others had. I was terribly worried about both Tom and the children and felt guilty, despite wanting this baby, for again taking on more burden than I could responsibly manage. These worries were mine alone, however. Bearing and raising children were the roles expected of women both in my family and among the Junior Leaguers I'd come to know.

Even before our return to Raleigh, my parents had begun visiting Hilton Head, S.C. several times a year. In 1963 they built a house on the beach there. And not long after Jonathan's birth, they decided to sell the Raleigh house in preparation for moving to Hilton Head permanently when Father retired. Barely two years after our return from Indianapolis, they were spending weeks at a time in South Carolina, leaving Tom to handle *The News and Observer* editorial page pretty much on his own. It took months to prepare the big house for sale and to sort out and dispose of the childhood belongings of all us sisters. In that period Mommy and Father talked to Tom and me about buying the house and living there ourselves. Only the grace of God, in the form of not having the money, saved us from doing so.

Father's final departure in 1966 left Tom alone to deal with both the editorials and the bitterness of family politics, a task that most outsiders would have failed to handle. Our living in the family house when Tom was feeling so abandoned might have been the straw that broke the camel's back. As it was, Tom took up flying and was away more than ever at various political events. That also used up any extra hours that might have been our family's and, again, any extra money that could have been available for therapy. His drinking increased as well.

By the time Jonathan could talk, I was deeply troubled that Tom kept labeling my complaints about his drinking and his absences "selfish" and "righteous," in the same way Father had criticized me. But I didn't yet doubt he was right. I was just terribly discouraged that I hadn't been able to improve myself and didn't know how to even then. I also blamed myself for being a nag and not finding more tactful ways of approaching him. After much effort to understand what was making Tom so angry, however, I gradually came to believe it was more than just me. By our fourth year back in Raleigh, I wondered more and more whether his deprived childhood was making life harder for him in the present. But Tom would never acknowledge being upset by anything specific. So in time, my two competing theories were that either anger was driving him to drink, or alcohol was making him angry. Pondering those possibilities was probably the closest I ever got before Benjamin was born to facing the failure of our marriage.

Ben's birth in September 1966, did begin the end, however. It drove me to work harder than ever to be a good wife and a better mother. And having four children without knowing how to raise them kept me feeling terribly guilty. "I can't do it!" I used to cry alone in the bathroom. "I should've stopped myself before there were innocent children to suffer!" Then I'd go back out and continue trying.

My only dreams then were of wandering lost. And awake, I literally felt so. Tom began disappearing at night and drinking more heavily at home from the moment Benjamin arrived. In fact, because my labor started early one Friday afternoon when Tom was making up the Sunday editorial page, he lambasted me for not being more patient before he finally came to drive me to the hospital. Afterward, his frequent absence, sullen moods and vicious, loud, angry behavior made my depression that time worse than ever. I couldn't sleep; I wanted to die; I hated myself for having brought children into this mess. Then suddenly, out of nowhere, it dawned on me that this drinking problem and Tom's anger were hardships he put us through. After that I hated myself for not being able to work to earn a living and support the children without him.

That's when I made up my mind to talk to Wilmer about Tom's drinking and nights away from home. And I did try to. But by then Wilmer devoted his treatment to medications and did not want us to be distracted by other issues. "Take these as prescribed and come back in a week," he'd say with a benevolent smile. When I did as he directed and found myself thick-tongued, depressed, and literally unable to shut my eyes for several nights in a row, his response was the same: keep taking the medicine until our next appointment. This in the context of four children under eight; an alcoholic, angry, often-absent husband; and other situations that avoidance of people and feelings can cause to explode. So, one day, after calling Wilmer without success, I decided to stop all the medications. As bad as I might feel without them, while taking them I simply wasn't capable of the things I needed to do. The result was a seizure a couple of days later. Because, we learned at the hospital, after Tom had come home and found me unconscious on the kitchen floor, one of the medications had been addictive. As scary as that was, however, it ended the medications and left me, again, with depression and an unhappy life.

By that time Tom was into his hunting phase. The year before he'd bought a female sheep dog who was not gun-shy as his previous male setter had been. He had also had this dog spayed. But the male mutt of the incompetent vet (who lived directly behind us) had been able to span the fence and impregnate Tom's "spayed" sheep dog nevertheless. Her litter was born a few days before Ben. Then, one Saturday morning when Tom was about to go hunting and leave me with a month-old baby and the three other children (eight, six, and three), he reported to me that at least one and maybe two of the puppies had distemper. (The same vet had supposedly inoculated the mother against distemper!) Not that this stopped Tom. He told me to just leave dog and puppies in the basement until he returned and he'd do whatever was necessary then. I didn't really know what distemper was. Since I'd been saying for a long time that a dog was more than our family could handle, I took him at his word and put Jill and her pups out of my mind.

Not so three-year-old Jonathan, however. The baby was querulous that October morning. I fed him and he fell asleep in the process; soon after I'd laid him back down he was crying for more. It was in the midst of this second attempt to nurse Ben that Jonathan came to me saying, "The puppies are sick."

I replied, "Yes, Jonathan, I think some of them are. But their mother knows how to take care of them."

But Jonathan was then, and still is today, a determinedly independent soul. "I don't think she does. She's not trying to."

"How do you know?" I asked, trying to burp Ben.

"She doesn't go near them, and they can't walk to her."

"Jonathan, Father has the dogs in the basement so we can't bother them. I know Father told you to stay out of the basement."

No response. Just blue eyes provoking me with their unyielding stare from his sturdy face.

"Jonathan, I know Father told you to stay out of the basement. Have you been down there?"

Again no answer. Just unflinching ice-blue eyes.

With the nipple back in Ben's mouth, I suggested, "Jonathan, go get that new Richard Scarry book. I'll help you read it while the baby's feeding."

He got the book and we did read it together. But after I changed the baby and put him back down, Jon was nowhere to be seen. Searching, I found the basement door open. Down there, he was brooding over limp puppies. I couldn't tell if two were dead or not, but the mother had definitely turned away from them to struggle over the other pitiful three. "Jonathan," I said, trying to loosen his grip on the puppy he was holding, "Let me take the puppy and give it back to Jill. You and I have to go upstairs and let her take care of her babies."

Reluctantly he gave up the puppy. It felt lifeless to me as I placed it closer to the mother's bed. Then I took his hand to go look for another book to read. Upstairs I looked for the key to lock the basement door, but it was missing.

"Those puppies need to go to the doctor," Jonathan said as we sat down to read. But we didn't get far into it because Lucy came in screaming that Pat had hit her and taken her ball. With Jonathan in tow, I went with her outside to deal with Pat who was being so obnoxious that I sent him to his room. And by the time we got inside, the baby was screaming again. I believe I tried to get Lucy to play with Jonathan while I went to tend Ben; maybe I put a record on for them both to listen to.

But while trying to rock and then feed the baby, it occurred to me that the record had finished downstairs and that aside from the baby's crying, the house was quiet. Not long after that, Jonathan appeared in the bedroom doorway with another puppy.

"This puppy won't wake up," he said.

The baby was crying again. I could feel my insides washing away like sand before ocean. "Jonathan, I told you to stay out of the basement. Put that puppy down and go back and play with Lucy."

But Jonathan was impervious. "This puppy's too sick for a doctor. He needs Jesus."

The baby's crying eased a little. "Jonathan, put the puppy down and go play with Lucy till I can quiet Ben."

He did. The baby began to guzzle the milk. And in those few moments of peace, I struggled inside myself for whatever I could do to help Jonathan. I was floored by what he'd said about Jesus and figured that because of his determined realism, he even knew the puppy was dead. But I didn't know how to deal with a three-year-old about death, and. . . I was still in this quandary when Jonathan appeared in the bedroom doorway with yet another limp puppy.

The rest is less clear in my memory and even more upsetting. I've felt guilty over it for years and talked about it with Jonathan more than once in his adulthood. I'm not sure which one of us declared the puppies dead. But I was the one who suggested that since not even a doctor could make them well, the only thing we could do to help them get to Jesus was bury them. So, together, we took Tom's big shovel and a small one from the sandbox to the wooded area in the back of our lot. It was hard. The earth was barely penetrable. I was thin, weak, and clumsy in chipping away at that dry, unyielding dirt. Then, together Jonathan and I laid a limp puppy in each hole and covered them over with as much earth as we could.

Afterward, Jon kept asking questions like how long it would take for them to get from these holes to heaven, while I worried for fear we hadn't buried them deep enough. When Tom came home late that afternoon, he took care of the rest and was angry that I was still worried about the possible effects on Jonathan when, in his opinion, I'd clearly taken care of it.

I did not agree with Tom about that; then, as at other times,

I thought he was being callous and blindly unwilling to consider the child's emotional vulnerability. I saw that as due to his own hardening by the pain of childhood—which even after nine years of marriage he hadn't told me about in any detail. Still, his conviction that I had taken care of everything as well as anyone could was tempting to accept.

"I hope you're right," I said. "I felt utterly helpless with all those dying puppies and Jonathan so determined."

"Well, it's Fred's fault. Damn him any way. Sorry excuse for a vet! I'm glad I didn't let him make me miss dove hunting."

Anger shot through me at those words. "When you say that, Tom, I can understand. But it makes me feel like Fred's not getting the best of you is more important than the children and me."

"Oh, come off it, Lucy! It worked out okay. I've buried the rest of the pups! Do we have to run ourselves into the ditch over this all night?!" He wearily wiped his sweaty face.

"No. But I want you to understand that it angers me that you knew those puppies were dying and still went off and left me to deal with it."

"The basement door was a problem. I'm sorry; I didn't know it. Aside from that everything could have waited till I got back. Can't we just be done with it, Sport?"

"Sure." But I really couldn't, because things like that seemed to keep happening.

The next nine years are hard to separate from one another. There were two or three trends that grew constantly in one direction over that period. But the events and dilemmas which part of me likes to consider influential don't always stay in the proper sequence. I better understand my bout of depression after Ben's birth because midway through it, I changed psychiatrists. Tom's drinking and volatile anger got so much worse that with my threats to end the marriage, he eventually did see a therapist. The drinking did not improve. But giving more thought to what in the present might be aggravating the problem, allowed me to think of his drinking and my depression less rigidly. They could be separate phenomena. Or his drinking and driving under the influence could be depressing me.

Thinking about the possibility of ending our marriage steadily increased my concerns about my lack of education and inability to earn a living. In time this drove me to action. College seemed the most essential but also the most terrifying route to self-improvement. For years I'd clung to my novels for protection against the shame of being a high-school dropout. No longer considering myself a writer made that shame all the greater. But when I called N. C. State, I found you could take courses as a special student without ever having to apply and risk rejection. So I audited an English course.

It was in the fall, a year after Ben's birth that I met Dr. Mitchell. Covering for Wilmer during vacation just to do a med-check for the new antidepressant I'd started, he was the first psychiatrist I met who actually talked about feelings. Discussing my fear and despair with him gave me hope I'd never had before—that somehow there might be a way to understand and work out my problems. Of course, I didn't talk to him about no longer being a writer any more than I had to Wilmer. By then NOT-A-WRITER seemed just one more effort that hadn't helped. When Wilmer returned, I gathered up all the courage I could muster (against memories of Father's ridiculing his ears and his kindness to me after New York Hospital) and told him I wanted to switch to Dr. Mitchell. He was as genial as ever without any signs of feeling hurt. We both spoke to Dr. Mitchell, and the change was made immediately.

chapter eighteen

WAKING UP

Dr. Mitchell was quite different from Wilmer. Today I would call him "engaging." Back then I just thought he, unlike the other doctors I'd known, had access to feelings. Besides being in practice with his psychiatrist wife, he referred to himself as a psychoanalyst. Furthermore, he talked about feelings on a regular basis — his as well as mine — in a way that I found disconcerting but heartwarming. I told him right away about my loss of sexual desire for Tom and concerns that it might relate to the qualities in me that had caused Father to say I had no sexuality and no other feelings as well. One of his earliest responses to this was startling and disturbingly similar to Father's criticisms: "It does seem to me significant that despite having felt sexually alienated from Tom for a while, you haven't had an affair." From time to time Dr. Mitchell also made remarks about having followed my car out Highway 70 after our previous session and the problems of having one's car identified at a motel. Such statements made me uneasy; I felt I was hearing things I shouldn't hear. Afterwards I'd worry and wonder why Dr. Mitchell had said them. But a day or two of thinking would bring me back to the "realistic" position of recognizing my own priggishness and that Dr. Mitchell's therapeutically touching off some sexual feelings had frightened me. One day he told me that he wanted to become a training analyst even though his wife was critical of psychoanalysis. At the end of another session, he held out his thumb for me to grasp in response to my having said that I felt like touching him.

As comments like that continued, I found myself in a quandary. Why did Dr. Mitchell make them? Since I had such a marked reaction to his being familiar and subtly sexual, was I frigid like Tom accused me of being? But gradually, with much thought and soul-searching, I came to the conclusion that doctors who could really deal with feelings showed their own to help patients recognize and deal with theirs. As our work continued, there were also long periods when either he didn't say such things or I didn't catch them and react. Also, after about a month, Dr. Mitchell took me off the antidepressant and increased my sessions to twice a week.

But aside from no longer feeling drowsy and having a little more hope, nothing about me changed. Though continuing to timidly pursue friendships with the Evanses and Dee and Tom Haizlip, who lived two blocks away and had a little boy Ben's age, I still felt like a scared rabbit whenever I had to talk to most people! I'd shake so hard inside I could hardly hear what they said. Though "fat" often still bothered me alone and at home, with other people my thinness felt like neon evidence of inadequacy. At conferences with the children's teachers, I felt like any failings of Pat, Lucy or Jonathan were due to my mothering and that the teacher knew it. If she smiled at the end, I took it as her pitying me and left the school with tears in my eyes, thinking, "I cannot go on like this!"

In those days I almost never dreamed. And when I did it was always the same:

I was wandering alone and lost across a barren landscape, unable to find my way because there was nothing to see.

By then, Tom worked at least as hard at fishing and hunting as at the newspaper. After starting therapy, he told me about how his father had never helped him participate in those activities and about discovering how weak and ashamed that made him feel. So I could empathize with his need to pursue these activities even when they became a relentless drive. But Tom was also more frequently acting bitter and drinking. Tires crunching the gravel driveway became a common early-morning wakener after worried nights of useless waiting up. When he got upstairs, he'd look and smell awful and be unsteady on his feet with his suit all wrinkled. Too scared to cry, I'd ask what was wrong and where he'd been. And he'd yell back loud enough to wake the children, "Well, don't you wonder?! Work? I bet you wish!" Falling weak and reeking into the bed beside me, he'd be asleep when I tried to speak to him again.

"What's there to talk about?" Tom said the night I tried to confront him while he was still sober. "It's the same old story. You're unhappy. I'm not." When I insisted that he'd been drinking too much and not coming home some nights till morning, he got silent.

"I'd like us to talk to somebody," I said.

"Well, I wouldn't," he snapped back. And before long he was accusing me of nagging again and saying, "Why do you have to assume that getting drunk or staying out late means I'm unhappy? You know, Lucy, you have some pretty narrow views. Would it ever occur to you that I'm just bored? That you bore the hell out of me?!"

When he went to the kitchen to pour another drink, I thought about Father.

Somehow — I don't understand it — but despite everything, I've always kept a strong hold on my inner self. Long before psychoanalysis, or even George School's emphasis on the Inner Light, I was intently focussed on trying to find the answers to life's questions for myself. This has also felt a bit like clinging to (perhaps relying on, perhaps straining not to lose) innermost me. Sometimes this need to figure things out is comforting; sometimes it's desperate. Nowadays it can be dogging. In those days of Tom's worsening anger and abusiveness, that innerness was frayed not only by concern about how to deal with Tom, but also about how much I should tolerate without separating from him; what could happen to the children's sexual identities without a father present; how I would ever manage financially and as a parent without Tom's help; what would happen to his job at the paper if we did split.

First off, these ruminations drove me, when Ben was about two and I was thirty-four, to investigate and finally enter North Carolina State University as a freshman to prepare myself to earn a living if the worst came to pass. Only after completing two semesters of math and chemistry with A's did I believe I was capable of college after all. That relief empowered me to think more assertively, as a real college student, about what I might be able to do. Up to then I'd planned to be an English major since that seemed the least intimidating route to a degree. However, some English professors had embarrassed me by talking about my novels in class. Their doing so had also made me realize that their ambition was only to do what I'd already done before going to college. As a result of such experiences at a time when I felt increasingly capable, I began to consider what I would most want education to prepare me to do that wouldn't be possible without it. Investigating, I learned that clinical psychologists did work that was interesting and effective in helping people. I also learned that the clinical psychology program at UNC in Chapel Hill was one of the most respected in the country. It was hard to get into, however, and one psychologist I talked with suggested that with the odds only one in fifty, it might make more sense for me to try for a degree in social work. It was also clear that if I wanted a competitive chance to be one of the ten in five hundred applicants to get into the UNC clinical psychology program, I'd need to enroll at Chapel Hill as an undergraduate.

Tom and my parents opposed each step in this process. Mommy and Father still insisted that college was a waste of time and that I should be writing. Mommy was angry, Father sad that I wouldn't come to my senses. Tom agreed with them but also understood how depressed I felt about not having a college degree and grudgingly went along. He may have compared it to the flying he'd taken up to feel more macho, equating my wish for a college degree to his for a pilot's license.

School did make me less depressed even though more beleaguered, because at least I was doing what I could about the current things that depressed me. I applied to UNC with my George School transcript, as well as the one from N. C. State, and being admitted made me realize for the first time how academically acceptable I'd been all along. Still, going to the university added a whole new set of stressors to our life. Besides the anxiety about higher level classes, commuting, and struggling to park, it was necessary to fit all this together with the increasingly active lives of the children. Furthermore, since by then my therapy with Dr. Mitchell had been converted to psychoanalysis, there was a conflict between my school and analytic schedules. Nevertheless, four sessions a week instead of two felt luxurious and made me hopeful that something could be done about how messed up I was. Analysis also relieved my loneliness; there, at least, someone did listen and sometimes responded reasonably to my pain and turmoil.

But how horribly confusing life remained! My succeeding in college to become a better wife for Tom only made him hate me more. After being treated with respect all day, I still went home to wait up for him most of the night. Nor did I feel that Dr. Mitchell really understood. He did listen. I did tell him about Tom's anger and drinking as well as the guilt I felt about my going to school and my lack of sexual interest hurting Tom. Yet if Dr. Mitchell really understood, why would he keep listening? I remember talking on the couch and searching myself the same way I did lying awake at night: What will I do if Tom kills somebody driving drunk? How can I manage if Tom and I separate? What kind of job can I get? Where can the children and I afford to live? Will I even get custody?

The sense of dignity that came with being accepted into clinical training overwhelmed me with gratitude. No longer a high school dropout, I might even have the opportunity to work for a living in a way that felt inspiring. In fact, just getting accepted gave a person honored status, my first evidence that my hard work and good grades and something about me personally had been valuable.

But the honor accorded those of us chosen for the UNC program had a price. We were required to carry five graduate-level courses each semester, one of which was a two-day-a-week practicum at one of the state hospitals. It was like going to school at night while working a fifty-hour-per-week job. Because of my responsibilities at home, I had to resolve to not worry about either grades or friends and just do the best I could.

Yet the second semester of my first year in clinical was devastating to other parts of my life. The grueling clinical schedule meant that some of my analytic hours were at night. And this, because Tom was away from home so much, meant sometimes having to get a sitter. It also meant going to Dr. Mitchell's office when no one else was around.

In those evening meetings, Dr. Mitchell talked more to me about the significance of my never having had an affair in the course of Tom's abusiveness and alcoholism. He spoke of this critically and suspiciously as though it was similar to my eating problems and low self-esteem and needed to be corrected. Sometimes these comments made me feel messed-up; sometimes they made me distrust Dr. Mitchell and then criticize myself for giving his remarks unorthodox interpretations. Then, exhausted and confused, I relegated them to the back burner in keeping with my strong belief that Dr. Mitchell was the good doctor I needed. Between children and clinical training, analysis had to remain a safe haven where I could talk about anything.

Somewhere in there, early 1973 I believe, sexual feelings for Dr. Mitchell began to stir in me. Sometimes I told myself that was foolish and uselessly painful and tried to make them go away. But most times I followed the rules of analysis and talked about those feelings the same as any others that came to mind. In a way, too, this increased sexual aliveness seemed an indication that the treatment was working. I worried a little more in that period that some of the things Dr. Mitchell was saying sounded un-doctorly. Words that I didn't even really know but that sounded too sexual. When I told him, though, Dr. Mitchell said it was just my distrust. And I knew he was right. He was talking that way on purpose — about my breasts and my "twat" — to help me with my sense of sexual inadequacy. Furthermore, his doing so was another indication of his own emotional freedom and strength of character. I pressed myself not to "chicken out" when I'd finally found a doctor who was able to help me.

My dreams had picked up a little as well. Every so often I would have one about Dr. Mitchell instead of about wandering lost on the prairie:

I had an appointment with Dr. Mitchell. But something had happened to delay me. My watch had stopped so that I'd lost track of the time. Or my car wouldn't start. I kept trying frantically to reach him on the phone. But the dream ended without me getting there or him answering.

Then one evening when I went for my appointment, the office was in disarray. The couch was over against the wall as usual, but his desk and the rug and the three chairs were all muddled up. Dr. Mitchell said something about repairmen and that there was little use to fix it since they'd be back the next morning. On the couch, along with strong sexual feelings, I felt extremely agitated. When I talked about all this, Dr. Mitchell wondered whether I would like to sit up. I did. In the armchair where I'd begun my therapy. But that night, that chair was directly facing Dr. Mitchell's chair and very close to it.

Sitting up was no help. If anything, both the sexual feelings and the agitation were stronger. And with Dr. Mitchell that close, my distrust and confusion mushroomed as well.

"I don't know what to do! My feelings are so strong!"

"The feelings in your twat?"

"Yes."

"What do you want to do?"

"I want to touch you . . . I want to sit in your lap."

Silence.

"I don't know why I feel so strongly now when I didn't before!"

Silence.

"Maybe this is the reverse of the same problem."

"Remember what you said you wanted to do?"

"Yes."

"What?"

"I wish you would hold me."

Silence.

"I still want to sit in your lap. I still want to touch you."

"Why don't you then?"

Silence.

I was sweating with confusion and excitement.

"Why don't you then?"

"Because . . . I don't think this is how it's supposed to be."

"But the feelings in your twat are strong."

"Yes . . . they make me want to sit on your lap."

"So, why don't you? . . . Are you still afraid of your own feelings?"

Thinking was no use. I could think and remain confused and agitated or take the risk as he encouraged. Earlier thinking about Dr.

Mitchell had taken days. Nor could I rely on any rules. No doctor before had done this with me. But neither had any doctor talked about feelings or said he could help with sexual problems. At the hospital, Dr. Wall had asked when I would commit myself to life. Wilmer had talked about the fat fear but never about the feelings inside me. In graduate school we hadn't got to therapy yet, just to statistics and theory.

"Since you want to, why don't you?"

Thinking was still no use. So I did it. Terrified, but still trying to trust, trying to let myself feel free to go to the point where he would say, "Okay. That's enough."

But he didn't. So I moved from the chair where my knees were already nearly touching his to his lap. There my excitement spiraled into a sirening war. As Dr. Mitchell pressed my hand against his erect trousers-enclosed penis, he asked, "Do you still want to touch me?"

I don't think I answered. I was too scared to speak.

"Shall I take it out?" he asked again as he undid the zipper, and I still can't remember to this day whether what I touched was a pants-enshrouded erection or bare penis.

He talked softly then about the pros and cons of whether we should have sex. It was something we'd need to think and talk about, but not act on that night. Because he had another patient after me.

chapter nineteen

ENDING AND BEGINNING

How does one go on living after an experience like that? I can only say, "with great difficulty." I held myself totally to blame for what had happened and feared that it might make Dr. Mitchell feel so awful that he'd stop seeing me. Also that this could mean that my character was too weak for this kind of feeling therapy; I should have been able to tolerate both Dr. Mitchell's words and my feelings without acting out. For years afterward it would not cross my mind that harm had been done me. My whole focus was on how guilty Dr. Mitchell must feel due to my irresponsibility.

Going to analysis became extremely difficult; when there I lay on the couch unable to think of anything to say. Dr. Mitchell just let me do that with only minor promptings about what I was thinking or feeling. When my answers were minimal, he inquired what my feelings were about having sat on his lap and touched him. I replied that I still had some sexual feelings but that I also felt very ashamed and guilty. When he asked if I wanted to sit up again, I said, "No." The office was back in order by then; his chair was in front of the desk.

Three or four sessions after that awful night, Dr. Mitchell announced that he had given it a great deal of thought and had decided that we should not have sex. I felt so confused by that statement that I still can't sort it out. Today's good sense comes loudest: what a son of a bitch! Knowing my pain and still hurting me again in the worst way! Yet only a few years ago I was still trying to imagine what in the world was going through his head. How could any bit of what he was doing and saying seem right to him as a therapist? In those days I had no capacity at all to realize that I'd been sexually abused again or see the similarity of the lap scenario with Father's seduction of me in the near-death stages of anorexia. I only knew that I'd once more been unable to keep myself from being very destructive.

As my first year in clinical labored to its end, I was buoyed by passing the second of the two horrendous statistics courses and by receiving positive evaluations of my clinical work. These successes would have made me feel almost fully capable of what I was doing if my pride and personal confidence hadn't been eroded by what had happened with Dr. Mitchell. Furthermore, on the first of April he told me that he would have to stop seeing me on the first of May. He did not say so, but I had no doubt he was closing his practice and that it was my fault. I continued going four times a week till the bitter end, and my grief was devastating. I didn't know how I would bear life without Dr. Mitchell and analysis. I also gathered in this process that a further reason for ending the treatment was that he had concluded I was not analyzable. In trying to determine what I could do about my dashed hopes for finding help, I asked Dr. Mitchell to give me names and advice. He told me I shouldn't seek treatment again for at least eighteen months. I took that to mean that since I'd been so destructive in treatment with him, I needed to wait to return to analysis so I wouldn't act out again.

One night that same spring, Tom never did come home. He'd been arrested for driving drunk and called from the courthouse early the next morning, to get me to come post bail. As a result, he lost his license for six months; or rather, had a limited one which permitted him to drive to and from work and nothing else. But even though that stopped his driving under the influence, it caused still more strife between us. To hunt or fish, Tom needed me to drive him to rural areas and later come back and pick him up. But with my packed schedule, including a full-time job that summer at a hospital thirty miles away and being the sole chauffeur for the children (aside from whatever carpools we could arrange), it was very difficult — both practically and emotionally — to take Tom fishing. I was angry, exhausted, and feeling unfairly treated even as I helped him. Tom's anger about this would have taken a much greater toll if I hadn't been working with psychiatrists and psychologists who taught, encouraged, and praised my initial efforts with patients.

Grief dogged me that whole summer. Sometimes I felt I couldn't bear to wait the eighteen months to see another doctor. It never occurred to me then that Dr. Mitchell had only said that to protect himself. I longed to call him at home, but stopped myself. Instead, I did write to him a couple of times. He never answered. Looking back now, it seems what most held me together in that period was feeling responsible for others and having too much to do and too little time.

In addition to the same grueling five-course-per-semester curriculum, the second year in clinical drove us relentlessly toward doctoral writtens in the spring. That October Tom did get his license back, but despite his continuing therapy, there was no letup in either his anger or his unwillingness to talk with me about our dilemma. He seemed constantly on edge, and in those months of late 1973 and early 1974, breaking things in anger grew more common — perhaps because he was drinking at home more. Braced to survive, I clung to a few "truths" as guiding principles: as awful as the drinking was, it was better in the house than on the highway; not driving under the influence might be evidence of Tom's trying to do better; with writtens scheduled for that spring, I could do nothing substantial about the situation at home until they were over.

But my inner calculations about whether or not to stay with Tom never ceased. Nor did my loneliness and depression. Besides feeling that Dr. Mitchell had ended my treatment and even left his practice because I was as terrible a patient as Tom said I was a wife, I had tried a few times after Tom's arrest to communicate to my parents that his drinking was a serious problem and that I might need financial help to leave him if things didn't improve. They responded by saying that most people drank and that I was exaggerating the problem, I should be grateful to have Tom, and I should stay with him no matter what. That didn't lessen my despair, but it did make it clearer that there was no alternative to my determined effort to survive.

Up to then, I'd been putting my *News & Observer* dividend, which we'd begun receiving about three years earlier, directly into Tom's and my joint account. With it (probably totaling about $6,000 per year at that time), I'd been able to feel I paid my own tuition as well as part of Juanita's wages. But in December 1973, I decided to use the $3,000 dividend to buy a VW Beetle. I did so because of the gas shortage, and because Beetles were in short supply. Twenty-five miles to the gallon felt like security itself. But of even greater significance was that, on the advice of our insurance agent, I did not put Tom's name on the title. Tom was livid. Now, buying that car stands out as my first conscious step toward freedom. I devoted Christmas vacation to learning to shift its gears.

As soon as doctoral writtens were past, I began work on the proposal for my dissertation research. The third year in clinical was typically devoted to the dissertation and the fourth year to clinical internship away from the university. But except for the research proposal, my main plan for summer 1974 was to devote myself to our family and see how my not being in school or on practicum affected our spirits. I had a friend who was divorced and going to law school; she urged me to take that summer to separate from Tom. But I rejected her advice, hoping to make a more reasonable and less traumatic decision in the fall.

That summer's experience was just more of the same, however; my freedom from schoolwork only seemed to exacerbate Tom's belligerence. Nor did our having finally become financially able to rent a little beach cottage for two weeks instead of one make us adults any happier. And because the children were old enough to enjoy themselves pretty independently, it was hard to deny our misery by playing "family." On our return home, Tom disappeared and called me from a motel to say he'd left. That again set me wondering how the children and I would manage, but less desperately than before. Finishing my doctorate seemed a realizable possibility, and I found the absence of Tom's rage a relief. He came back in six days, however, wanting us to see a marriage counselor.

But marriage counseling didn't work either. At the third appointment, Tom failed to show. When I questioned him about it that night at home, he spoke disparagingly about professionals being able to help us. Asked if he was going the next time, he said, "Probably."

I did go, and he didn't. But I learned something valuable there on my own. That too-familiar psychiatrist and his soft-spoken, long-eye-lashed female assistant weren't good enough for me. If they had been, they'd have smiled less and let me talk more. I began to think of getting more substantial help for myself.

After all, it had been nearly eighteen months. I decided to resume psychoanalysis if an evaluation by a respected analyst showed it to be the appropriate treatment. By then I had clinical classmates who were in analysis and analyst mentors at my practicum sites, so I also considered that a personal analysis could be good for me profession-ally. From the three names given me, I chose Dr. John Howie, because he was the only one located in Raleigh and because I was already commuting seventy miles per day. At that point, because I'd blamed myself instead of Dr. Mitchell, I had no conscious distrust of analysts.

That same fall brought a momentous crisis for the Daniels family, crisis which felt particularly devastating for me because of the problems in my own life. Cleves and Derick had used their *News and Observer* stock (which could only be bought and sold within the family) as collateral for funds to establish restaurants in New York. When that enterprise failed, they needed to sell their stock in order to pay off their debts. They arrived at the special stockholders' meeting, called to consider this, with a New York lawyer to help them get as high a price as possible. Our father did not come to the meeting; Derick's father, Big Worth, was there in the early stages of dementia. Most of the family was determined to keep the price paid as low as possible to diminish the inheritance tax problems expected with the deaths of the second generation. Because of my personal dilemma, I felt only slightly torn as I spoke and voted against paying a higher price that would have further threatened my own security. There were no glimmers then of the life-enhancing opportunities Cleves and Derick's example and the experience of that tense meeting would ultimately open up for me.

The prairie again. Tall grass waving as far as I could see. I was trying to get to Dr. Mitchell, but there was no path. I'm a lost waif, but with Jonathan and Lucy traipsing behind.

"So that's why I'm here," I said to Dr. Howie. "All I've told you, plus seeing no way out. . . My life has been ruined. I hate that, but I can stand it. What I can't bear is hurting my children. And Tom. I wish I was a better wife to him, but the children are helpless and need me to be much better than I am. Because of them, suicide's no longer an alternative. But how can I help them get out of the mess I brought them into?" He seemed more a statue than a man. A statue in brown cords and cowboy boots. Shoulder-length hair, straight and graying brown. Weathered face deeply lined and fringed by a long mustache. Craggy, angular features that barricaded any thoughts. Brown eyes that penetrated without feeling, while he sat there motionless. Ironically, in a rocking chair. A wooden Indian. Or stone. Relentless. Also ageless and unfathomable. A living riddle. With one gold earring. In the tiny waiting room and on the answering machine, his somber voice echoed with distance and irrelevance. But inside that consulting room, the distance was so great that I strained to see him across a desert and through clouds.

At best, he might be a Buddha dedicated to guiding others toward the truth. But he seemed a genie that existed in and only in that room. Or whose existence depended on the virtue of the beholder. So that again, I might not be good enough.

By comparison, Tom seemed the epitome of security. Yet, wanting Dr. Howie's help, trying to get it, I'd told him all I could. About the hospitalization and doctors who'd forced me to eat but couldn't help the rest; about being incurable and trying to live the best I could on my own but, deplorably failing Tom and the children. He insisted on specifics. When I told him I felt guilty about how these people had been hurt by the way I was, he said, "And the way you are is?"

Which was when the tears first spilled over. Silent, blurring streams that I couldn't stop. His questions caught me off guard and made me feel intruded upon by his staring, ruthless, maybe even treacherous, eyes. Still, my voice was docile as it replied from somewhere inside me: "Empty. . . no, not just empty. . . a sham. Someone who has led other people to believe she is someone she isn't. A person who has published novels, but who never even finished high school. . . who has children, but doesn't know how to be a mother. . . is married, but disappoints her husband."

There were long stretches when he said nothing and I waited. During those silences when he seemed to have a nervous habit of sniffing, I thought that in spite of what I'd been told about his being an "astute and dedicated analyst," he looked as strange as anyone I'd ever seen. In a way, sad and alluring, like that "Sweet Sir Galahad" Joan Baez sang about. But he might ride a motorcycle. He might hang glide. Could rob banks. Could easily seduce women. Could try to seduce me. Or turn out to be homosexual. Like a woman without sexual feelings. And his appearance didn't even attempt to deny any of that.

That day, my third visit, I felt desperation building. "Is this all?" I kept thinking, despite saying out loud, "Perhaps there's no use in my coming here. The other doctors couldn't help. But because the university doctors did once recommend psychoanalysis. . . I guess what I want to know is do you think you can help me?"

"That depends on what you want."

So, I listed: "To be adequate, to stop being a hollow sham. To be a good mother, a better wife to Tom. Maybe, to be helped by somebody competent."

He said nothing.

Waiting. Then, desperate to shake something out of the silence, I pressed, "Is that too much to ask?"

"Obviously, you feel it may be."

I was crying so hard that his eyes and mustache seemed weak and water-logged staring blankly back at me. Like the mottled grimness of bobbing ocean buoys. Echoing eternity.

Finally he said, without any change of expression, "I would be willing to work with you."

chapter twenty

THE TRUTH

From the patient's point of view, psychoanalysis does several things you can't get any other way. It provides support during the process of working through conscious and deep unconscious separations and for bearing the pain that such losses entail. It maintains a sense of being listened to intently by a thoughtful person who will not let you be self-destructive without at least asking a question, but who will also, unblamingly, let you accept the consequences for your own mistakes. An analyst is ethically barred from repeating to anyone else what you say. This results in something I've labeled "the chamber of truth," a condition where thoughts and feelings expressed freely allow reality to emerge. The truth is not magic, however; it is self-evident. The search for it amounts to just trying to see it when it's voiced. That is not easy, because the truth is too large to be contained in words. It's also so pure, as to be invisible.

Probably truth is best recognized by the sensations that accompany it — silence, awe, a certain sinking in the gut, the sad whisper of feeling touched. Sometimes clues to it appear as images in the shadows on the blank wall facing the couch or as sounds snatched out of silence, which simultaneously reduce distractions and magnify reality. Psychoanalysis is an affiliation of innerness — the patient's and the analyst's — exploring the patient's. The inner coming out is what reveals the truth. Relief accompanies that revelation at times because of its solidity. But anxiety is its usual precursor. The whole experience might be best described by a saying I once saw in a Buddhist bookstore: "The truth will set you free. But it will make you miserable first."

The first time I used the couch at Dr. Howie's, I told him that I'd reached the point of feeling there was nothing left to do but tell Tom I wanted a divorce.

His response was, "Do you think you will?"

I did tell Tom that night. We agreed we each needed a lawyer.

My first session with Dr. Howie had been on October 24, 1974. On the Sunday after Thanksgiving, Tom and I talked to the children together.

He moved out the second week in December, about a week before Pat turned sixteen and got his driver's license.

This states the facts, but also demonstrates the dissociation with which we "realistically" dealt with these cataclysmic life events without fully registering their emotional impact. For instance, for Pat, as a junior in high school, to become the second driver a family like ours needed had both positive and negative implications. I worried about accidents and his having to put our family ahead of himself in a crucial period of development, but I saw no alternative to worrying and relying on him. Since Pat and Lucy were unwilling to visit their father, my concerns mounted about how to manage being the only parent in their lives. And they were both of an age and attitude that made me know better than to simply trust them. Juanita's presence each afternoon made me more grateful than ever.

Having wheels that I needed him to have, Pat was the one whose behavior first caused conflict. As a conscientious and sensitive "A" student, he felt he deserved more freedom than I allowed. Sometimes he just defiantly took it. After he was late coming in several times in a row, I told him that if he didn't observe my 11:00 p.m. curfew, he'd lose the use of the car except for school and work. When I followed through with that consequence, he was so enraged that he slammed his fist through the wall of the upstairs hall. Then I told him he'd have to repair the hole before he could use the car to get to his job. That made him madder yet, and I felt guilty, because I didn't know how to repair the wall myself.

Pat himself made me feel better by repairing the wall himself. He also respected curfews better after that. But then despite not abusing alcohol or drugs himself, he wanted to sleep in the living room like

Tom had when drunk. And my not allowing him to made for another round of rage.

Probably, standing my ground over issues like these was only possible because of Dr. Howie and analysis. I drove to his office regularly from the far corners of my life at the odd hours Howie had available. Mostly he'd just listen to me, sometimes ask a question that set me thinking hard in a new direction, and occasionally he'd offer an interpretation that allowed me to feel heard and sometimes understood. I came to know that Howie's praise was usually expressed by silence, and that his questions were intended to be a stronger intervention than they seemed. His sensible remarks sometimes helped me feel grounded with kindness. For instance, when I worried about my inadequacy to meet the children's needs for a father as well as a mother, he said, "And, of course, you can't." For years, I wept there and recounted my failures while he listened with minimal, but apt comment. The issue there, too, was not so much fixing myself as surviving.

In those days, the cars and the house were continually requiring repairs for which I lacked the money. But problems like that were at least less shameful than divorce or a drunken husband. I was able to ask friends for help. Besides keeping me in touch with people, sometimes the help I got was very good. One day, for instance, I came home to find water pouring through the dining room ceiling. And my neighbor Murphy Evans not only advised me on how to deal with the insurance company about a leaking shower, but persuaded me not to sell *News and Observer* stock to put my house in good working order. I probably wouldn't have talked to anyone else about that possible source of funds. But had I talked to less-knowledgeable people, they might have encouraged me to sell without understanding the self-destructiveness of doing so with closely held stock in a family determined to keep it devalued.

Given all these problems, I began to dread — as soon as I'd found a lawyer I could work with — what would happen when our divorce did go through. We had $10,000 per child from my parents put aside for college educations, so the future was not a major worry. But I would have felt like a thief to touch any of that then. Instead, I earned a little extra money by teaching more sections of psychopathology at the university, and pondered what to do after the divorce about paying for my analysis and for a housekeeper to supervise the kids after school.

Knowing that I'd be losing Tom's health insurance with the divorce, I asked Mommy and Father for a loan.

"Are you sick?" Father demanded when I called long distance. They'd been in South Carolina several years by then. "Are you crazy?!"

"No," I answered softly, shocked and hurt. "I'm not sick or crazy. But I do need help. I never saw a doctor before who could understand me, not until this one. And now that I'm separating from Tom, I especially need his help."

"Better you should use your money to put divorce out of your mind. . . Lucy, you are crazy if you think you can look after four children alone."

I can still feel myself disintegrating as he said all that, the reality I feared myself, and in his cruelly critical way that brought out my sense of worthlessness. But, for once, I did like I'd talked about with Dr. Howie — pushed the inhibiting feelings down and spoke back pretty straight. "Father, I've told you why I have to get a divorce. Also, why I need some financial help now."

"Lucy, everybody drinks. And cops wait to pick up somebody for drinking because it's an easy bonus. Nobody's perfect. You need to remember how fortunate you've been to have Tom. This is one instance in which greediness will get you nowhere. You could end up alone with a mess."

I hung up the phone on him. And before long Mommy rang me back: "Your father and I are so worried about you. We can't bear to think of you working so hard and the children going without nice clothes and piano lessons." The upshot of it was that they didn't want to help me with the doctor because Father didn't trust doctors, but would help me with the house if I got an appraisal.

I was still so blind then! Because later, their reaction to the appraisal surprised me too. "You should have considered needs like these before you up and got rid of your husband!" Mommy scolded. "To help you with this kind of money we'd have to pay penalties on CD's."

"Lucy," Father added from the other extension, "Life has some hardships that have to be tolerated and even tolerated with good cheer. The ability to do this, to live life to the hilt in whatever circumstances, is a valuable life force you've never seen fit to strengthen in yourself. But you need to. Life is not one bail-out after another!"

It still amazes me that despite streaming tears, my voice answered directly: "I don't want a bail-out, Father. I need you to lend me the money to buy the house from Tom."

"How do you propose to raise four children alone?" Mommy asked. "Do you know about the consequences for the children of divorced parents?"

"Your mother and I do not have the kind of money you're asking for. $25,000 indeed! And Lucy, this wild goose chase of yours into psychology. If you're really going to go through with divorcing Tom, you need to go to work, and not let some shrink eat up the little money you have. If you're so sick, how can you take care of your children?"

Crying hard then, I said: "I don't need your cruelty any more. I'm at least well enough to tell you good-bye."

"What's this about 'bail-outs'?" Dr. Howie asked. "When have they bailed you out?"

I scrutinized the wood paneling at the foot of the couch. The answer to Dr. Howie's question seemed obvious in all the things I'd already told him. Did he mean for me to think deep inside myself and discover a more obscure but significant piece of information? Finally I said, "I think Father was talking about their paying for my hospitalization and helping me with Wilmer when I first got out."

"How was any of that a 'bail-out'?"

My throat was dry and knotted. The last thing I needed was for him to not understand. "That's just what I think Father was referring to," I said more haltingly.

"But would you call that a 'bail-out,' paying for a child's treatment, even with a long-term illness like anorexia? If it were your daughter, would you call it a 'bail-out'?"

"No." But I realized in saying that that I did feel differently about myself personally. And in the long silence I finally found the courage to say, "But I do feel about my anorexia and its treatment — even though I understand from you that some of that treatment was bad and inhumane — I do feel that all that was part of my greediness."

"In other words, you still haven't accepted that anorexia was a disease outside your control."

"I guess not."

For days afterward, that conversation echoed through my thoughts. Especially the part about my not being responsible for the anorexia. But I couldn't see myself as not to blame — in that or many other issues. Even though standing up to Mommy and Father felt good, I also felt like I shouldn't, at 40, still be asking them for help — no matter how rich they were or how big my problems.

It seemed natural to turn to my sisters after that, even though analysis made me recognize their blindness. I knew they still talked to Mommy and Father. I wanted to trust them, but I felt they couldn't understand. Not even Cleves, whom I'd helped go through her own divorce.

"It does sound pretty grim," she said when I called her one morning. "Thank the Lord I've never felt like I had to put myself through the things you struggle with. Divorce is deadly, makes people ugly to each other. When you most need somebody to hold and stroke you and tell you you're beautiful and everything's going to be all right, the people you need either disappear or start being critical. What I don't understand is why in the world you're trying to get a doctorate in the midst of this shit. And why you expose yourself to something as ghastly as Parents Without Partners."

"I need to go somewhere. Neighbors and the younger students in my program don't help. I think I need to face being single and needing other single people. I've talked about it in analysis, and that seems to be where I'm at."

"Well, I've always preferred bars. You do run into an occasional lush. But they're usually harmless. And the other men in bars are at least there to have fun and forget their troubles. Which is a hell of a lot better than being dutiful."

Feeling weak and even lonelier after hanging up, I blamed myself for not having predicted Cleves's scorn of my struggling. I dialed Bibba for comfort.

"Hello!" she chimed cheerily as if it were Christmas. "Oh, yes,

I know a few people who go to Parents Without Partners here. Sounds like a worthwhile organization that's helpful with the problems of single parenting. I've heard it's a place to meet people in the same boat and to help each other with things like babysitting and loneliness."

"Perhaps," I answered her. "I don't know if I can stand it though. The people seem so boring. And I'm not very good at being single."

"Maybe you don't have to."

"Don't have to what?" I asked, confused.

"Be single."

"I don't know what you mean."

"Maybe you and Tom can work things out."

"But I told you before. We've already tried. I've had professional help. And we can't."

"Don't give up too easily. Remember that loneliness may be harder than living with Tom. And you probably still have time to change your mind."

"After all I've told you," I sputtered, more surprised than I should have been. "After the drinking and the way he treated me, us, you would still say that?"

"Well, yes." Long, breath-holding silence before she added, "Remember, Lucy, anything's better than nothing."

The divorce went through on April 15, 1976. Tom had wanted me to get it in a county other than Wake (the state capital and location of *The News and Observer* and both our residences), and my attorney, Sam Johnson, suggested that getting it in Orange County, which held one of its courts in Chapel Hill, might be an easy solution. As things turned out, it was.

The judge was blind. I didn't realize it until we were just a few people from the front of the line. A whole crowd was getting uncontested divorces! I'd thought "in his chambers" meant something personal and private. Instead, it meant "at his desk." Robes and all, but at his desk instead of in the courtroom. He talked to no more than two people at a time — a lawyer and a plaintiff — but looked out blankly over the crowd as he spoke just loud enough for those two to hear. At first I thought his looking out that way had to do with pondering, but then I realized he couldn't see.

"Who is representing the plaintiff?" he questioned the air in front of him. His big dog scratched.

"I, Sam Johnson, am counsel for the plaintiff, Your Honor."

"Are there dependents?"

"Yes, Your Honor: Patrick, seventeen; Lucy, fifteen; Jonathan, twelve; Benjamin, nine.

"Is there legal provision for their support?" he asked the air behind us.

"Yes, Your Honor. The father, Tom Inman, is legally bound to provide support."

"Granted. Next case. Who is representing the plaintiff?"

The first courage was making myself tell the whole truth. And despite my first impression that it bored and alienated Dr. Howie, I did come to feel more brave and honest as a result. I told him again and again, word for word about how Tom had treated me and about how angry the children were and how I knew I really wasn't giving them all they needed. The more openly I talked, the more I dreaded going there and being surprised when Dr. Howe still came out to get me. I guess I believed I was hurting him with my words or horrifying him with my life because I kept expecting him to look old or ravaged by disease. At times I thought of holding back again, but realized it was no use because he already knew too much. Also, because he did keep listening, quietly and respectfully, as if nothing had happened. When I got silent, he'd still ask, "What are you thinking?" And if I said, "Nothing," he'd answer, "I think you mean nothing you feel you should say." So I'd go on.

How the idea of getting to be a psychologist shamed me there! Because I realized I could never be a good one if I stayed as messed up as I was. I came to understand, too, that Dr. Howie had been right all along about my problems being much more anger than craziness or stupidity. I could no longer escape the fact that I couldn't be a worthwhile mother, psychologist, or woman unless I let myself claim that anger and learn to manage it.

The further I went, the closer I got to revealing the terrible badness that I'd tried to convey to him and to Dr. Mitchell before him, the more he refused to see. One day, after describing the time I'd lost my temper with Tom for wanting me to take him fishing, Dr. Howie's silence made me desperate. "Will you never hear me?!" I shouted at him angrily. "How can you help me with my badness if you won't acknowledge it?"

More silence. But after a while, he said, "I think your need to make me believe how bad you are is terribly complicated, an issue that we'll have to keep confronting over time. For the moment though, while I don't want to be mistaken for agreeing with you, I'd like to join in your conviction long enough to look at something I believe our disagreement about your 'badness' obscures. . . Let's assume for the moment that you're right. You are the most evil, depraved, greedy person imaginable. Was that reason for Tom to drink? Or drive around drunk, running the risk of killing other innocent people?"

The divorce was the first of a barrage of changes. Pat graduated from high school and went off to Bowdoin College in Maine. Tom remarried. I completed my dissertation on adolescent pregnancy and began a year-long clinical internship at the Durham V.A. Hospital, the last requirement for the doctorate. Following the divorce, Sam Johnson was able, after considerable protest, to persuade Mommy and Father to lend me $25,000 at 10% interest to buy the house from Tom. And through that struggle, I learned from the example of Derick and Cleves that I could borrow money using my *News & Observer* stock as collateral. This discovery greatly increased my sense of security and capacity to endure.

Of course, the ultimate change came one year later when, having successfully completed both my dissertation and internship, I got my doctorate and went to work. As director of psychological services for Lee-Harnett Mental Health Center in Sanford and Buies Creek (each about an hour's drive south of Raleigh), I began valuable training in reality.

But the divorce's most harrowing change was that I could no longer afford Juanita. This was sad for us all; she had become like a member of the family. But she needed to earn a living, and, besides not having the money to pay her, I could no longer spare the hour required each day to pick her up and take her home. Between my efforts and her own, Juanita found a very good job with a wonderful family who taught her to drive. But I was left with the formidable issue of how to find an adult I could trust at the house each day when the children came home from school.

Since I was doing my dissertation on adolescent pregnancy, I knew it would be courting disaster to leave them on their own. But I also lacked the wherewithal to seek out the high-caliber people I needed. As a result, I had a series of women, who did provide a semblance of the protection we needed despite having a variety of shortcomings that I could not tolerate once I recognized them. The best one was a pleasant and sensible matron who said she just wanted a few hours work each day to supplement her husband's income. She quit the afternoon of the day I got my divorce. Then there was a 65-year-old white woman who went into a frenzy over the boys' long hair and Lucy's black friends. By then conflict was not something that worried me. But when I discovered that she firmly believed she had the right of way when turning left on a red light and tried to practice the switching she thought appropriate to punish misbehavior, I let her go. Next came Sadie, a black, middle-aged mother whose hair bushed out on end as though she'd been plugged into an electric socket. She lasted the longest, and we all liked her because she kept family uproars to a minimum. It was fortunately not until years later, near the end of my single-parenting, that I learned she kept peace by conspiring with the children to hide all transgressions—hers as well as theirs—from me.

In my newspaper life, largely rural Harnett County had been called "the murder capital of the world" because of how judges and jurors there had tended to let murderers off. And Lee-Harnett Mental Health Center lived up to this reputation by providing a most humbling enlightenment regarding the extremes possible in human rage and politics. Like other rural communities, Lee and Harnett counties wanted to export their "crazies" to the state hospital in Raleigh and, therefore, provide services only to alcoholics and individuals with grief reactions. Their area directors tended to be alternately psychopaths and manic-depressives, each correcting the mistakes of his predecessor. Though the clinic needed me as a Ph.D. psychologist in order to operate with federal funding, my degree did not require them to respect what I did, nor to follow my directives. Rather, they pressured me to use my credentials to certify what the non-professional staff wanted.

It was a grueling job. But I still appreciate how, in my three years there, that clinic made me labor in pursuit of competence and find it because I had to. Frequently that meant doing only what one reasonably could in an impossible situation. Tremendously valuable education for a former anorexic!

chapter twenty-one

CONNECTING AND SEPARATING

At the time it felt like Dr. Howie was a slave-driver. Maybe even an intrusive sadistic slave-driver. Because no sooner had I settled down from the divorce and become established at Lee-Harnett than he started in about my writing.

"One thing we've never thoroughly discussed," he said one day, "is you as a writer."

"That's right," I shot back after a stunned silence. "Because I'm not one."

Silence behind me. Then, "I think I understand what you're saying. But evidence in the world disagrees."

I waited. But after he just sat there, I went back at him hard. "I've told you I stopped being a writer because I was no good at it. And you know that I stopped for my own good, to not live my life as my parents' pawn."

"I do know that's what you've said. And we're in agreement that it would be destructive for you to live your life as your parents' pawn. But I also think there is more to your writing than that and that not considering it neglects important issues here."

So he hooked me. First, into talking about how I'd decided to put writing out of my life and then about what that decision meant to me.

"I think I've understood why you decided to stop," Dr. Howie went on a few days later, after the smoke from his original foray had cleared. "But I don't think you've told me how you felt afterward."

Silence, while I tried to remember.

The creak of his rocking chair.

"Exhilarated first. Stopping felt like a load off my back. No longer keeping myself ashamed. Free to just be a mother."

Silence.

"Father didn't like my stopping. Neither did Mommy. But they also may have thought it was just a temporary interruption, almost a necessity because of the children."

Listening without a creak.

"I don't think either of them took it seriously until I entered college...My deciding to become a psychologist and starting graduate school was what really upset them. Maybe because it actively abandoned the writing."

Then, later that night, not in Dr. Howie's office but when I was locking the door before going to bed, the conversation I'd had with Father about becoming a psychologist came back to me as clear as life:

"But you're my boy," he said. "The wise one who can understand me. . . Surely, then, you don't mean this."

"I do, Father. I've searched my soul and talked about it for many weeks with this analyst I see."

"A fool like that has convinced you to study shrinking instead of writing?" Cigarette haze encircled his face.

"No, Father. Dr. Mitchell's not a fool, and he didn't convince me. I've been seeing him a while now. Because of the depression and — ."

"How can you say he hasn't convinced you?"

"Because he didn't. I haven't been able to write since the children. And I've felt depressed and inadequate. So, I decided I did need to go to college after all. And now, if I can, graduate school."

"That is foolish, " he scolded. "Lucy, you are a writer. And you don't need college or graduate school to write." Reaching over, he put his large gnarled hand on top of my trembling thin one.

"But you don't understand, Father, I'm not going to write. I want to be a psychologist."

"Another one of those pretentious degrees," he chided, dragging again on his cigarette. "But you'll learn in time. Lucy, you are a writer. You can't help it."

When I told Dr. Howie about that conversation, he asked, "How do you think what he said affects you?"

I didn't know the answer. "In one way, you could say I didn't let him stop me. I became a psychologist anyway. But I can understand his saying what he said."

Silence. Sniffing.

"He wanted me to be his writing heir. Whether I have it in me or not."

"Though you have to admit he had reality to back him."

I was silent then, feeling suddenly dropped. "What do you mean?"

"With two published novels and one of them as successful as *Caleb, My Son*, there is evidence of your having writing ability."

I had no answer.

Not long after that I gave in to Howie and the remaining flutterings of my wish to write and started a short story. But with commuting to Lee-Harnett and having to struggle with the children as well as seeing the few private patients I had in Raleigh, it was some time before I had the wherewithal to really work at writing.

Another top priority then was doing what I could about my loneliness. As it became possible to reduce my days at Lee-Harnett and increase my private practice hours in Raleigh, my search for friends proved more fun than I'd ever imagined, because of all the other people looking for somebody, too. Mary Huelsbeck, whom I'd met as a student when I was interning at the V.A., was a psychologist who was anxious to marry. A Catholic girl from Iowa sixteen years younger than I, she had the advantage of my being a friend, mentor and quasi-mother without being in competition for boyfriends, while I had the benefit of a bright friend who could value what I had to offer. For a while she also leased space in my office. Another significant comrade at that time was Allan Bloom, a social worker in private practice who later became a psychologist, and, ultimately, a psychoanalyst. Allan was also about fifteen years younger than me. Both he and Mary, and a few others, had many of the qualities the people in Parents Without Partners lacked. They were both therapists who were in treatment themselves and who were working hard to improve all aspects of their lives, including their singleness.

Allan was a tall, dark, rather burly Jew with a hearty, somewhat hostile sense of humor, a big heart and relentless ingenuity. For a while he tried to get me to fix him up with Mary. But after I did and it didn't work out, Allan and I settled down into a few years of helping each other. Because of Allan's warmth and ingenuity, this sometimes felt a little like being partners in crime! We read and criticized each other's singles ads. We listened to each other's accounts of new efforts at relationships. We would go to parties together—I would take him to the homes of my new acquaintances and he would do the same for me. At parties we'd split up, each pursuing our own course, while keeping an eye out for possibilities for each other.

But my other experiences alone continued to be difficult. One night I had to go to a P.T.A. meeting at Ben's school directly after my last patient. I never liked those meetings, because at Ben's private school I felt socially shabby as well as uncomfortable as a single parent. When I arrived home very tired at about 10 p.m., I found a note from Ben on the kitchen table. I was surprised and dismayed: fourteen-year-old Ben was not only grounded at the time but knew very well from previous groundings that leaving home for any reason under those circumstances was a major violation.

The note said he'd gone to his girlfriend Zelda Johnson's house because she was depressed. Zelda lived fifteen miles away, and as I looked up her number in the telephone book, my mind was storming through how he might have gotten there.

Mrs. Johnson answered the phone and I asked to speak to Ben. He came on right away in his hesitant, manipulatively nice way, "Mom?"

"Ben, what are you doing over there?"

"I wrote you a note, Mom. It — "

"Yeah, I've read it. But you are grounded. You shouldn't be away from this house right now for any reason. How did you get there?"

"Mrs. Johnson came and got me."

"Well, please get her to bring you home right now."

When Ben got home, he and I talked about what had happened and what his punishment would be. He and Zelda were supposed to spend the upcoming weekend in South Carolina with his father. I decided cancelling that weekend would be his punishment. With Ben there, I called Tom to tell him and for once he understood.

But the fallout from this punishment was one of the greater

surprises of my singlehood. As I was driving in from work the next night, Sadie, the afternoon housekeeper, called to me from the door to say a lady wanted to speak to me on the phone.

The lady was Mrs. Johnson. She wanted me to change Ben's punishment because Zelda had said that if they couldn't go to South Carolina that weekend, she'd kill herself. I couldn't believe my ears! But I told her, with Ben sitting right there to hear me, "I'm terribly sorry Zelda's so upset. I hope you're getting help for her because that's a very desperate reaction. But I'm not going to change Ben's punishment. It's appropriate given what he did. Besides, Ben's not trained to help people who're depressed, and trying to isn't good for him." This was just one of the many encounters of single parenthood that showed me my strength. By doing what life required, I learned about capabilities I never would have believed before.

Then, on New Year's Eve, 1977, I met Thad. He was a long-divorced recovering alcoholic with twelve years of sobriety who was also in psychoanalysis. Before becoming an alcoholism counselor, he'd nearly earned his doctorate in classics and was still devoted to reading Latin and Greek. Warm and playful and much brighter and more imaginative than any other man I'd met, he was impressed by and appreciative of my being a psychologist. I also enjoyed being introduced to the things he valued, including ways to make coffee and green salad. We had lots of fun, though that was the first relationship in which I really had to struggle over the conflict between boyfriend and children.

When I talked to Dr. Howie about my concerns over the children seeing my affection and physical closeness with Thad, he said, "Have you considered the effects on them of not witnessing these things?" We also talked about the ways Thad was like other men in my life: angry, rebellious, maybe even defiant like Tom, but with a manner that was childlike and playful rather than hard and belligerent. Very like Father in his charming way with words, but also, honest and seriously conflicted about achieving. And, of course, in time Thad also became ambivalent about me: if I was valuable enough to be attractive to him, I was too good for him and therefore bound to regard him as inferior.

By Christmas 1978, I had grown alienated from my whole family of origin and was not especially sad about it. My sisters clearly didn't understand my situation. And although Mommy and Father had canceled the note for their loan to me after I went to work at Lee-Harnett, our relationship was more polite than dependable. Then, in early January 1979, Mommy developed a life-threatening illness. That was a shock then, but from today's perspective, clearly one due in part to our blindness. Mommy had worried about age and death for a while and had taken measures to designate to whom she wanted to leave what. But that December — even before becoming sick — she did more. Heavy cardboard boxes addressed in Mommy's script were delivered to my office by certified mail. Heavy like lead. Surreal.

Silver. Box after box of it, each carefully sealed with its own detailed list in the top. Why? I wondered for days, waking in the night, looking at my tired face in the mirror. On the telephone she said, "Your father has not been well. Drinks too much. Smokes too much. He's depressed about his eyes going bad and about being old. Putting things in order, dividing up the silver, takes my mind off it." So in my office I pursued the Rorschachs and the Draw-A-Persons, the weeping and the rage, the dreams related without concern for my unconscious. After an incredibly few days Father left a message on my machine: "Lucy, your mother is gravely ill. There is a problem with her liver. I'll be with her at St. Joseph's Hospital."

That drive down to Hilton Head was like all the others. Too long, too laboring. But also suspenseful and worrisome because the doctor had refused to tell me whether to come or not. His unhelpfulness had ultimately been why I went — in order to not feel guilty later. So, I was doing what I felt was required, but also with the vaguely irritated expectation of finding her much improved and given over to nagging instructions about how to care for the silver.

But the woman in the hospital bed did not recognize me. She stared blank-eyed, insulted by a stranger's intrusion. Also humiliated, terrified by her own loss of control. I, in turn, was shocked to see her ravaged, jaundiced face and clung numbly to disorientation. Until her flaccid lips slurring garbled worries about checkbook and taxes jarred me out of doubt. Then I looked to the slate-colored eyes for confirmation and found with relief that, in spite of being glazed over, they did still condemn the world.

Sitting there alone with her through the night, I realized I had never known her. Nor she me. And now, there wasn't time or consciousness. A part of me angrily blamed her for arranging it that way, for sending the boxes of silver ahead as a front to be seen in her place. But I remained there beside the bed in order to not desert her, and to know for myself that I'd not run away; probably, too, I stayed to make up for not having heeded the silver's message to come earlier.

Mommy's death stays as distinct in my memory now as if etched there by acid. By the time she died I had come to understand that she'd never really comforted or protected me. But she had controlled us all and provided the only order our early lives had known. Therefore, even though Dr. Howie and I had not yet reached the point of dealing with my role as her appendage, I reeled with the incredible shock of her loss at least as much as Father and my sisters. Could life itself continue without her?

When we arrived back at the Hilton Head house the evening of her death, a drawn and plaintive Father tugged on my arm and said, "Lucy, I want you to sleep in my room tonight."

"Let's see, Father," I replied. "There are so many of us here. Let's see how it works out."

"Well, I want you. Surely, Cordelia, you won't make an old man sleep alone tonight."

I held my tongue for the moment even though his request stirred dismay and anger in me. After all the talking Dr. Howie and I had been doing about his sexual abusiveness, his request that night brought back the memory of his kiss on the back of my anorexic neck and his gift of Babs's books in the hospital. That night was when he started frequently calling me Cordelia. The name made me feel worse about sleeping with him. However, with all the other beds filled, there was no way out of it. So I slept that night in the bed that had been Mommy's. Without a single protest, but with my mind focused on feelings to discuss with Dr. Howie.

By that time, because of the interaction of my life and psychoanalysis, I'd begun to get the hang of change, to almost expect it and to know that it could only be weathered, not stopped. As I faced the continual crises of adolescent children growing up and leaving, there were also issues between Thad and me. That spring after graduating from high school, Lucy moved out to an apartment with a friend, in large part because I refused to continue struggling with her unsavory friends and her refusal to apply herself academically.

Then during a weekend at the beach in early summer, Thad and I had a confrontation.

"It's not that I don't love you," he said. "But the idea of committing myself to you or to anyone makes me feel trapped."

I knew I had to face reality. From what had happened in my marriage, I knew I could. But I kept hoping reality could be different. Also, when Thad talked that way I could see traces of sadness around his eyes and in the way his lips strained against his teeth to make a smile, but couldn't. "Do you think you'll come to feel otherwise?" I asked. "Do you think you even want to?"

"Sure," he replied thoughtfully, pulling me close with that wonderful long-armed hug of his. "I want to. Or at least, if I have to to be with you, I want to. . . Lucy, I think I really do love you very much."

I still dreaded loneliness. But gradually, over the next few weeks, I came to see that because I needed more than Thad wanted to risk, and because he was intimidated by the work that fulfilled me, we would be doomed to loneliness even if we stayed together. My attempts to discuss this with Thad only irritated him. By the time we made an appointment to settle things, I'd also realized how unlikely it was that talking would help.

On the agreed afternoon, Thad made a pot of tea. "For coziness," he said. But I knew that he meant "to prevent getting too serious." He knew why I'd come, had resisted at first, and then agreed, knowing my persistence. I was direct and explicit, despite crying as I watched his face and eyes that, in time, cried too. His fingers fidgeted around his teacup. At one point, he said, "If you haven't found someone else who wants the permanence of marriage, why can't we continue as we are till you do?"

"Because I have to be alone to find the person I'm looking for."

The sunlight was fading when I left. We were both crying. His arms encircled me and we kissed. As I turned to look again before driving away, he was grinning and crying.

Just rocking and listening, rocking and listening. Perhaps the most remarkably helpful thing about Dr. Howie is that he's never forgotten his place. He's been the doctor, listener, human presence, sometimes the interpreter. But it's always been *my* life with failures and successes, good fortune, stupid mistakes, and sad losses. Mine to feel and come to terms with.

That year he was more help with Mommy's death than with either Lucy or Thad. In my last session before driving to South Carolina to evaluate the seriousness of her illness, he'd said, "You may want to take your appointment book and patient telephone numbers with you. In case your plans change."

Whereas his response to both Lucy and Thad was, "What were your options?"

I imagined him still-faced and not missing a beat as I tried to list them: "Thad would have continued, but — he doesn't want what I want. . . . Lucy continues not taking care of herself and blaming me. But — ." The longer I stumbled through such statements, the clearer it became to me that as much as those outcomes pained me, I'd chosen the only acceptable alternatives.

Dr. Howie's silence echoed my own sad lack of guilt.

Then, too, there was Father. Alone in South Carolina, depressed, legally blind, and suffering from emphysema but refusing to move to be close to any one of his daughters. Because of that there were his frequent phone calls and his insistent pleading for visits. I eventually made a plan to deal with this — I drove to Hilton Head one weekend every month and talked to him on the phone two or three times a week in the interim.

In the spring of 1981, all four sisters gathered at the Hilton Head house to settle Mommy's estate. During that meeting I asked Father for a loan against his estate to help me buy a smaller but nicer house in town and nearer to my office. When he jeered at this, saying I should "be grateful for what you have," I reminded him that I was only asking for a loan.

"What do you want with another house?" he countered between drags on his cigarette.

"It would make people and all the things I need to do in town much easier to get to."

"How much does it cost?"

"About $225,000, I think."

"Phew!" He took another puff. "You don't need a house like that!"

His sneering tone made me angry, but I persisted, while Bibba, Adelaide, and Cleves gaped in silence. "I just want to make the rest of my life easier than the past. There will only be twelve houses in this project, and that's why I want to try to get one early. If I could borrow, say $40,000, against my share of your estate."

"So, Cordelia, you, too, want to strip me before I'm dead!" His blind eyes looked hard; his voice was sneering again. "As selfish as ever!"

I waited while my sisters watched. Then I said, "Father, you've been cruel enough to me in my life. You don't need to talk to me like this now!" I rose and left the room.

That night there was a page for me at the restaurant I'd gone to with my sisters and their husbands. When I got to the phone, Father's voice was huskily sweet on the other end, "I love you, sweetheart," he said.

"I love you, too, Father, but I don't like it when you humiliate me."

Later visits with Father were heavily influenced by what I'd learned working with dying patients at the V.A. I urged him to take walks, to drink less, and to listen to the recorded books for the blind which arrived regularly but enraged him. Besides assisting with paraffin soaks for his arthritic hands and the late afternoon visitors who came to drink Bourbon with him, I made a point of talking to him about his feelings and about death. I still recall one of those conversations which took place after his emphysema was so advanced that he needed oxygen.

Breathing the oxygen frantically at first, then more easily, he finally gasped with impatience. "Give the poor old man a cigarette!"

"Father, you have to wait ten minutes after the oxygen."

"Ten minutes! Scientific torture! Mercy! Have mercy on an old man."

When feebly puffing again, he first joked about "coffin nails," then added, "This is damned hard, Lucy. Old age is the worst of God's pestilences." Tears filled his blue eyes.

"I can see. I'm sorry."

His face was ashen. His blindness gave it an averted, blunted tilt. "Father, are you afraid of dying?"

"Not entirely." He hesitated. "I have some longing. . . I expect to see Mother and Father again. Also, your mother and Babs."

"You do believe in heaven then?"

"More and more every day."

I did not speak. My eyes studied the wall at the foot of his bed where a resurrected photograph of Babs had been hung beside the familiar one of Mommy.

"For psychologists, heaven is an illusion. . . But don't scorn an old man, Lucy."

"I don't, Father," As I reached to relieve him of the still smoldering cigarette butt, he slipped his hand around mine and squeezed it.

When his death did come, it seemed long overdue. He went to the hospital one more time, and the doctor said he would never go home again. But, thanks to the strength I had developed in analysis, I did not rush down. Rather, despite my sadness, I set myself the plan of talking with him on the telephone every day but not going again until his death. Oddly, this seemed to increase his trust in me.

I called several times during that last day only to be told by his favorite sitter that he was sleeping. Trying again near bedtime, another sitter I didn't know said she thought he would speak to me.

Then his voice — gasping, choking — gurgled words I could barely make out as resembling the way my son Jon had called me "wow dow" for "I love you" until he was four.

"I love you, too," I fell into the childhood ritual.

"I love you . . . I love you . . . I love you," his words spluttered.

"Good night," I said. "Sweet dreams." Hearing the sitter hang up, I did, too.

Later, as I was coursing south on the snowy interstate, my old feeling of lostness loomed huger than ever over the awesome knowledge that I would never again hear Father's voice. The large flakes plopping on the windshield insulated against the traffic, but inside my head his thunder continued. I repeated the same words that, despite feeling blasphemous, I'd once discussed with Dr. Howie. . . "a stone, a leaf, an unfound door." Those words had come from Father's friend Thomas Wolfe:

". . . a stone, a leaf, an unfound door; of a stone,
a leaf, a door. And all the forgotten faces. . .

Which of us has known his brother? Which of us has
looked into his father's heart? . . ."

I believed I had. More than once.

When the wet snow gave way to rain that trickled and then poured, I reflected on us sisters. How would we be without the screen of dying parents? How would I be? Idealized big sister? Martyred confidant made official by the "Dr." in front of my name? Or the harsh and hated purveyor of a blasphemous "false" truth about childhood abuse that not one of them was willing to acknowledge? It seemed defensive to think of them in their childhood roles. But even if they'd changed too, how could we know each other except as Nobody, Intellectual, Pagan, Baby. Competitors for love and personal worth in a circus contest where those prizes were nonexistent. Competitors who, though unable to win, could look as though each barred victory from all the others. Baby, Pagan, Intellectual, Nobody; would we, indeed, still exist with the namer dead?

". . . a stone, a leaf, an unfound door . . ."

In the church our positions were unchanged. Adelaide and her husband Bobby were in the pew nearest the front; with their sons' wives, they filled it up. I sat in the third pew back, in the middle, with Bibba and her husband Chick on my left and Cleves with her second husband Steve on my right. The midday sun streaked through the stark, modern, unstained windows, illuminating the whole church with unexpected purity. I studied it all, trying to memorize the very light rays, the organ swells, the sea of faces. So intent on preserving that, I was surprised by the most penetrating detail of all — the grandchildren as pallbearers. Adult men and women who should have been jabbering, giggling, fighting each other in pursuit of crawfish and lightning bugs; girls against boys, but all united in their fear of disapproving grandparents. Instead they solemnly carried the casket to the front and filed into the pew reserved for them.

> The Lord is my salvation;
> Whom then shall I fear?
> The Lord is the strength of my life;
> Of whom then shall I be afraid?

At Mommy's funeral despite my own voice rising with others, those crystal words had seemed to ring out from a distant choir. Evoking her decorum with its promise of salvation or retribution. Father had been hunched beside me in the pew that day, trembling and shrunken, in the tasteful, too-big grey suit provided by the same expedience as had produced the cardboard boxes of silver. Weeping openly, blundering loudly through the parts of the service he remembered. Father never could carry a tune, but never let that stop him. Then, as always, he'd sung the beloved hymn full-voiced and confident. While at his funeral, as the motley congregation sang his favorite — "Father, the tempest is rag-ing . . .," I was jarred back to the present by the absence of both his off-key croak and my child-hood embarrassment. Also, by the aching sense of waste that both the angry man and the frightened developing girl had vanished without resolution.

". . . Which of us has known his brother . . . "

Or her sister?

chapter twenty-two

LOST AGAIN

"Freedom's just another word for nothing left to lose," Kris Kristofferson crooned over the tape player of the Toyota I used to chauffeur kids in those single parent days. Still, before the deaths of Mommy and Father, my own view was that FREE and LOST were equivalent. There was bountiful evidence for this perspective from my life experience—confinement to yard and mental hospital; the draining disoriented "lostness" of both leaving the hospital and separating from Tom. But after Mommy and Father, life opened up in many ways I'd never expected. In fact, I'd say now, it kept opening up in ways I couldn't anticipate.

Money came first. Father's life insurance and *The News and Observer* dividends from the stock I inherited enabled me to buy my house in town after all. In addition—perhaps just due to luck or to my no longer working so hard to deal with both life in Raleigh and Father in South Carolina—there was love. Maybe a year or so after private practice allowed me to work in town, Allan Bloom introduced me to Rudy Schmidt. And for the next eight years, this warm and charming though petulant literature professor filled my life with excitement and adventure. In that period, too, the children kept leaving—both physically and philosophically. With Lucy and Pat already out on their own, Jonathan and Ben went to the University in Chapel Hill where they both became Christian fundamentalists.

But I experienced the most significant and sustained release in the arena of writing. I began keeping a copy book, one of those college composition books with a black and white speckled cover and lined pages. Ultimately it took a whole string of them — for my dreams at first and later, for important thoughts that bubbled up out of my unconscious. I referred to it as "my copy book" for years before it ever dawned on me to question why. When I did, my first thought was of the notebooks I'd used as a reporter.

Maybe that book prompted Dr. Howie to talk more about my writing. In 1982, compared to the copy book, my other "real" writing was still limping along at a half-hearted pace. By then Dr. Howie's pursuit of me as a writer had shifted to my pursuit of the writing I'd always wanted to do. But it was a discouraging quest, because whatever I produced had the same wooden quality I recalled as having discouraged me into quitting twenty years earlier. The only saving grace was that Dr. Howie helped me turn the hunt inward to explore why I would write that way when I didn't want to. I had already freed up early clinical hours so I could write from 5:00 a.m. till mid-morning before going to work. I'd also come to require a minimum number of words per day. Still, in 1982, working at writing made me feel slow-witted, as I produced little. Continuing would have been hard without the support of analysis.

That summer the struggle behind the meager output was vividly revealed in a dream:

The setting was an institution. A mental hospital. And I, at once a doctor and a patient, was sitting on the toilet in a bathroom like those on the acute wards with no doors on the cubicles. But the commode was much further off the floor than normal. I was trying to urinate. . . trying. . . trying. . . but couldn't. My name was announced on the loudspeaker. My name, but the wrong one for me as a doctor: "Lucy Daniels. Dr. Lucy Daniels, please call 2973." I didn't know the way, but at the nurses' station, the telephone told me that my family doctor was waiting on the chronic ward. To get there I had to go out the locked door of the acute ward and in the locked door of the chronic ward. Also, my clothes were wrong. I was wearing one of the white gowns acute patients wear. I tried to stand behind a window curtain to hide this, but no one seemed to care. And even though I had no keys, everybody else there did and was glad to unlock the door for me. The nurse on the chronic side had a twitching dimple; she nodded as she let me in but did not speak.

Thinking about this dream on awakening, I could see several things about myself I'd never have thought about otherwise—the way I confused writing and urinating, the way writing was elevated and inherited like a throne for me, the way I felt ashamed in the world as though my having been a mental patient still showed. And as other dreams as equally full and complex as this one kept coming, I began to wonder about the differences in myself these seemed to manifest. No longer just dreams about wandering lost. But why?

I couldn't answer that question then. But today I associate my dream world opening up with resuming writing. By 1982 I was also much more aware in many aspects of my life than I could bear to be back in 1963, the year I gave up writing. Perhaps, the years in between, I acquired the capacity to "act in instead of out." Acting out amounts to acting on unconscious feelings without knowing you're doing it. Repeated acting out also helps keep the trauma that drives it forgotten while momentarily reducing the tension of keeping feelings repressed. Probably I had, without knowing it, stopped writing for the same reason I couldn't really dream: to maintain the "bliss" of ignorance.

The problem is—as my life kept showing me—such "not knowing" is both painful and costly. Acting out by not eating had mutilated my life. While not writing had felt "free," a rejection of my parents' enslaving me as their favorite son, it had also ditched my lifelong wish. "Acting in," in contrast, allowed me to see such unconscious conflicts and errors in dreams so that they could be thought about rather than acted out. But the main reason for this was something I could do but not think about in 1982: depend on a reliable other to listen and witness my pain.

Different from earlier experience, meeting Rudy Schmidt aided rather than interfered with my writing. At the brunch my friend Allan gave to introduce us, Rudy's warmth and wit radiated throughout the room. Allan had told me all about him— a divorced, brilliant literature professor, writer, and gourmet cook who'd come to Raleigh from California after growing up in New York. Allan also said he thought Rudy was a little arrogant and prissy, but I could decide for myself. Talking with Rudy about his children and mine, about Raleigh restaurants and concerts compared to those he knew in Italy, Vienna, Lyon, and Munich, I could see how worldly-wise and discriminating the man was. I wondered if Allan mistook those qualities for arrogance. Because they complimented his Jewish warmth and use of Yiddish phrases, characteristics that I found most appealing, I wondered if Allan disapproved because he felt intimidated or comparatively less sensuous. I hoped Rudy would like me enough to ask me out.

He did. And that was the beginning of what turned out to be a long and exciting relationship. Rudy was writing his own book, a biography of Trollope. Furthermore, he delighted in my being a therapist and a fiction writer. He too was in analysis and could therefore understand my concerted efforts to overcome conflicts, peer into dreams, and strive for the good life I'd been deprived of earlier. His warmth and power as a person, his experience as a world traveler, and his lack of inhibition about expressing his feelings made me think he would be a wonderful mentor as well. How much fun we had! Rich in the best sense! Talking for hours, trying out new restaurants, comparing the pain and increasing freedom of our lives. Even when Rudy lied to me, I could confront him and felt both effective and relieved for doing so. He'd told me he was 56 and hadn't mentioned the first of his two marriages. Confronted, he said he'd forgotten he was 57 and had been afraid I'd reject him if I knew about the other brief marriage in his youth.

Rudy talked to me about many subjects. And when he did, all of him entered into the story: his warm brown eyes, his expressive face lighting up with enthusiasm, his large hands gesturing, and especially the drama in his voice laced with its New York accent. His excitement made me feel valuable myself for having found such a relationship, and this seemed proof of how my analysis was paying off. By late spring, we were clearly in love. . . with an intensity that was hard for Ben to take. In early summer, Rudy persuaded me to go to Europe with him.

That was terribly exciting. Money-conscious, overworked and inhibited, I'd never been anywhere outside the U.S. To travel abroad, and especially to do that with a warm and knowledgeable man who found me a "mensch," felt like truly and wonderfully coming into my own.

But in the process, something else happened that made me feel even closer to Rudy. Ben came home one night and said, "Mom, my friend Joe told me his mother said you'd been in and out of institutions."

The hair stood up on my arms as he spoke. I felt briefly angry at Joe's mother and threatened by the unease in Ben's voice, even as I recalled how a therapist we'd taken Pat to as an eight-year-old had said to me, "He doesn't need to know that." Now I still didn't want my life or my behavior to hurt my children.

"What did that make you think?" I asked Ben. "How did it make you feel?"

"I told him she was wrong. I knew you hadn't been in and out of institutions. But he said you had, before I was born."

"And now you're asking me?"

"Yes." His young face was sad and tense with reluctant dismay. We'd been in that same position many times with me confronting him about skipping class or staying out too late. This time the tables were turned.

"I don't think the phrase 'in and out of institutions' is correct," I said. "But the truth is that I was hospitalized as an adolescent due to a disease I'm sure you've heard about — anorexia nervosa. I couldn't eat because of psychological problems."

No answer. Just somber blue eyes holding onto mine.

"Maybe you're afraid I was crazy?"

"No. . . I couldn't think of you as crazy." His face still looked troubled. "But I'm sorry you were so sick. I feel mad at Joe's mother."

"Sure. But she doesn't really know. She was probably just repeating some rumor she's heard."

Ben still gazed back.

"Is there more you want to know? Are there other things you've heard?"

"No."

"If there are, now or later, please ask me."

"Okay."

I felt so lucky then that Rudy loved me. Sitting on the patio afterward, he held my hand and talked about my courage. I can't recall a time — before or after — when I felt as genuinely appreciated.

"I can't get over what a mensche you are," he said softly. "I've never known anyone who could so steadfastly maintain her integrity when attacked like this."

"Ben wasn't attacking. He was just talking to me about what he'd heard."

"But Joe's mother was. What a terrible thing for her to tell her son!"

"Maybe she didn't mean it that way, Rudy. Maybe she's even admiring of me."

"There you go again!" he almost shouted, hugging me tight preliminary to a kiss. "Honest. Decent. Able to consider the other person's feelings even in the midst of your own pain! How lucky I am to have found you, Lucy. I love you!"

Later I worked out private times, as they became possible, to talk to the other children about Ben's discovery. Before each conversation I was a little anxious and had to remind myself that there was no actual reason for guilt. Not only was I not responsible for the anorexia and the hospitalization, Ben was the youngest child I was sharing this information with. I needed to share it and thus invited each of them to talk with me about it directly. And sharing my history was not unnecessarily intruding on their feelings.

"Oh!" Pat sighed on the other end of the telephone. "That's terrible! I knew your family was bad. I knew you didn't eat a lot, but — Mother, I'm so sorry!"

In my mind's eye I had no doubt about the kind, pained expression on his 24-year-old bearded face. I didn't mind that, but I didn't want this news to undermine his feelings about himself. "It's long past now," I said. "But I wanted you to hear it from me firsthand rather than from Ben or someone else. When you all were little, I was advised not to tell you."

Lucy and I were able to talk about it during a walk. As a 22-year-old summa cum laude college graduate and newspaper reporter, she'd resumed a more comfortable relationship with me. Her long blond hair shielded her face on first hearing. But her response was like she usually is — matter-of-fact, less emotional than Pat's, but as direct with kindness as with anything else. "I'm not surprised," she said. "I've always known your life was hard. It probably makes me prouder of you." Then she turned her head to meet my gaze. "Did it make you ashamed to have to tell us?"

Jonathan was more problematic. A twenty-year-old college junior, he was hell-bent on shedding a rock-music ROTC-leader identity for a born-again Christian one. In keeping with this, he'd moved into a group living arrangement called His House. But when I spoke with him about my hospitalization for anorexia, he said, "I'm sorry, Mom," without a muscle stirring in his stalwart blond face. Then he added with blue eyes piercing mine, "But there is one comfort, Mom. You won't go to hell for that."

Through all this — confrontations with children and writing struggles — Dr. Howie kept sitting there listening. Listening. . . Listening. . . LISTENING in a way that filled the whole room with me. Making me what mattered, in pain and confused at first and then later clearer and more confident or sometimes even amazed at hearing myself. As in the earliest days, he still greeted me by sticking his head out into the waiting room and saying, "Hey! Come on back," while standing behind the door to hold it open for me with both hands. Some days he wore plain cowboy boots, some days the ones with gold toes. I didn't know about the earring. Maybe it was always there, maybe it wasn't. I very early stopped looking close enough to see. But his long mustache and ponytail were constants. Inside the office itself, of course, I couldn't see how he looked or what he was doing because I was lying on the couch, facing the empty wood paneling opposite him. Sometimes I thought he was taking notes; sometimes I wondered if he was filing his nails. I usually couldn't hear him rocking, but my fantasy was always that he did — ever so slowly. And he listened very closely. Always.

Over time the office had changed. Also, I'd gradually become comfortable and curious enough to take in more and more of its unconventional treasures. The waiting room was dark and small, the only natural light coming from a very narrow window the height of the room, near the entry. Its furnishings were a brown couch and chair — each with upholstered back and seat and dark wooden arms — and a table between them holding an old metal lamp and *New Yorker* and *Southern Living* magazines perpetually askew. The pictures on the wall were intriguing, but so disturbing to me early on that I was satisfied to let them be submerged by the little room's comforting, gloomy seediness. It was not until years later that I dared to study the paintings of the crouching, clearly terrified dog and the rhinoceros in his hobbling coat of bronze mail. Beside these, the familiar print of Gainsborough's *Blue Boy* always seemed relieving, though out of place. In the beginning, these pictures looked like mistakes to me, leftovers from Dr. Howie's attic. Later I saw them as wise and confrontive references to the problems we all brought there. The bathroom off the waiting room was cramped and brightly lit. After hearing other patients in there urinating and splashing water to remove evidence of their weeping, I never wanted to use it.

Going from the waiting room to the consulting room brought a sharp contrast. The corridor between the two was not only painted white, but further brightened by both sunshine and overhead lights. Its wall displayed an awesome series of four unique and intriguing masks. The most distant, the one I never could see straight on, was light colored and, for some reason, reminded me of Caesar. Beside it was a rugged brownish face with a piece broken out, as though fresh from the archeological dig. Still another, bold, braced for battle, and vivid with stripes of black, blue, and red, seemed utterly impenetrable. The one that most often caught my eye exiting the consulting room was white, with open mouth and taut cheeks that made it seem to be hallowing into the wind. There was never enough time to really grasp the meaning of any of these, but I repeatedly had the sense of their being eternal. . . or immortal. . . like people who'd once seen Dr. Howie or been in pain long before me or him.

Inside the consulting room itself, the atmosphere was always serene and professional with subdued warmth. Over time I came to expect it to be a little too cool in summer and a little overheated in winter. I also got used to its dimness because the Venetian blinds were closed.

If trying to take it in, there was a fair amount to see, however. The Oriental rug on the floor was balanced by a smaller, darker version at the foot of the couch. To the left, if I glanced quickly while entering, there was a small chalkboard on the wall over a straight chair with Howie's jacket — denim in spring, leather in winter — over it. To the right at just about that same point at the end of his ponderous desk (like a banker's or a school principal's, I always thought) was a table with several large Indian medicine men or Cochina dolls equipped with a variety of colorful robes, masks and instruments. Some were near naked. I have the impression that these figures came to be there gradually over the years. But I didn't pay them much attention until there was a whole crowd. And even then I never deeply pondered them, because I considered them Dr. Howie's material, while I went there for my own.

Lying down on the Victorian chaise, all I could see was wood paneling straight ahead and ceiling-to-floor bookcases beside it. When Dr. Howie was listening and my gaze was fixed on that wood, I sometimes had the fantasy that he could see, in the paneling we both faced, the very images my unconscious projected there. With greater familiarity and ease, my eyes began to stray occasionally to the books and bric-a-brac that filled the bookshelves.

Because years passed before I felt the need or reason to visually consider the bookshelves, I'm under the impression that there were fewer objects early on than later. When I did look, I was reminded of Father's books and bric-a-brac in the library of my childhood, especially his Venus de Milo. Eventually I realized that a phrase came to mind when I glanced over there, "Look but don't touch," which probably came from that childhood library too. I could only see a couple of Dr. Howie's keepsakes clearly — an odd piece of glass and metal that looked a little like a bird and a ceramic dish that looked like Don Quixote. Much more obvious, however, were some tiny heads or masks which he had accumulated over time and tacked to the vertical edges of the bookshelf. For years, I believe, there was just one — a dark, somber, gaunt-faced Indian with pigtails.

Another fantasy I had a few times was the sense that if I should suddenly stand up and turn to face Howie, I'd see a listening expression on his face like that of my dachshund Hansel in the yard. This fantasy has been constant over the years. But Dr. Howie is not a fantasy. He is very real. And he has made changes over the years too. For instance, somewhere in there he largely overcame his nervous sniff. Besides working at the Alcoholism Treatment Center all these years, filling Raleigh with hundreds of recovering alcoholics who speak his name reverently, he has a beautiful blond, brown-eyed wife and two children, one Ben's age and one a little younger. I think of Sistie, his wife, often both in that office and elsewhere. She's a psychiatric nurse and also sees patients somewhere in that same suite of offices. When I see her at clinical conferences, I both hate and love to see her — because she's so pretty and seems so kind, but also has a look, or something, that makes you know she loves to dance. I'd love to be like Sistie. I'm sure there are many different fantasies behind that wish, especially those about wanting to be loved by Dr. Howie. But I value his sterner side too. And even his confrontiveness. He's been that way with my attitudes more often than with my self. Like how he's never given up on my writing.

"By the way," he'd say, "You haven't mentioned your writing lately."

Sometimes I would remain silent. Sometimes I'd make excuses or express doubt. But over time I came to welcome those questions and to feel grateful for Dr. Howie's "challenge."

In and out of the next few years, my relationship with Rudy alternated between glorious and heartless, with a rich mix of sensuality, affection, control, and outrage. We married in 1986 and divorced in 1991 with many adventures and much growth both before and after. At the time, the intensity of our relationship seemed a major propellant toward freedom in both my life and writing. But because of Rudy's compulsive need to control and his tendency to disintegrate when he could not, a more valid image of his power is a dream I had after one of our earlier breakups:

Rudy evaporating upward into steam like dry ice.

In fact, the tried and true freedom drivers proved to be writing and psychoanalysis. And dreams were the place where these two came together. As I moved into working on an autobiographical novel, I happened to read a paper in which J.B. Pontalis spoke of dreams as transitional objects like teddy bears. He explained that dreams are unconsciously shaped to allow the dreamer to continue sleeping due to the illusion of being safely in the presence of the mother. In this way, Pontalis described dreams as helping the dreamer symbolize feelings in a manner that allowed psychological growth and development. I'd already seen that the salient truths with which dreams confronted me showed progress over time. Where once I'd been lost on a prairie, I'd eventually become able to see myself as a therapist-patient with the wrong name, wrong clothes, and missing key, and for whom sitting on a high toilet (throne?) made urination (writing) impossible. So it occurred to me it might be possible to facilitate what Pontalis said took place naturally. Could I use dream images not only to chart movement toward resolution of life and writing problems but also to actually produce such movement?

Thus began what I now call my "mountain-climber's grapple" use of dreams. With it I learned to use dream images and situations to think about the difficulties I had with writing and in dealing with children, friends, and patients. It enabled me to see when an unconscious need to maintain or avoid a certain feeling prevented me from being free to speak or write or think or do something else in the way I wanted to. The solution to these life problems could then be seen as requiring the ability to tolerate dream circumstances not yet experienced. This would result in my thinking about what in myself (my feelings and fantasies) was holding me back from the more desirable dream situation.

I used this strategy with two dreams several years later. Both related directly to my writing problems, but the first was set in Dr. Howie's consulting room and the second in the room Father had used for writing after World War II.

On Dr. Howie's couch, telling him about having drunk two and a half glasses of wine. Suddenly I noticed that my right hand was in a cast and, then, that this was responsible for a good feeling all over my body, a kind of white-light goodness that enveloped me. I was lying on my side, though, my left side, looking at the wall beside the couch and turned away from Howie.

The second dream occurred six months later:

I went back to the Shamrock Drive house where we raised the children. It belonged to other people, and they had a team of laborers in there renovating it. I went in and up to the second floor. There I entered the writing room Father used after the war; a sunny, high room that had been the nursery before we went to Washington. There I found my own black analytic couch. It was under the window looking west and in the same position as my desk is in my writing room now. I lay down on it face down. Father was working away at his writing table across the room. I began to have strong sexual feelings in my vagina. This indicated to me that I had to leave. I stood up to do so, so sad that I was weeping. Father was Dr. Howie and with him was this smaller copy of Dr. Howie. It made me even sadder to see that his boy could stay while I had to leave.

By comparing these two dreams, I was able to think in an emotional and physical way about what might happen if my own writing room were to become more important to me than Father's. I was able to see that staying a crippled writer felt good at the unconscious level because it enabled me to remain cared for (but not recognized) by Dr. Howie as a stand-in for Father. And then, looking at the strong sexual feelings in the dream, I could see how being an expressive female (with mouth or vagina) would be associated with the pain of having to leave Dr. Howie/Father.

Dr. Howie's response to my dream drive toward writing freedom was the same as his reaction to my happiness and distress with Rudy — continual listening and rocking.

chapter twenty-three

WINNING AND LOSING

In July 1987, when Rudy and I returned from a trip to England and Ireland I found a letter from my cousin Frank, publisher of the paper, with attached copies of correspondence with Ansbacher Literary Brokers about an anonymous offer to purchase *The News and Observer* for $285 million. Frank's response letter said that the stockholders were not interested. His letter to me said "That's a lot of money! But the stockholders I've talked to don't think it's enough or the right time."

That was the beginning of the end of the Daniels family as we had all known it. And a blessing in disguise for me—both financially and in terms of character-building confrontation. Cleves and Derick, having sold all the stock they owned at a low price in 1973, were not about to be told that $285 million was too little. At that point, too, with my adult children wanting graduate education and feeling increasingly at odds philosophically with the newspaper as Frank was running it, I wanted more say or more money if either were possible. By then Father's estate had been settled, so all four of us sisters (even Cleves) had sizable portions of stock. Frank's father had died the year before, but his estate tax was still pending. I joined Cleves and Derick and Derick's physician brother, Worth, then Chairman of the Board, in calling for a special stockholders' meeting to explore the possibility of individuals selling stock at a reasonable price.

That meeting in October 1987 was the first of many over the course of the next two years. This arduous and sometimes stormy process made it possible for me, Cleves, Adelaide, and Derick, as well as our children, to sell our stock at a fair price. But all of those meetings were uncomfortable or openly unpleasant. "Entitlement," which I'd learned about clinically, seemed to predominate—whether over the "treason" of someone wanting to sell their stock at a fair price, or the "insult" of having to pay interest on money borrowed from the paper, or the insistence that, as family members, there was no justification to limit the amount borrowed. At the first special stockholders' meeting I was most impressed by two things—how much need for money each of my cousins and sisters had, and how little sense of personal worth the individuals assembled in that room seemed to possess. It was easy to see (even for me, who'd always worshipped *The News and Observer* and the strong liberal voices of Father and Grandfather) that each of us had always had little significance in the family compared to that newspaper. We agreed that "in the interim" (until a solution could be found, we hoped within two years), major stockholders could borrow $1,000,000 on their stock and minor ones $100,000. As a result, despite the bitter somberness of that meeting, most people went away happy.

I, along with all my male cousins, was appointed to the "Structure Committee" charged with working out a means for those who wanted it to sell their stock at a fair price. We met periodically over the next two years, sometimes as often as once a month. We also hired experts to help us gather information, examine possible ways of responding to it, and negotiate with each other. Derick, an experienced and savvy media person in his own right, and I were on one side. Frank and Edgar were on the other. Worth, decent and obsessive physician that he'd always been, fulfilled his role as Chairman of the Board with a much-needed reasonable demeanor.

Since we were all minority stockholders in a closely-held corporation whose stock could only be sold to family members or back to the company, all of this might have ended in frustration. Frank, as publisher, owned a slightly larger proportion than the rest of us: because his 12.5% (compared to my 6.25%) had been augmented over the years by cousins who needed cash and sold him a few shares from time to time. Initially I, with my still idealized attitude about the paper and its meaning to Grandfather, wanted to sell it outright to a topnotch publisher who could both do the newspaper justice and save it from the scrappings of fourth generation stockholders who'd never really known it or the powerful voices of Father and Grandfather.

Because of Frank's personal investment in the paper, however, as well as a feeling several in my generation had about not wanting to part from this great institution, that was never seriously considered. Rather, we first agreed to have the value of the paper and its subsidiaries established, and later negotiated how to allow people to sell for a "fair" value. These deliberations, which pitted cousin against cousin, sister against sister, also made it obvious that once the sellers were gone (it was early established that a shareholder would have to sell all shares to get the "fair" value), the stockholder balance of power that remained would be quite different from the one we were then negotiating within. Toward the end of the negotiations, Adelaide and her adult children joined Cleves and Derick and me and our adult children. And while those who stayed in considered the rest of us "disloyal," some of them also needed money and we agreed to let such "stayers" sell a few shares as well. Because of all this, the outcome of our negotiations would be that Frank and his children would own close to 20% of the old structure, or 40% of the new. Thus, ironically, Frank clearly stood to gain through those of us who sold and left. Never again would stockholders like me have the clout to command a "fair" price. But the most profound gain for me was the opportunity to stand up to the family and leave it constructively.

Rudy and I took advantage of my opportunity to borrow money by building a beach house on a beautiful, wooded ocean-front lot in Carteret County. A creative decorator and would-be architect, Rudy worked energetically and excitedly with the architect and contractor to make our wishes a reality. And the house plans, with our personal wishes and ideas inserted by him, were truly wonderful. We delighted in studying them and planning the fun we'd have there together and with friends.

But as the house went up, it also became more and more a slave-driving demon for Rudy. Not only did it have to be perfect, and built the way he wanted, but perfect details had to be added exactly the way he'd directed. Not long after the outer walls were completed, he became so angry that we fired the architect. And like many of Rudy's actions, that one produced both relief and a new burden. The contractor was excellent, but Rudy felt even more driven than before to supervise the work. When I urged him to be more laid back, he turned his anger on me.

"What is the matter, Rudy?" I pleaded time and time again. "What is upsetting you so?"

"There you go again trying to make me the one at fault!" His voice was condemning.

"But, Rudy, you're angry all the time now. And you weren't before. I wonder if all this money I'm getting isn't upsetting you. Money can be hard on people's feelings, you know. Like I've told you about with the children and my family."

"Don't psychoanalyze me!"

"I'm not. But I don't understand, and I love you."

"Well, don't psychoanalyze me then!"

In this same period, in order to be prepared to deal with the money that I seemed increasingly likely to acquire, I was working to establish the Lucy Daniels Foundation, through which I hoped to help other creative people blocked like myself. Rudy was enthusiastic about this, too. But again, his not being able to control it was more than he could bear. I've looked back many times since to see whether that, or the beach house, or the money, or just the continuing closeness of our relationship with his love for me undermining his need to feel in control was the straw that broke the camel's back. At any rate, rather quickly Rudy's anger became increasingly explosive, even over seemingly insignificant issues. Until nothing would help.

And, of course, life doesn't stop for marital stress. My children were having more graduations and weddings than ever before. In May 1989, Ben graduated Phi Beta Kappa from UNC, and in July he married Sara Bell. In May 1990, Jonathan received his Masters of Divinity from Westminster Theological Seminary in Philadelphia, and that same weekend Lucy graduated from UNC Law School. Despite the stress in our marriage, Rudy accompanied me to all those events and did not complain. He had become more angrily withholding, however, almost seeming to say, with his scowling silence, that he was being virtuous even though conditions were unbearable. I sometimes asked, "Rudy, is there something I can do to help you feel better?"

"You take care of you, and I'll take care of me."

So we kept trying. And because of Rudy's periodic warmth and excitement, I sometimes felt hopeful. Even when his anger did erupt, it frequently was so surprising and out of context that it seemed more like an irrational fit than an attack to be taken seriously. I labored, with all the emotional awareness acquired in my analysis, to attend to and consider his anger without being controlled by it. But Rudy, whom, I'd say now, had to feel in control in order to feel safe, didn't respond positively to that.

One Friday, when we planned a routine beach trip to check on the progress of the house, now remains a painful memory of rupture. We were both in good spirits that day, and Rudy, in response to my urging and his own better sense, decided that it would be all right if I relieved him of the task of making the sandwiches for our lunch. He wanted me to make them at 8:00 a.m. before I went to analysis and saw a patient. I told him I couldn't, but that I would make them at 10:30, in plenty of time for us to leave at 11:00. When I did as I'd planned—returned at 10:20 and slipped into my beach clothes while telling him how excited and in love I felt, he said nothing at first. But when he came into the kitchen and found me making the sandwiches, he bristled with rage.

"What are you doing?!"

"Making the sandwiches."

"Why are you making them now? I told you to do it at 8:00!"

"I know, but I told you I couldn't do it then. They'll be ready in plenty of time."

Rudy slammed a cabinet door and threw the kettle into the sink. "Why is it that you just have to spite me?!"

"Rudy," I stopped slicing the tomato to make eye contact with him. "I'm not trying to spite you. I'm making the sandwiches just the way you like. The timing—"

He opened and slammed a cabinet door three times while grimacing at me. Then he stomped out.

Dropping the knife and the tomato, I followed him into the bedroom. "Listen, Rudy, cut it out!" I shouted. "You're acting like a baby. I'm not going to the beach or anywhere else with you behaving like this."

He didn't reply, and I returned to the kitchen to finish the sandwiches.

Once they were ready, I went back into the bedroom and declared, "Rudy, we need to talk about what's happened. We need to talk right now, before we leave. The weekend will be miserable if we don't."

"There's nothing to talk about. As self-centered and spiteful as you have to be, how can talking help?"

"Rudy, you take my not being absolutely controlled by you as spiteful. It's not. It's—"

"See! How can we talk? If you won't take responsibility for your behavior, how can talking get us anywhere?!"

"Rudy! You interrupted me. Please listen!"

It went on like that for twenty minutes or more. Then my stubbornness about the need to talk and Rudy's worry that we'd be too late to meet the contractor collided. "Look," he said with sudden evenness, "We're not getting anywhere. Can't we just agree to disagree and go to the beach? We can talk about these things later when we're less upset."

"Okay," I agreed. "I just want us to be clear enough not to ruin the weekend."

So we departed, with Rudy at the wheel and me in the position of doling out lunch when he got hungry. But we weren't thirty minutes down the road when something I said triggered another explosion. I don't know what it was, so I can't claim or deny responsibility. All I can recall now is our flying down the highway with him screaming at me about my "mean mouth" and my "self-centered coldness."

"Stop, Rudy!" I shouted back. "Shut up!" It took three blasts like that before he quieted down to hear the rest. "It's not good for either of us for you to be abusive like this. But doing it when you're driving is dangerous."

Rudy drove on in silence after that, stony silence that lasted through the weekend.

Saturday night I dreamed:

In the kitchen of the house of my childhood. I was married to this long-haired dark lady who looked like a witch or that schizophrenic woman with a crooked walking stick I once tested for Dr. Lawrence. She was sitting at the kitchen table playing solitaire. I wanted to play UNO, and she agreed. But then I saw that her deck was made up of cards from lots of other decks. I said, "We need to get a straight deck." But she refused. Then I said I wasn't going to play unless the deck was fixed. She didn't budge. I said, "Well then, I'm not going to eat any of your food. I'm going to just drink coffee. You can eat your food yourself!" And I left.

On Dr. Howie's couch, I said, "While I may still be ambivalent about my sexuality, I'm not at all ambivalent about enjoying myself." Dr. Howie rushed over and threw a rug on top of me.

Our troubles didn't get better.

Because Rudy's anger spiraled, we separated while Howie was on vacation.

Yet the end itself was quiet and deliberate. I told Rudy I couldn't take his continuing abuse. He told me he'd made a mistake in marrying me, that he'd been trying to love me the way I wanted to be loved but couldn't. He even added that he couldn't be married to anyone, that dating and affairs were as close as he could get. Since he also said he couldn't afford to separate, I agreed to help him. He moved out.

By the time I told Dr. Howie, I was calm. Despite depression over again having chosen a mate who'd become abusive, I didn't share Rudy's view that our marriage had been a mistake. I'd really loved him. I still did.

When I finished talking that first day, Dr. Howie was silent before he remarked, "Well, I'm certainly sorry. But sad and lonely as this decision naturally makes you, it may open the way for considerable growth."

Confronted again by the unnerving abyss of aloneness, I strained to keep my focus on patients and writing. Then several weeks after Rudy had moved out, I dreamed:

The light was flashing on my answer machine. Pushing its message button, I heard Dr. Howie's voice terribly upset, talking about canceling two of my appointments. I recalled the time his brother died and that his message then had been calm and businesslike. He was much more distressed now. Why? His voice screamed: "I am NEVER coming back!! NEVER!!" God! I thought, he is upset! What's happened?! In my mind, the idea came: his wife ran off with Tom Inman; he feels betrayed. Next his voice shrieked, "And you can just take that furniture back to Wilmington!" So upset he was talking crazy! I marveled in pain.

Why Dr. Howie screaming? And what was all that about taking furniture back to Wilmington? I recalled having gone to Wilmington once for the funeral of Bibba's Aunt Emily. In the cemetery there, because of what Wilmer had told me after I left the hospital, I'd made it a point to seek out the grave marker of Babs and her infant son. Still, why now? Of course, I was angry – at my lot, at Rudy for not being able to continue our life together, at Dr. Howie and analysis for not fixing my life after all these years. Then I realized that Howie's screaming was like Rudy's had been at the end, and that both had filled me with the same disintegrating distress as Father's voice had in my adolescence.

By the next day, Howie's talk about "growth" set me pondering how becoming hurt and angry enough to "erase" Rudy might help my writing. I never could do either, but a month or so later I had another dream that seemed to insist I stay on task:

12/10/90

I was in a dormitory suite with several other people the morning of exams. My exam was at 3:00, but the others left me alone there long before that. Sitting in this church pew, facing high-up sunshine, I realized I'd urinated on my beautiful red dancing skirt. I got up and decided to put a white skirt over it to hide the wet. But standing in front of a long mirror to see how I looked, I realized that the white one wasn't long enough to cover the red one. Also, that below those skirts I was wearing high black walking (or riding?) boots that were real stolid and businesslike and ruined the dancing effect of either skirt. By then it was nearly time for my exam, and I was worried because I hadn't prepared in the usual way. Because I was already experi-

enced and proficient in the subject matter, I hadn't studied like a greasy grind. And that made me anxious even though I'd made a deliberate decision not to. Suddenly I got frantic about having nothing to write with. But in the bathroom drawer in the packet that used to hold my diaphragm, I found two substantial black pens. Black and plain-looking like the boots.

Entering this dream in the copy book quickly to ward off forgetting, I knew that the urinating and the red dancing skirt had to do with both writing and sexuality. Odd, though, anxiety about not being anxious. Were those pens the penises Mommy and Father had pushed off on me after all? Or perhaps, this dream, occurring on Adelaide's birthday, connected today's hurt and "test" with how Father's snapping, "You're big enough to walk," while carrying Adelaide, had kept me "walking" self-sufficiently ever since to avoid more hurt. I decided Pontalis would have seen the walking boots as transitional phenomena. But what would be required to trade them in for dancing shoes? Only while pondering this did the auditory similarity of "riding" and "writing" come to mind.

chapter twenty-four

UNPROTECTED

I never did ask Dr. Howie what he meant about "opportunity for growth." But I now believe he understood something I was still blind to then. Though feeling lost because the person I loved most had again turned against me — being outside my family, less confined by guilt than after Tom, and occupied by the demands of the Foundation and the Lucy Daniels Center for Early Childhood (a psychoanalytic pre-school I funded), I was shedding invisibility for the first time since *Caleb* was published.

But even without guilt, my return to loneliness was hard to accept. Once again, it felt like a permanent sentence. My only companion was writing, which didn't assuage the misery but did keep me occupied. And when I did write, thirst for the freedom to do it well drove me fiercely. By then, both dreams and Dr. Howie's listening had made seeing myself in the presence of an accepting other something I could count on. And dreams were no longer my only windows to the unconscious. Using the same deep concentration useful with dream associations, I'd become able to reach unexpected insights during such mindless activities as walking on the treadmill, driving, or taking a shower. In this way I began to grasp the power of fantasy in my life.

The dictionary defines fantasy as "an imagined event or condition fulfilling a wish." From my perspective, unconscious fantasies are self-concepts and ways of perceiving that we put on, like costumes for a masquerade ball, so we can survive in places we feel require disguise or tolerate ourselves in unbearable roles. They differ from conscious disguises in that the main person fooled is oneself and in that, since they aren't recognized, there is no choice about wearing them.

Sometimes such fantasies originate from pressure outside the individual. In our family, for instance, Father made it seem lovable to be self-destructive, and girls were expected to be powerless and unintelligent. At other times fantasies spring forth defensively inside the individual in response to unaccepted drives or feelings. Thus, a very angry person may feel and act like a wimp, or a terrified person may feel and behave like a menace. Or a starved anorexic can feel fat. Such fantasies are accepted as facts like all the other forgotten facts we carry around in our heads. Yet, being dynamically unconscious, these fantasies have properties that ordinary facts lack: they can contain opposite attributes side by side, as in bisexuality or a menacing wimp; or one fantasy can represent several beliefs at once — a child suffering from a learning disability may unconsciously be refusing to be murderous, avoiding repeated sexual attack, hiding an unacceptable identity, and more, all in the single symptom. Robert Stoller (in *Sexual Excitement*, 1979) compared fantasies to microdots, the technique developed by the Nazis during World War II, which made it possible to print an entire photograph in an area no larger than a period. Stoller's comparison speaks to one of fantasy's most salient characteristics — the fact that a small mannerism, idea, image or remark may be the outermost trace of a much more fully developed belief.

By the time I lost Rudy, despite my failures and continuing neurotic limitations, I had developed comfort with and capacity for self-observation that it is impossible to acquire without the assistance of an accepting other. Furthermore, given my inheritance, I could keep pursuing my voice without the interference of an insurance company refusing to pay when my problems were no longer life-threatening. Thus, even as writing, working as a therapist, and increasing adventures in the world confronted me with my limitations, being well educated and relatively free of anorexia made me able to hope that other self-imposed smallnesses could be given up as well.

Gaining awareness of beliefs that have previously controlled one's life from the unconscious level makes it possible to examine these fantasies, including their underpinnings and destructive "benefits," and, thus, acquire the capacity to shed their unconscious bondage. But these fantasies feel like reality itself. Recognizing them as only illusion can seem as devastating as an earthquake. Or as shocking as recognizing the emperor's new clothes when you are the emperor. In my case, however, the shift was just as often from negative to positive — I discovered that I was not really as helpless or evil as I'd always believed. Sometimes dreams were the windows that revealed these fantasies; sometimes a waking experience would trigger a moment of remarkable insight.

These discoveries came in two main forms. The first involved suddenly recognizing an uncomfortable state I'd never perceived before. For instance, standing in the supermarket line one afternoon I had the horrible sense that if anyone looked at me, they'd see my body was riddled with holes. The second form, though less upsetting initially, required much more emotional work. It involved feeling miserable about some current condition, such as inarticulateness, loneliness, or resistance to some expected activity, and looking into myself for what felt-to-be-essential fantasy was being maintained by this debilitating and confining behavior.

In the first case, the shock came from recognizing that a fantasy had already been given up — that, in fact, other people could see my needs; the emotional work required was to get more comfortable with the fantasy's absence and to use this release to seek even more freedom. For instance, what could account for my body feeling riddled with holes? How could I have benefited from such a belief? Or what had hidden the belief from me before? How did this limit me? In the second case, my misery came from a cruel but felt-to-be-necessary fantasy still intact; the work required was to oppose it and get to where it no longer shackled me.

Being able to think about feelings, fantasies, and dreams together also allowed me to recognize and remove writing impediments much more easily. By then I had come to understand that problems and fantasies in one area were likely to be active in others as well. For instance, during some of my wonderful travels and happy times with Rudy, the feeling of being repulsively fat had loomed large. Indeed, during a stay in a magnificent Irish castle, I'd had to admonish myself, "If you're going to keep on having good times like this, you're going to just have to put up with feeling fat." My writing difficulties were harder to deal with. But I gradually began to see that my unconscious was striving to starve and constrict the writing much as it had done to my body. My issues then were how to recognize these constrictions and how to deal with my unconscious to relieve them. None of this process was easy, but it did allow me to stop writing "crazy," that is, to see what the problems were and begin to see that the saboteur in me created them on purpose. Only later did I become able to see the crucial part this played in my sense of self.

Dreams were how I first came to see that for me eating, speaking and writing were equivalent. Later they also showed me that clothes and writing were both ways I presented myself to the world. In addition, I came to understand that unpleasant dreams often accompany a positive change in waking life and that pleasant dreams sometimes reflect the unconscious's comfort resulting from a conscious loss or failure. And from Mort Reiser's *Memory in Mind and Brain*, I learned about how our experiences are filed in memory according to feelings present at the time. As a result, I began to learn that I needed to take small details of dream settings and dilemmas seriously in order not to continue painful acting out in the form of wooden writing.

All of this led to a new realization about the interaction between internal and external events: that dreams affect behavior and interactions in the world just as life experience produces dreams. Also, that just as unconscious fantasies are expressed in dreams, a dream and its conscious processing can alter unconscious fantasies. Inner and outer are not nearly as separate as most people assume.

In those early days of floundering alone in the rich life I'd expected to share with Rudy, the everyday personal me plodded precariously between the often surprising inner world of dreams and fantasies, and the sometimes overwhelming outer arena of public recognition. Staying the same in the eyes of others had always been a comfort I needed. Having it ripped away again with my sudden changes in fortune produced a far-reaching insight: not staying the same in the eyes of others, feeling unrecognized, or, worse still, rejected where once I'd been warmly accepted, or important where once I'd been insignificant, all brought on the same blurred, draining-away sense of lostness I'd dreaded since early childhood. Dr. Howie was the one person with whom this dismaying disorientation did not occur. Talking with him, I felt most changed but still myself. Writing in the copy book was a close second.

Ironically, my own consulting room, where I could usually count on patients' need for me to remain constant, was the setting for several confrontations. Fortunately, by 1990 I'd already had enough such surprises that I knew how to weather them. But I learned an important lesson from the publicity I received when I established the Lucy Daniels Foundation and the Lucy Daniels Center for Early Childhood: dealing with patients about my being a millionaire is little different from dealing with their discovery that I've written novels or that I was once institutionalized.

Years earlier, after about eighteen months of therapy, a depressed patient made a passing remark about "your having been institutionalized with anorexia."

When I responded with, "How did it make you feel to hear that?" she'd replied, "I'd heard it before."

"Oh? Still, how did hearing it affect you?"

"That's really why I chose you. . . I mean. . . I figured if I was going to do this, I'd want someone who could understand, someone who'd seen the other side and got better."

In 1990, when the Foundation paid half a million dollars for the land for its building, The News and Observer's business story described me as having endowed both Foundation and Center with millions obtained through sale of the newspaper's stock. My patient, Roger Troxler, couldn't bear it then, and every so often now he tells me that he still can't. How unfair it is that he has to work two jobs to see me twice a week at a reduced fee! That I came from such a wealthy and respected family and can have anything in the world I want, while he's never been able to! I agree with him about the unfairness and assure him I don't see how he could not be angry. Also, that it's an inequality we're stuck with and therefore will have to keep talking about. But oddly, though essential for his therapy, these repetitions benefit me as well — by making name, family, money, and anorexia just details of a life.

In 1991, the American Psychoanalytic Association voted me a Distinguished Friend of Psychoanalysis. Besides being a great honor, that felt a gratifying turning of tables since I, years earlier, like many other psychologists, had been denied analytic training by The American because I had a Ph.D. rather than an M.D. degree. Once, that exclusion had weighed heavily on me — exacerbating my life-long experience of being locked out. Later, however, Bryant Welch, a lawyer friend and clinical classmate of mine, had won a restriction of trade suit against The American. Along with other evidence, he'd used my two rejection letters from the Duke-UNC Psychoanalytic Institute.

Anger about being barred from analytic training had driven me to attend clinical conferences wherever they were in the country and to buy psychoanalytic supervision in order to learn as much as possible from the cases I was treating. I'd also read up clinicians like Winnicott, Guntrip, Fairbairn, McDougall, Kubie, and Schafer just as I'd once devoured Hemingway and Faulkner. As a result, when Bryant's suit removed the barriers to psychologists, I no longer wanted psychoanalytic training. Acutely aware of life's limitations, I wanted to devote whatever time I could to reclaiming the writing I'd abandoned earlier.

Nevertheless, an honor is an honor. Genuinely pleased to receive notice that The American would honor me at its December 1991 meeting at the Waldorf in New York City, I privately resolved to send my autobiographical novel to my old agent, Brandt and Brandt, before then. This felt like a conscious effort to ward off "lostness" and to not remain invisible and silent while taking care of others: I wanted to remain true to my writing. In fact, I decided to send the novel to another agent as well as Carl Brandt.

Sometimes it felt eerie the way life kept clipping right along as I labored to integrate both external changes and new insights into my identity. Aging and medical research required me to add lifting weights to my calcium/treadmill regimen. Ben and Sara moved to Philadelphia so Ben could pursue a Masters of Divinity at Westminster Theological Seminary. Pat was earning his doctorate in history at UNC, but seldom saw me because of his pain and anger about my divorce from Rudy, repeating his despair about the failure of my marriage to his father. I wondered if Pat felt that he couldn't be a man without being abusive. Whenever I saw Jon, who was still at Westminster pursuing his Masters of Theology, I sorely missed his childhood realism and sense of humor. Lucy, who was clerking for the Chief Justice of the North Carolina Supreme Court, fell in love with a flamboyant but salt-of-the-earth Catholic newspaper reporter named Billy Warden. In August they staged a more fun wedding than I'll likely ever see again. Billy had "Billy Loves Lucy" painted in pink and white on a Wade Avenue billboard. And I had a wonderful time dancing at their wedding, more spiritedly than ever before, with Billy and all three of my sons.

Before and after the wedding I worked determinedly, sometimes urgently, to get the novel ready to send out by mid-November. During that time, too, my divorce from Rudy was finalized. Consciously neither of these was upsetting. The end of Rudy had been final from his leaving. The issue with the novel was to get it out in completed form so that I wouldn't have shortchanged it for Lucy's wedding or The American's award. But unconsciously a storm was raging. And the mixture of unarticulated anxieties about recognition of both my book and myself only trickled into awareness through dreams. The most salient one occurred over Thanksgiving weekend:

I went to see Murphy Evans. Standing directly in front of him (like he was a Buddha), he seemed fine. But looking closer, I could see his wrists were bandaged. . . Then I was in my office (only it was in our house on Garfield Street in Washington). I was going out at 6:00 p.m. to play with the analysts. But I stashed my wallet in the back of the bottom desk drawer along with my pretty blue denim dancing bootlets. There was clear, maybe bullet-proof, plastic over this drawer. Outside I could see the analysts I normally didn't know because this was the only time they came out of their offices.

I thought Murphy (who had recently been attacked by a thief) represented me with still-damaged (though out-of-the-cast) writing. Washington really had been the place I'd gone out and made friends of my own. "But, now that I have them, why leave those dancing boots hidden in the bottom drawer?" I said to Dr. Howie.

"Maybe to deny your power?" Howie asked.

Made sense to me. But then I had another hideous idea.

"Would you say I'm doing what my parents wanted — having power or a penis in my drawers that I don't want the analysts to see?"

"That would be a problem. Your parents' basic problem — their belief that all power and worth came from penises. But do you need to hang onto it?"

Later, at home on the treadmill, I recalled how, in Washington, I hadn't felt isolated after the first year. But why not bring my power and the analysts together? Why not go everywhere with everybody in those pretty denim bootlets?

The terrifying dream that followed probably answered those questions. But I couldn't recognize that then.

Terrifying. I was standing on a hillside, and took a risk — something as simple as breathing in (or speaking?). Anyway, when I did it I was obliterated; my insides, especially my mind, were blasted to emptiness.

Awake, I connected the feelings in the dream with ECT. On the treadmill, "untouchable" kept coming to mind. In analysis Dr. Howie suggested I might have a fantasy that being "untouchable" could preserve me against the double jeopardy of Carl Brandt's response to my book and The American's honoring me. That's when I decided to consult another literary agent as well.

But in the end neither terror nor fantasies saved me.

One of my most painful conscious experiences of positive and negative affecting me at once happened at the meetings of The American that December. On the day I received my certificate as a Distinguished Friend of Psychoanalysis, two different agents told me my novel wasn't publishable. Both said, with slightly different wording, "You really have two stories here, and they interfere with each other. . . A memoir might work better — if you don't mind the work and the exposure." But as disappointing as that was to hear, my tears only started in the elevator, in response to an unknown gentleman's saying, "Dr. Daniels, congratulations on your honor for all the fine things you're doing. Your moving remarks on receiving it made me proud to be an analyst."

Back in Raleigh, the holiday season felt miserable, even with the children present and Ben and Sara's announcement that they expected a baby in June. But again the place where I could see the misery close enough to try to understand was in a dream:

An old lady was kept in solitary confinement by a sinister old man who may have been a doctor. I visited her. She was not only old but in poor health; she may have been crotchety. When I left, I realized that her keeper was going to kill her. Perhaps out of rage or exasperation or to get her money or to just get rid of her. I was horrified, but didn't know whether to tell anyone or not. If I did, the hateful keeper might deny it or charge me with libel or get me charged as an accomplice. I was also afraid that if I didn't and they found out I'd known, they'd charge me with murder, too. And not telling would make me feel terribly, terribly guilty.

Such intense, inescapable fear and guilt were the very same feelings I had struggled with in anorexia.

"Who do you think the keeper is?" Dr. Howie asked.

"Father maybe. Or both my parents. . . It is like me held prisoner, like you've said, by the way they fought through me. Who do you think he is?"

"Well, I don't know. I wonder if it could be me?"

"How? I don't get it. The man looked more like Rudy."

"Well, I wonder if part of you doesn't feel like I'm killing the you that belongs in solitary confinement?"

Later, it occurred to me that both Tom and Rudy had been people who'd helped me maintain an isolating envelope of fear and self-denial. Thinking that made me hopeful that having been able to shed those external skins, I could also shed some internal ones. I could see that staying dead was a painful but high priority for my unconscious. Even the revised and shortened novel manuscript, I was beginning to see since its rejection, had had an outer wall that killed its inner vitality. But could such deadening skins really be discarded? Or would they inevitably be replaced by duplicates?

Life doesn't stop while such questions are addressed. But sometimes its movement can provide the same distracting external engagement of consciousness as the treadmill or driving. Unable to decide about the book — whether to hunker down and convert it to a memoir or stash it in a drawer to be forgotten, I moved ahead with plans to renovate the upstairs library where Rudy had wanted me to work beside him. Rudy had liked the library's seedy darkness. Maybe the dark shadows with just an overhead light over the writing table had made the idea of us writing together feel cozy or romantic to him. I, on the other hand, had not been able to do that because it made me feel controlled and boxed in. That had been a major disappointment for Rudy. But with him gone, the idea of making the library a bright, cozy, even exciting room for me alone took on surprising importance. With the skylights, cathedral ceiling, and white paint the contractor promised, I anticipated a wonderful, bright sitting room and possibly an alternative to the upstairs bedroom which I'd already converted to a writing room. Both felt considerably more expansive than the copy book or the yellow pad on which I did my other writing.

It was also that winter that I discovered Dr. Howie had a motorcycle! Distressed by both the surprise and the fear of his being injured, I expressed my anger and disappointment to him directly. But of course, he just listened and went on riding. Nor did he let this distract him from referring to the copy book as a container that interfered with me doing my real writing. Sometimes that made me angry too. I told him so more than once.

By late spring, 1992, I was consciously trying to decide whether or not to convert my novel to a memoir. There was still Dr. Howie's gentle nagging, and the beckoning of the new shining writing room. But the strongest motivation was my own frustrated sense of being bound and gagged. The more I tried to decide, the more I knew that what I wanted was release — escape from the book in any way possible. Once again, dreams showed me the emotional chains with which I needed to grapple. By July the main issue was no longer whether converting the book would be good or bad for me. Going public like that with actual names was a definite dare. But showing myself by speaking out had become something I absolutely had to do to be free. Deciding I was up to a memoir if the manuscript was, I began re-reading it. In the process, along came a dream packed with clues:

I gave up an important suitcase or pocketbook — like my neat, versatile roll-aboard suitcase-luggage carrier. . . Then I was kneeling down naked and folded up on myself on the floor of Dr. Howie's office. All wet and weeping mightily about this loss, with my back to Dr. Howie. I was scrunched-up, as if I'd been inside the suitcase myself. . . Next, I was with my artist friend, Eleanor, outdoors beside a pair of trees a few feet apart. There was a board nailed to and joining both. Looking at the board, she saw this scary children's art work (clay monster faces) on it and loved them. A little boy who lived with elves under the roots of one tree had made this art. Eleanor wanted to leave a note to him on the back of one of her pictures to say how much she liked his work. I knew this boy and suggested that she tell him in her note that she was a friend of mine. But Eleanor didn't want to. . . Then I went out in the garage of our Shamrock Drive house in a nightgown you couldn't see through to meet a friend. But before she arrived, a cute little four-year-old blond girl came up with this long-haired, pimply-faced, flaky-looking pedophile I once evaluated. He introduced both of them to me, "I'm this bigamist who lives up the hill there by Adelaide, and she's the daughter of my neighbor, the kidnapper.". . . Then riding to the airport at night in a van with lots of other people, I thought I might have forgotten my bags. The others said they'd seen me with them. We stopped and turned on the lights to look. I had left the roller one but still had the red canvas carry-on with two handles.

It thrilled me to see myself out of the "suit" case which had confined me to being my parents' perfect, endlessly versatile little extension! Even though I could also see and feel in my body that this loss and freedom were painful. The two trees recalled the trees for the hammock of my childhood; the board between them was at the height we'd swung to when it was pushed highest, so that we could bring back "money." Did Eleanor represent Bibba or the artistic part of me? Was the boy under the tree roots me as my parents' boy or

Caleb? His being under the roots made me wonder if I feared losing myself if I became artistically successful. It seemed clear that the man who called himself a bigamist represented my view of Father's sexuality, taking advantage of all kinds of people, children as well as wives. But I knew, too, that me in a nightgown you couldn't see through must be me not able to see a lot due to still not being awake. Clearly, there was more that I knew and didn't know that I knew. Pondering how to exchange that nightgown for the gold dress I'd liked in an earlier dream, it occurred to me that the nightgown could also be a shroud or "denial of life" that I'd always needed to be like Babs. Or to conceal my feelings and, thus, be acceptable to both my parents at once. Then I suddenly realized that the board must represent "bored," my defense against exhilaration!

Comparatively, the decision to change the genre of my book turned out to be easy. Anyway, I did decide; not in Howie's office but before my first session back after Labor Day. After a dream about having to choose between flying down off a cliff directly onto a major highway or taking the long, safe road around to it.

"How did you feel?" Howie asked.

"Scared."

"About?"

"Crashing, I think. It was Highway 70 West."

"Your route to Chapel Hill?"

"Yes."

But, as hopeful as Dr. Howie's question made things seem in referring to my route to the university and freedom, my fear turned out to be right. Though the final decision to use my own voice to tell my story had seemed as easy as flying, the emotional consequences of doing so soon felt as cataclysmic as those from jumping off a cliff. As I got under way, the most pervasive consequence of working on the memoir turned out to be physical and emotional pain. After removing the book's outer shell, I began to industriously fill out and connect its inner portions in a way that appeared effective. But this was accompanied by relentless physical aching and uncomprehending emotional anguish. One afternoon in early December, while feeling shaky and weak, I suddenly realized: maybe I have to write ineffectively in order to stay in solitary confinement. Maybe this pain is due to losing that preserving isolation. That night I dreamed:

It was on the news that the earth had grown larger. This meant to me that it could barrel out to the edge of space and fall over the side. I was too terrified to read any more about it. But then I was relieved to hear other people talking who'd read in Newsweek *that space was infinite and that, therefore, barreling out to new parts of it didn't mean falling over the side.*

The "largeness" made me think Dr. Howie had been right about his being the "keeper" who was going to murder me, as that woman held hostage. For my unconscious, the only alternatives seemed to be solitary confinement or growing so large that I'd be lost over the edge of space.

chapter twenty-five

CHANGING SKINS

Dr. Howie still came to the door every time and stoically leaned his mustached face out to say, "Hey. Come on back." And inside it was almost the same — him rocking and me talking. Only I couldn't hear the rocking and he was saying even less than before. Sometimes I talked a lot, trying to make him hear the severity of my suffering. But sometimes, without my understanding why, all the words left my mouth. I'd still be full of things to tell him, but not able to. In those periods I'd study the wall paneling and the books in the bookcase beside it. A couple of times I had to laugh and tell Dr. Howie about how the shrunken Indian head on the bookcase resembled him. Despite that, analysis felt terribly lonely. I knew Howie was back there, and I had no doubt he believed my pain. But he didn't understand it. Sometimes he'd just sit there almost the whole session, while I was silent. Until near the end when he'd say, "Although I know it's little compensation, since your pain is accompanied by productive writing and dreaming, there does seem reason to hope for relief. . . I'll have to stop us there and see you back next time."

Days later when we were talking about my self and my writing needing me to separate from Father, it occurred to me that because of having wanted Father's voice, I might feel I'd stolen it.

"The problem isn't that you incorporated his voice," Dr. Howie said. "For a little girl to love her father and to have that experience of taking him into herself is entirely normal. The problem is that other things happened around that as well."

My eyes walked up and down the shelves of books. "Like what?"

"You're the person who's labeled it stealing. Do you understand why?"

"Probably, like you've said, because I feel it would be wrong to be a writer whose success overshadows Father."

Silence.

"But I can't bear to be a writer who's not that good either."

Silence.

"What do I have to do to get out of this bind?"

"It's much easier to say than to do."

"What?"

"Reject him and join him."

The next week I bought a small stereo system for the renovated room and began writing there most of the time. The writing went well but aroused new guilt.

In analysis Dr. Howie asked, "Are you aware of feeling a traitor?"

I had to think. "Yes. Maybe not believing I'm a writer is a way of withholding the full force of my voice so as to not feel a traitor."

The sound of rocking.

"But that just keeps me enslaved by Father. Probably I've also crippled myself so as to not murder him."

"Yep. . . But there's more to it than that."

"What?"

"Children in families like the one you grew up in do not feel they can go on existing separated from their parents. They know unconsciously that their parents do not really care about them, that out of sight means out of mind. You remember. What happened when Bibba was sent to boarding school?"

"Her place was empty at the table. And, you're right. We didn't talk about her."

"Well, that kind of not mattering feels worse than death. Children will do anything to avoid it. I'm sure you've seen it clinically. Children whose bodies bear the scars of violent parents still cling to those parents for dear life."

"Yeah. I do know about that."

"What they dread is nonexistence. . . Your existence in your family depended on remaining your parents' good child whose achievements reflected glory on but did not surpass them."

"In other words, I'm afraid that if I become and feel a writer who's successful in her own right, I'll cease to exist?"

"Right."

"I know that feeling. It's connected to vanishing. Popping like a soap bubble and leaving no trace."

"Pretty scary."

"How can I stop this?"

Rocking.

More rocking without an answer.

"By seeing it for what it is?. . . By claiming my anger? Or? What would have happened if I'd been able to say to Dr. Mitchell, 'You are being unethical. Behave yourself! I'm not going to put up with this another minute!'"

"I don't think you could have said that then."

"I didn't. But why?"

"Because if you'd said that, you'd have felt like you had to leave. I don't think you could have stood that then."

Later, on the treadmill, I thought about whether I could bear to leave Dr. Howie. In analyzing my losses, that issue had come up many times — a separation that I would need and want to make at some point in order to fully claim my own life. It pained me to think of that, but it also made me feel good to know that I could. And to have the answer that Dr. Howie and I had discussed more than once: the time to leave would be when I was ready and when not losing him would interfere with my growth.

Continuing to write in the renovated room, I became consciously aware of wanting to put myself out there IN PRINT in order to claim my own existence. And one day, working in this manner, hatred of Dr. Mitchell soured my mouth. What a horrible person! A doctor who, knowing the terrible pain and crippling problems of my life, had taken advantage of me in the most damaging way possible! Should I confront him even after nearly eighteen years? Not to impact Dr. Mitchell, who by then was old and probably retired, but to free myself?

Then, too, Father's cruelty loomed larger than ever. Almost as if the words streaming out of my pen fueled those feelings. What a terrible thing to say to a three-year-old: "You have no feelings or sexuality!" How horrible to ridicule a little girl's fear by calling her "Casper Milquetoast."

None of this anger seemed to interfere with the writing. Rather the two felt unrelated. The words and pages poured out of me while the anger about these separate issues seemed felt, voiced, and unloaded. Trying to be observant, it occurred to me that I might actually be doing something I'd long aspired to do — using my anger to write. The Irish jig on the stereo swelled strong and stirringly as I continued, swinging my foot in time. And it was at that moment, as I was musing about the wonderful lack of weakness and the intense sense of pleasure in both myself and the story spilling out of me, that a new idea came to mind:

Oral rape. A large penis jammed down my throat as a little girl. So huge and brutal that I could neither breathe nor swallow! The gagging, choking sensation of this monster forcing me into oblivion for his merriment. I was shocked by this apparition and dismayed by the sensations accompanying it. Finally, when able to breathe again, I tried to understand. Father had done many cruel things to me. But never that. Still I knew the penis and the cruelty to be his. My numb throat and tongue were well-remembered from my place at the dinner table. And though he'd never done that, he might as well have. When he'd ridiculed me into eating tongue, fish eggs, brains, leg of lamb, liver, why not penis?! Also, all the cruel names that had made me feel weak and bad for trying to make something of myself!

Related or not, that day I actually wrote and mailed off letters to the hospitals asking for copies of my records. That didn't seem particularly brave or earth-shaking. But it did feel assertive in terms of finally doing something I'd been thinking about for a while.

Someone who hasn't experienced analysis might think that this oral rape fantasy marked a place where treatment was getting tough. But in fact, the opposite was true. By the time of this grim fantasy in

March 1993, I had become grateful for any awareness that gave me the sensation — even if painful — of definitely being alive. Furthermore, this gratitude may have been a facilitator because recognition of my fantasies gained momentum after that. Some of these were not terribly surprising, but experiencing them physically, whether in dreams or awake, allowed clearer ownership of how they had distorted my life and perhaps were still doing so.

In one dream, for instance, there was a doll with a removable head. And as Dr. Howie and I compared that decapitation to the function of anorexia as a remover of awareness, I realized that the doll herself was shaped like a penis. Through another dream, I came to understand that I'd needed to stay small and not leave a tiny man I was married to in order to keep him from exploding. In other dreams I realized that seeing myself as sexual made me feel crazy, as though I were in someone else's body; they also revealed to me that some of my pain in writing had to do with Mommy inside me losing me (like an amputated leg) as her physical extension.

And of course, Dr. Howie kept saying useful things along the way. For instance, one day after silent rocking, punctuated by an occasional sniff, he clarified, "After all, your being your mother's 'heart strings' or an object that gave her power, those were her fantasies, not yours. . . In fact, I think we could say you nearly killed yourself to avoid fulfilling them."

Silence.

"Could that be the key to the anorexia? At menarche, no longer able to be the boy who could give Mommy power or the 'sexless intellectual' Father said I was, I couldn't bear to think of myself as turning into either an unlovable woman like Mommy or a lovable dead one like Babs."

"Not much of a choice."

The relentless thoughts about all this pursued me everywhere. Like a mystery driven to solve itself. Asleep or awake. Writing. In the shower. Lifting weights. Driving or waiting at traffic lights. Talking to Lucy on the phone. With patients I had to sometimes jot down my own thoughts to free my head. . . What powers an illusionary penis can have! Father's calling me his "boy" when he was caressing me as a nearly dead anorexic had "protected" me from realizing consciously that he was being sexual or that I was having sexual feelings. Feeling like their "favorite son" had been a fantasy I'd dragged around all that time to protect myself from other people. Even Dr. Howie! While all that dismaying fantasy had actually accomplished was to keep me from knowing I'd been abused and, therefore, from being able to do anything with my anger except mutilate myself.

In time I felt driven to shed the illusion of being their "favorite son." Deliberately trying to give that up would feel brave, somehow, like standing up to Father.

"Sure. But do you understand why?" Howie asked.

"Maybe it's like removing camouflage. Standing up to him with my true self showing. My sexual self, I guess. Or would it be my 'fat' self?"

Silence.

"It's almost like the two are the same for me. Or for my unconscious."

"Yes."

"So. I have to be able to bear the negative to get to what I want."

"Or as you said, see the negative for what it is, a camouflage. 'Favorite son' is no different from the other roles their pathological narcissism forced on you — anorexic, nurse, scapegoat. In childhood you had no choice. Now you do." The rocker's creaking resumed.

"But you know I tried to give this up before by stopping writing! Since I saw being their favorite son as the way to be worth something in childhood, can I really give it up?"

"Or can you stop fighting with it? Which is really what's maintained it all this time."

Other dreams led Dr. Howie and me to talk about my having been treated like a prisoner or a pet by more than one person — my parents, my husbands, and the hospitals, but especially Mommy.

"Probably being Mommy's perfect little cripple was a way to make her take care of instead of kill me."

Silence.

"But she couldn't ever really protect me because she was using me as her cover. Praising me to other people, showing me off to make herself look good."

Silence.

"I suppose we could say Father made me a pet by caressing me as his boy when I was anorexic. Is that what you meant when you said he didn't want me to ever leave him or have another man?"

"That along with other things," Dr. Howie replied. "Your father's attacks also made it harder for you to leave him."

"I know the pattern, of course — being attracted to abusive men like him. Is that what you mean?"

"In part. But also, if they were abusive, how much could you love or be loved by them or anyone?"

"Maybe with Tom — or especially, with Rudy, I confused being a pet with being loved. I don't think I was aware of either with Dr. Howie. I mean Dr. Mitchell. . . You know Mommy could do everything. And I felt helpless — really, I believe now, due to both her need to dominate and my straining not to be like her. Probably feeling an inadequate underdog contributed to my attraction to people like Rudy and Tom. But Dr. Howie was different from them."

"Dr. Howie?"

"No, I mean Dr. Mitchell. . . Somehow I keep mixing you up."

Silence.

Rocking.

After several minutes Dr. Howie asked, "What do you suppose it would take to sort us out?"

I had no idea.

Seeing and discarding fantasies set the stage for considering what they had been used to confine and conceal — mainly my sexuality. So the reasons my unconscious needed me not to feel sexual became the focus of numerous analytic hours. Again, this simply involved looking more closely at aspects of my life discussed many times before. But now I could see and not believe these fantasies, having grown free enough to be able to distinguish between feelings and facts about myself. Father's telling me that I had no sexuality and his having attacked me when I was excited, sexual, or successful took on new significance. So did the more subtle details of Mommy's desire for me to be a boy to make Father love her, not me.

Dr. Howie spoke in a variety of ways about how my experiences with men — including Dr. Mitchell — still made me fear disaster if I were to feel and voice my sexuality. Also, about how that fear would be even greater with him because I was trusting and accustomed to saying whatever came to mind in his office. This talk led me to focus afresh on what Dr. Howie had said about my needing to "reject and join" Father in order to be free myself. Only now I rephrased it to address the existing problem rather than the desired solution: what unconscious fantasies was I still dressing myself in to prevent loss of Father? What isolating self-deceptions would I still need to shed to be able to walk away and forget him? To be able to write with a voice that pleased me?

Eventually, I had a dream about flying with the analyst who was serving as the Foundation's research-education director, which I knew had to do with sexual feelings for Dr. Howie. In it I was feeling terribly sleepy, misplaced my ticket, and got confused about whether I was on a plane or a train. All that defensive muffling to conceal the exhilaration I'd have felt otherwise! Still, the dream had ended with me opening the little blue bag I often travel with and finding it full of things that delighted me — a tiny, dollhouse-sized dachshund puppy; magically strong eyeglasses; sheer, brightly colored dresses in the pouch I'd once used for my diaphragm.

In time I came to understand that because sexual feelings were unacceptable, all other good feelings about myself were forbidden as well. This was hard to grasp. Even after I thought I had it, I'd discover I didn't. The paramount importance of maintaining low self-esteem came out in a 1993 dream, which I never could have understood without Dr. Howie:

I lost all my money. It was awful! Devastating. Because losing my money was retroactive. It wasn't just becoming poor now. It was like dominoes falling backward. Without it I couldn't pay for education or analysis or have children or be a psychologist. I was nothing. My life was empty and ruined.

"Are you worried about losing your money?" Howie asked.

"No. I wouldn't want to be self-destructive with it. But being lonely feels a lot worse to me than being poor."

Silence.

"All I can think of is that the dream is somehow about losing my value to myself."

"How would that be?"

"It doesn't make sense. But what comes to mind is all the writing I've done."

"Why doesn't that make sense?"

"It's not logical."

"Sure. But it does fit with your experience with your father — losing his love if you worked hard or were successful."

"I know you're right. But I keep thinking I've somehow given you the wrong impression. I still can't see how writing relates to losing all my money."

"The way I'd put it," Howie answered after another silence, "is that your unconscious is worried about your losing the life-long negative concepts it's valued you for. You'll lose them if you fully claim your voice."

But it took strong dreams to show me that Howie was right and that his interpretation had far-reaching implications. Two of the dreams presented Dr. Howie very negatively. In one, he was a kind of disheveled oaf who used the toilet at the same time as me, sitting behind. In another he was represented by a critical professor whom I felt attracted to, but whose course I'd failed to attend all semester and who'd found my writing crazy.

"What do you think about that?" Howie asked.

He rocked while I racked my brain. "I guess . . . since my writing's going okay right now, maybe I'm afraid you'll think it's crazy."

"Because?"

"I don't know. Maybe because most therapists I know would never be this open, might even disapprove. Maybe I confuse you with any judge."

Silence. Then, "What about the course? What would you say that represents?"

"My sexual feelings are what come to mind. Here and for you. . . I'm sure I have them, but I'm never aware of any."

"Do you suppose that's related to your viewing me so negatively?"

"I like you."

"But you felt bad about the professor in the dream."

"Yeah."

"And I wonder how that may be related to how bad you've always felt about yourself."

"I don't follow you." That surprised me. Dr. Howie has always impressed me as extremely wise. So when I had trouble understanding something, I assumed he was right and strained to see it. But this time, I decided he was showing his dumbness.

"Do you remember how you said to me once early on, 'How can you help me if you can't even understand how bad I am?'"

"Sure."

"And would you agree," he continued, "that your feeling of being a bad person has previously been pretty persistent?"

"Of course."

"Well, I'm wondering if there isn't some connection between the badness you gave me in the dream and your badness."

While there, I still couldn't see a connection. Even though Howie stopped seeming dumb, I couldn't get it. Only while driving to the Foundation office did I realize: Father's sexual badness had been considered "good" in our family growing up. So maybe. . . it was hard to get it, because doing so required thinking logically about the black and white illogic of our family. . . what had been "bad" in me as a child had been opposing Father by being "intellectual" and "the boy," and not taking care of his sexuality. I'd also held that "badness" responsible for my having been attracted to men who became abusive once my strength and sexuality showed. So, if Dr. Howie were "bad," and I was sexually attracted to him, he'd be like Dr. Mitchell and all the rest and my analysis wouldn't save me. But if, instead, Dr. Howie was good, then my being attracted to him could make me feel good instead of bad. And if he was good, he wouldn't be abusive, and I'd feel differently about myself.

What a struggle! Yet only in discussing this with Dr. Howie did I understand that this "badness" was a removable fantasy that kept me tied to Father through straining to simultaneously please and oppose him. And that insight flooded me with the realization of how terrified I was of Dr. Howie's liking me.

Not long after that, I went to Los Angeles to visit Lucy and Billy. While there, I had another dream about going back to New York Hospital:

To find the corridor that led to my room was a little tricky. You had to go through the dining room and also discover that this bookcase wall was really a sliding door. A pretty nurse was about to show me when I figured it out myself. Then she helped me take a bath in this old-fashioned bathtub. I couldn't find the big white towel I was supposed to use. But high up in the bookcase wall I saw a stack of pretty little pink towels with a floral pattern in the texture of their terrycloth. I took one and undressed. The nurse stood by as I squatted in the tub on my hands and knees and washed myself. The soap she gave me was brown. As I rubbed it on my arms and legs, it made a powdery coating the color of molasses. But when rinsed off, my skin was smooth and clear. Getting out, I confessed to the nurse that I had taken a pink towel. She thanked me for telling her and added that I wouldn't get in trouble. I felt clean and at peace.

This dream was followed by intense worries about again being taken for crazy if I put the story of my anorexia and long hospitalization out for everyone to read. In focusing on these worries to try to sort things out, I decided I didn't really feel it was crazy to write my story; I wanted people to know both about how a person can get damaged through abuse and how it's possible, with appropriate help, to get beyond the confinement caused by such injuries. Still, the fear of being seen as crazy didn't let up.

"Even you," I said to Dr. Howie. "Sometimes I think you can't understand the things I discover. And that makes me feel you think I'm crazy."

Silence.

"I do have this sense more and more lately that you'll think I'm being loud-mouthed or self-destructive if I actually put this book out."

"And the self-destructiveness?"

"That if I were reasonable, I'd just keep all this stuff to myself."

"In other words, that all this should be a secret between you and me?"

Of course, a light went on when he said that, recalling how my feelings that he didn't want me to speak out repeated the secrecy after talking to Father when I was four.

But Howie was no help with one element of the dream that plagued me as insistently as the worry about speaking out. Only that night driving home from work did I suddenly recognize a relationship between the bookcase wall's being a sliding door and my having helped Father hide his Bourbon from Grandfather. That memory of Father's cowardliness made me ask, "Are you now doing the same thing without knowing it? Trying to hide your writing behind craziness like Father hid his whiskey behind books!?"

Deadness was another self-concept that it pained me to relinquish. The dream put it this way:

An orange cat, like Ben's Thistle, had died. But I was keeping it around for a while. It didn't smell yet, and I knew I'd have to give her up before she did. It made me sad to think of that though. She was just lying around curled up like a fur piece. . .

At Dr. Howie's, discussion about this dream led us through such issues as my being a "dead pussy," a woman denying sexuality, in order to be loved, and the resemblance of that condition to being a pet on a leash. That reminded me again of having been Mommy's precious pet and that both Tom and Rudy had become abusive when I stopped staying small and crippled.

"I can imagine you'd think that feeling dead is feeling like Babs, the woman my father loved," I said to Dr. Howie.

"Sure."

"But somehow this deadness feels urgent. Like something terrible will happen if I don't keep it."

Silence.

"Or if I speak out."

I expected him to comment. But, instead, the room was still, without even a creak. My eyes studied the sunlight on the multi-colored miniature mask which had been added above the somber Indian one. And somehow, that made what he finally did say startling: "I think you knew that for your father Babs was not dead. You heard it in his voice."

That night I had a terrible dream that was mostly just feelings:

I was horribly injured and mutilated in my mouth, neck, chest and arms. Like I'd been bludgeoned with a club. All this had to do with my voice. I was trying to decide whether to speak out and feel the pain of struggling toward recovery or just remain silent. Speaking out would both hurt to the quick and display my mutilation.

chapter twenty-six

MY HOUSE

New York Hospital's response to the request for my records surprised me. After such a long time, I half-expected to be ignored or refused. But instead, the hospital's letter asked for $136.24 to copy the records. I laughed out loud writing the check because of how much easier being a psychologist, and being rich, made that feel.

For some reason, mailing that check brought *Caleb, My Son* to mind, too, and the conversation in analysis about Father's response to that accomplishment. In my imagination, the package with the hospital records resembled the 1955 package of *Caleb, My Son*'s manuscript, both being shabby parcels containing life-transforming significance.

"*Caleb* really was different," I told Dr. Howie. "Father seemed to have only positive feelings about it and about me related to it."

Silence.

"And, you know. . . I understand that it was my own defensiveness that made me feel so fake after that book. But Father's excitement and pride did give the sense of his claiming it as his own."

"Do you think that in some way it was?"

Hearing that, I could still feel the fakeness. Part of me wanted to ask, "Do you think he wrote it?" But instead, I said, "Well, my reason for writing was to be like Father and to make him love me. So, to that extent it was his."

"A natural wish. But in your family, I suspect, a very complicated one. Even the book's title might stir some feelings."

And that's when it came to me — out of nowhere, a flash of clarity blowing everything else away. I understood that what had made *Caleb* different was that its success had fulfilled Father's fantasy. In that one instance, he had delighted in being in my shadow because its radiance had fulfilled his dreams. In more than one sense, he had gained a son.

Christmas, 1993 was somewhat subdued even with Lucy and Billy home for two days. Ben and Sara didn't come because their second child, a boy named Jesse, had been born a month earlier. So over New Year's I went to Philly to meet him. And during my visit there, I observed a kind of stifled uneasiness in myself. I'd known for some time that Ben and Sara disapproved of several things about me that I couldn't and/or didn't want to change — my being divorced, a psychologist, and not an evangelical Christian. These "sins" had been openly acknowledged among us for a while; once their being so regarded had hurt and angered me. Since Kathryn's birth, those prejudices had made me sad and had inhibited my behavior when I was with them. The associated uneasiness was because I had to restrain myself in order to try not to break any more of their evangelical rules and cause useless open conflict. It was uncomfortable, and I wouldn't visit often.

But visiting Kathryn and Jesse seemed well worth a little discomfort that time. Kathryn was still darling and had become precociously talkative. Changes since the summer included her being able to call me "Wucy" and wanting to sit in my lap to read books. Jesse was solid with a steady dark-eyed gaze and lots of thick black hair. He mostly nursed and slept. But when he smiled, it was delicious.

The night after returning home I dreamed:

Ben and Sara and their kids had left messes all over my house. When I confronted them, they didn't seem to care. One of the things they'd left around was an ornate rectangular saucer of milk with an oriental design around its edge. I found it on the top of the built-in bookcase in the back upstairs hall of the house of my childhood. . . What was odd, though, was that the bookcase was otherwise totally empty. In fact the hall was, too — all glaring white and clean with that beautiful window over the back stairs that I've copied in the beach house.

On waking I kept mulling that over, especially the saucer of milk.

The best Howie could do with it was wonder if visiting Ben and Sara hadn't made me feel the same sense of being personally unacceptable and coldly controlled as I'd felt with Mommy in childhood.

When he said that I was reminded of the sadness I'd recognized coming back from L.A. and Philly. Given my increased sense of adequacy and self-respect, and the absence of my old shyness with strangers, returning home to a life without anyone to care about me felt bleak.

"Somehow the hall's whiteness feels alone like that, too," I said to Howie.

"Cold?"

"Maybe. But it also makes me wonder if I'm to blame."

"I don't understand. How would that be?"

"Maybe my fear of lostness makes me hang onto myself too tightly."

"In other words, does having to be controlled keep you alone?"

"I don't know. Maybe. I guess I'm wondering if I may not have to lose myself to be able to write fiction the way I want to. . . Doing so would require a large voice."

"Or perhaps — " Howie paused to clear his throat as he does sometimes when he's thinking. "Saying it slightly differently, you may need to allow yourself to accept and enjoy your strength in order to speak the way you want to."

That night I dreamed:

It was the middle of the night. I was a child being forced to say the "right" thing in a way that I wasn't capable of, a way that would kill me. I was strangling on those words while my parents stood over me demanding that I say them perfectly, even though they could see I was going to die from trying.

Facing that dream, I tried to fit it together with reluctance I was having about both returning phone calls and answering letters. Straining to record a phone message from an unknown colleague from another city, I suddenly understood: I was afraid to be heard because of a fantasy that I didn't have a voice and that if I spoke I'd be humiliated by others seeing that I wasn't entitled to speak!

Continuing to mull this over, I imagined my throat like the dark and empty basement stairs of my childhood. But the thoughts that followed were: Why? What happened to it? The usual answers came first: I was still small and silent, afraid of setting off alarms and feeling to blame for Father's attacks, still paralyzed by the terror associated with feeling that my four-year-old voice had killed Babs and destroyed our family. Then a new answer came with a brand-new feeling unrestrained by reason: my voice box was missing because Father had ripped it out!

Reason is valuable, however. Knowing that I really did have a voice, but also that I felt Father had ripped it and my sexuality out of me, presented yet another scenario to fit together with that of his voice having impregnated me. Both had been maintained by my blind belief that Father was right. Whereas, in fact, he had been wrong. His hostility from feeling overshadowed and castrated by his father's moral stature had led him to ridicule all conscientious industry and to hate anyone whose power, success or sexuality made him feel the painful deficiency of his own. Due to my own deprivation, his exciting dance had won my heart even as it brutalized my soul. But thus setting my two fantasies about him side by side allowed a separation I had never been able to imagine before. My love of Father's warmth and excitement, my longing for his voice still burned in me as intensely at that moment as at age four. Only now, beside it and distinct from it stood an equally intense hurt and outrage over his brutal crippling of my own voice and womanhood. And in that moment I understood that these two experiences could never be reconciled. Rather, the difference between them was as important as the two feelings themselves. Father had been both my most nurturing and my most murderous parent.

"Absolutely," was all Dr. Howie said. "I totally agree."

A few days later I dreamed:

I was facing baby Jesse and started talking to him playfully. He was so lovable and when I smiled and said his name, he said, "Hello! I love you, too," in this amazingly grown-up way. Then I realized he had a mustache!

This dream seemed connected to that other one about Ben and Sara leaving messes in my house and the image of the saucer of milk I'd never figured out. Probably it related to the pain of loving them and their children when they were so unaccepting of me.

It was hard to get started at Dr. Howie's that day. I felt a reluctance to talk without knowing why.

When my eyes went to the bookshelves for distraction, they found still one more little mask. A white one with black eye sockets, black and white feathers fringing out all around, and black rings at its neck. Alone. . . or starting a column on the other bookcase edge. Looking at it, I suddenly understood the saucer of milk. The music of the snake charmer came with it: da da da dadadadada. Something like "In the southern part of France where the ladies wear no pants. . . ." According to Bibba, the snake charmer always had a saucer of milk to get the snake back under control if anything went wrong! I felt myself get hot telling Howie.

But, of course, he just listened. And, while he was listening, I realized that the empty whiteness of the upstairs hall and the bookcase in that dream were probably a very early memory of Mommy's house. From way back when we were just moving in. "Me moving into Mommy's house!" I announced, laughing. "Making it my own in every sense of the image!"

"Sounds positive."

"Yes. And for some reason, I don't feel fat!"

Rocking. "How do you feel?"

"Excited." I felt very serious saying that. And then sad thinking about Dr. Howie back there turned white-haired from rocking. But next, laughter took me over again as I thought about the baby Jesse dream I hadn't told him yet.

Same old Howie, though: "What did you think was the significance of the mustache?"

"I feel quite comfortable loving Jesse so much I could eat him up." Rocking.

"Because of the mustache, I know that, despite the lack of comfort, I feel like that about you, too."

He did not answer. I'm not clear whether he was rocking or not.

There were a few silent minutes before he said, "I need to stop us there and see you back next time."

Perhaps it was talking in that session about the huge issue of my love feelings, but after the laughter, I felt this intense need to not lose Dr. Howie, to memorize the positions of all the little heads and the things we said. As I stood up from the couch and walked toward the door beyond him, Dr. Howie's face came into clearer focus than usual. Also, I had the definite impression of our eyes making contact.

"Good-bye," I said like always, deliberately noting gold boot toes, earring, and bone tiepull. Also, a certain almost dancing vitality that I'd never noticed before in his gray mustache.

"Good-bye," he replied, standing there facing me as still as ever.

Only as I closed the door and was passing the hallowing mask in the hall did a new question rise to haunt me. Why at that moment did I have the fantasy that Dr. Howie was wearing a black leotard?

That weekend I had two dreams that felt both sad and jubilant. In the first:

I was in a compartment on a very old, run-down train. On the seat opposite me, I'd placed my green tweed jacket from the Guggenheim trip. When the train stopped, I put aside writing in my copy book and got off. Only outside, walking across the barren weedy land surrounding the tracks, did I realize I'd forgotten both the jacket and my copy book. I went back to get them. But it was the wrong train. Getting off again, I asked these young men in the railroad yard if there was some way to retrieve things left on the train. They laughed as if I were crazy.

The dream the next night began with the sound of glass shattering:

I couldn't see where at first. Then I noticed something like a fence of gray and purple glass all shattered and falling down on the beach. I — at my present age — walked over and stepped through where it had been standing between me and the ocean. A little breeze was blowing on the other side, a sweet little breeze. And there was my small blue bag again. Open, with stuff falling out. Pretty, sheer dresses that I loved at first sight; denim bootlets; storybooks with colorful, glowing covers; a miniature motorcycle; other things I can't recall. And music was playing somewhere. It made me start to dance. A Willie and Waylon song that I love. . . sad and sweet: ". . . like an old stallion who's longing for freedom trying to outrun the wind." Glancing down as my toes tripped across the sand, I realized that the dress I was wearing was tissue-sheer white with purple words printed all over it.

I STILL EXIST!

Saying this evokes a mixture of relief and dread made conscious in me by my previously unconscious belief that finishing this story would cause me to vanish.

This dread of imminent erasure is probably a memory of how I felt as a little girl confined to the yard. I had to be silent and invisible then to prevent the devastating disapproval of parents who found children's needs and power equally horrifying. So I'm still afraid to let those same aspects of me show today. And the obverse is true as well: as a little girl and sexually developing adolescent, I managed to stay connected to Father by hiding both needs and strengths. Perhaps voicing them now threatens my existence, because it will sever those ties. Speaking out does bring to mind Father's bellowing explosions and his dread of being overshadowed by me as he was by Grandfather. Maybe the nonexistence I fear is really fear of Father's absence, of being left utterly alone once Father is blotted out by my shadow.

But I am no longer locked out. I have learned that needs can be the roots of power. As an adult, my childlike anorexic body, along with guilt, shame, and continuing terror, drove me to pursue the "miracle" of reasonable and effective treatment, which in ten years of suffering I had never received. The wonderful thing about this is that, despite terrible accidents along the way, I did eventually find that treatment and relative freedom.

Still, this thrilling freedom has been costly. Besides coming late in my life, it has brought a new form of aloneness. Claiming my voice has separated me from people with whom I once had a semblance of belonging. From sisters who, themselves, never knew to want this freedom. From children creating their own futures in ways that are sometimes at odds with my values. And thinking of them reminds me sadly that the time is coming when the next step in this freedom march will require me to leave Dr. Howie.

So, what am I to do? How can I benefit from such solitary freedom? I've asked myself and Dr. Howie many times. Howie usually doesn't answer. The analyst's role is to listen and not deprive the patient of feelings or ingenuity. Also, he cannot know for me. My answer, while not unique, seems workable: "The best revenge is a good life."

Therefore, this is my intention: certainly I cannot have at sixty what I missed out on at twenty. But I can claim life today in its fullness. That includes writing stories that were once silenced inside me, dreaming, working as a psychotherapist with adults and children whose emotional problems compromise their lives, lecturing on parenting and creative freedom, and enjoying children and grand-children and friends.

Yet, of course, I want more. Time. Fun. Love. I am not lonely, because I've come to enjoy solitude. Still I would feel tremendously lucky if I could have a relationship with a good man, one who can love me as a woman with power and needs because he also appreci-ates his own. I know that finding him will not be easy. I don't expect to. Especially at my age, women outnumber men. And most older men want younger women, a prejudice I have no wish to challenge. Besides, my man would have to be pretty remarkable to fit with the standards I've internalized from Dr. Howie. Also, recognizing him would scare me again due to severing more ties with Father. Nevertheless, I stay on the lookout and sometimes even daydream about the man — while lifting weights to stay fit, skimming the singles ads which I aged out of years ago, or putting on makeup before the bathroom mirror and noticing both the deepening lines around my eyes and how my right eye still strays slightly out of focus.

In these reflections, pain and pleasure often come together. For instance, I most miss a good man when I feel pretty and excited. Sometimes then I dance, with tears in my eyes, to Elvis turned up loud on the stereo. This is not because of nostalgia; I didn't like Elvis or his music when I was young. But I love the music's rhythm in my body now. Tripping through "Nothing But A Hound Dog" and "All Shook Up" in front of my grandmother's full-length mirror, I can almost imagine that my spirited reflection is me being seen by a partner.

Oddly, though, sadness can soon return me to a quietly hopeful expectancy. Often mixed with appreciative thoughts of my children, both now and in the past. Hindsight suggests that rising to the challenge of their births and lives is what converted my anorexia (fear and denial of my needs and power) to depression (unaccepted anger about unmet needs and suppressed power). This painful but useful conversion eventually allowed me to use Dr. Howie to restore my personhood. And doing so has both required and resulted in reclaiming myself as a writer. Indeed, with my children grown and gone, now substantial people in their own right, I need writing. Besides, despite the fantasy, stories do not kill you coming out. Rather, working at them can delight and, like Elvis's music, make me want to dance.

Sometimes, all this is still briefly amazing. But also thrilling and hope-inspiring. Such unexpected blessings make me wonder what else can happen.

LUCY DANIELS is a writer and clinical psychologist based in Raleigh, North Carolina. A Guggenheim Fellow in literature, she is the author of *Caleb, My Son* (1956), a best-selling novel about a father-son conflict intensified by racial inequality, and *High On A Hill* (1961), a fictionalized account of the life struggles of patients and doctors inside a mental hospital.

In 1977, Daniels received her doctorate in clinical psychology from the University of North Carolina at Chapel Hill and started a private practice that provides psychotherapy for adults, adolescents, and children. Daniels credits her own psychoanalysis for freeing her from both chronic anorexia and a debilitating writer's block that followed the publication of her second novel.

In 1989, she founded the Lucy Daniels Foundation, a non-profit organization dedicated to fostering emotional and creative freedom through education, outreach, research, and psychoanalytic treatment; and the Lucy Daniels Center for Early Childhood, a preschool program that uses psychoanalytic principles to promote the emotional development of young children and their parents.

Daniels has also supported art exhibitions that illustrate the relationship between psychology and creativity. In 1998, she co-curated and sponsored "Sacred and Fatal," a solo exhibition of the sculptures and drawings of Louise Bourgeois, at the North Carolina Museum of Art in Raleigh. She was also a major sponsor of "Dreams 1900-2000: Science, Art, and the Unconscious Mind," an international exhibition of twentieth-century art about dreams that was shown in New York, Vienna, and Paris in 1999-2000.

Daniels was named a Distinguished Friend of Psychoanalysis by The American Psychoanalytic Association in 1991 and an Honorary Colleague of the Association for Child Psychoanalysis in 1995. Both her foundation's ongoing seminars on creativity and dreams and its annual conference attract diverse audiences that include artists, writers, therapists, and accomplished psychoanalysts and researchers from throughout the world.

Daniels has four children and six grandchildren.